THE COMPLETE IDIOT'S GUIDE TO

Speed Reading

by Abby Marks Beale with Pam Mullan

ALPHA

A member of Penguin Group (USA) Inc.

ALPHA BOOKS

Published by the Penguin Group

Penguin Group (USA) Inc., 375 Hudson Street, New York, New York 10014, USA

Penguin Group (Canada), 90 Eglinton Avenue East, Suite 700, Toronto, Ontario M4P 2Y3, Canada (a division of Pearson Penguin Canada Inc.)

Penguin Books Ltd., 80 Strand, London WC2R 0RL, England

Penguin Ireland, 25 St. Stephen's Green, Dublin 2, Ireland (a division of Penguin Books Ltd.)

Penguin Group (Australia), 250 Camberwell Road, Camberwell, Victoria 3124, Australia (a division of Pearson Australia Group Pty. Ltd.)

Penguin Books India Pvt. Ltd., 11 Community Centre, Panchsheel Park, New Delhi—110 017, India

Penguin Group (NZ), 67 Apollo Drive, Rosedale, North Shore, Auckland 1311, New Zealand (a division of Pearson New Zealand Ltd.)

Penguin Books (South Africa) (Pty.) Ltd., 24 Sturdee Avenue, Rosebank, Johannesburg 2196, South Africa

Penguin Books Ltd., Registered Offices: 80 Strand, London WC2R 0RL, England

International Standard Book Number: 978-1-59257-778-1
Library of Congress Catalog Card Number: 2007941352

14   8

Interpretation of the printing code: The rightmost number of the first series of numbers is the year of the book's printing; the rightmost number of the second series of numbers is the number of the book's printing. For example, a printing code of 08-1 shows that the first printing occurred in 2008.

Printed in the United States of America

Note: This publication contains the opinions and ideas of its authors. It is intended to provide helpful and informative material on the subject matter covered. It is sold with the understanding that the authors and publisher are not engaged in rendering professional services in the book. If the reader requires personal assistance or advice, a competent professional should be consulted.

The authors and publisher specifically disclaim any responsibility for any liability, loss, or risk, personal or otherwise, which is incurred as a consequence, directly or indirectly, of the use and application of any of the contents of this book.

Most Alpha books are available at special quantity discounts for bulk purchases for sales promotions, premiums, fund-raising, or educational use. Special books, or book excerpts, can also be created to fit specific needs.

For details, write: Special Markets, Alpha Books, 375 Hudson Street, New York, NY 10014.

Publisher: *Marie Butler-Knight*
Editorial Director: *Mike Sanders*
Senior Managing Editor: *Billy Fields*
Executive Editor: *Randy Ladenheim-Gil*
Production Editor: *Kayla Dugger*
Copy Editor: *Amy Borrelli*

Cartoonist: *Shannon Wheeler*
Cover Designer: *Bill Thomas*
Book Designer: *Trina Wurst*
Indexer: *Brad Herriman*
Layout: *Chad Dressler*
Proofreader: *Mary Hunt*

Contents at a Glance

Contents

Introduction

People think of many different things when they hear the phrase "speed reading." Some might think of Evelyn Wood, the woman who pioneered speed reading in the 1950s, who offered free sample classes across the United States. Others might conjure up the vision of a finger zipping down the pages in record time while the other hand turns the pages. Many envy the thought of being able to speed read. Some just can't figure out how it can really be done.

In this book, Pam and I have combined our more than 40 years of speed reading experience, both doing research and training others, with information gleaned from reading over 30 speed reading books and experience with over 10 speed reading software programs to come up with *The Complete Idiot's Guide to Speed Reading*.

The Complete Idiot's Guide to Speed Reading enables you to see and experience ways of getting through your reading workload with speed and efficiency. If you practice with the suggested strategies, you can easily double or even triple your current reading speed. In addition, you might find you concentrate better or understand what you read with greater ease.

As you go through the chapters, you'll quickly learn that there are many simple options available to you for reading better and faster that you probably didn't know existed. Once you know, I think you'll enjoy putting them into action.

Because each reader comes into this process with varied levels of education, vocabulary, background knowledge, experience, and motivation, you learn how to speed read in your way. I present a buffet of proven ideas. Some will work for you better than others. There will be a lot you will want to keep and some you won't, but the only way to know what's best for you is to try everything, figure out which one(s) are best for you, and have fun along the way.

If you try something once and you feel it's not working, consider trying it several times before deciding it's not for you. I encourage you to experiment—or play, if you will—with the ideas in this book so you can come away with the most useful strategies to read faster and better to get you where you want to go. Remember, there is no *one* best way to read, just the way(s) *you* find most useful.

If you have any questions or want to send me your comments, please do so. I'd love to hear from you. (My contact info appears on the inside back cover of the book.)

Have fun speeding through your reading!

How to Use This Book

This book is divided into four distinct parts. Each chapter in each part builds upon the next with an opportunity to practice your speed strategies to solidify your learning. Here's what you'll find:

Part 1, "Getting Up to Speed with What You Read," puts you directly in the speed reading driver's seat. In these chapters, you first evaluate your current reading speed and comprehension using the One-Minute Timing Exercise. You are then introduced to several proven speed strategies, including using your hands and a card, reading key words, reading thought chunks, and spreading your peripheral vision to see more words at a glance. Another timing exercise, the 3-2-1 Drill, is also introduced as a way to challenge yourself to read faster than you might normally feel comfortable. Because comprehension is the biggest concern new speed readers have, I have included an entire chapter on helping you understand how comprehension is affected when you first learn to read faster and what you can do about it to secure it.

Part 2, "Get In, Get Out, and Don't Go Back," starts with helping you know how to best set yourself up for reading success. Good concentration is essential for reading with speed and comprehending most easily. The "getting in" part deals with the differences between nonfiction and fiction reading. It uncovers where the writer's outline is located in nonfiction so you can quickly find the most important information and not waste time. "Getting out" guides you into thinking about how you are going to literally get out of what you're reading as efficiently as possible through skimming, scanning, skipping, summarizing, and understanding the organizational patterns of most nonfiction. "Don't go back" provides ways to keep your keepers and reduce your natural tendency to forget. To put all this into practice, I also share some of the best ways to read each different type of material.

Part 3, "Tuning Up Your Speed," takes what you know about the speed reading techniques and the other effective general reading strategies to discover what to speed read and what not to. Included here is a fabulous chapter on speed reading on screen, which, as of this printing, is not found anywhere else. You learn how to adapt the hand and card methods for paper onto a computer screen as well as get some insights into how to print less to save trees and time. And finally, we look at how all readers can learn how to reduce daydreaming, back-skipping, and subvocalizing while reading to help their reading speed, concentration, and comprehension.

Part 4, "Overload Management," deals with your piles of reading, both on paper and on screen, and some commonsense strategies for managing them both.

In the back, Appendix A is a glossary of some of the most important terms listed in this book. Appendix B and C are sections you'll frequent because they contain the timed reading exercises (in Appendix B) and the personal progress charts (in Appendix C). Appendix D contains detailed information about how to figure words per minute on your own reading material.

Extras

Throughout, I've included some tips, techniques, insights, inspiration, definitions, and things to watch out for that will support and complement your speed reading efforts:

Speed Tip

Check these boxes for information you need to know as you go about your quest to read faster.

Speed Bump

Read these boxes for warnings all readers should be aware of when it comes to learning to speed read.

def•i•ni•tion

These boxes present definitions of words and concepts to expand your knowledge base as it relates to speed reading.

Speed Secret

Read these boxes for interesting nuggets of information or trivia about speed reading you might not be aware of.

Acknowledgments

Every time I write a book I remember that I don't really love to write (I really love to teach!), but I love to have written. To get this book to fruition, I couldn't have done it without the support and patience of my husband, Chris, and my boys, Jonathan and Michael, who understood my early morning wakings and weekend office hours to get this done. I am ever so grateful to have them in my life.

Heartfelt thanks to Pam Mullan, who is an expert in speed reading as well as being an extraordinary educator. Her assistance with this book has made it top-notch. In particular, her contribution of Chapter 12 should be read by all, as it's not found anywhere else. We engaged in some healthy intellectual debate and had a lot of fun putting this together.

I want to thank Narda Gruver for her supportive service to me and for her love of my speed reading programs.

I asked the subscribers of my monthly e-zine what questions they have about speed reading, which prompted me to include the responses in the book. I thank all the respondents, and you know who you are!

Thank you to the entire team at Alpha Books whose guidance and talent helped make this the best book it could be. It was a pleasure to work with them.

I am indebted to those who have written books in this field, as they have expanded my horizons for becoming the best speed reading educator I can be. I want to express my gratitude to all those people in the last 20 years who have attended my workshops and gave me feedback, either verbally or in writing, which confirm I am helping others in a positive way.

Trademarks

All terms mentioned in this book that are known to be or are suspected of being trademarks or service marks have been appropriately capitalized. Alpha Books and Penguin Group (USA) Inc. cannot attest to the accuracy of this information. Use of a term in this book should not be regarded as affecting the validity of any trademark or service mark.

Part 1

Getting Up to Speed with What You Read

When the last book in the *Harry Potter* series came out in July 2007, Anne Jones, a five-time world speed reading champion from England, read the 750-page book in just 47 minutes, 1 second! That's a world record–breaking 4,244 words per minute. In 1999, *The Guinness Book of World Records* included Howard Berg from Texas as the world's fastest reader, clocking in at 25,000 words per minute—that's 80 pages per minute—with comprehension to boot!

Still, you might be surprised to learn that fewer than 1 percent of the adult U.S. population reads at speeds above 400 words per minute, and the average person reads around 250 words per minute. You don't have to be one of those statistics! With this book; a timing device; a blank index card; a favorite magazine, newspaper, or book; a pen and some blank paper; and an eager frame of mind, you can join the ranks of the record holders—or at least get closer to their words per minute!

Chapter 1

Getting Started Speed Reading

In This Chapter

- Who are *you* as a reader?
- Speed reading: a conscious choice
- Your reading "gears"
- The discomfort zone—the place to be
- Speed looking versus speed reading

If you're like most people, you've probably never had the opportunity to take a speed reading course or otherwise test your reading speed and comprehension. And if you did, it was only a snapshot in time given the conditions under which you read: how easy/difficult the material was, how tired you were, why you were reading, how interested you were, how hungry you were, how many distractions surrounded you, and so on.

It's time to remedy that and take a closer look at how you read now. Wherever you are, give yourself credit for how much you have achieved and how far you have come with the skills you currently possess.

After a few simple reading exercises, you might find that you're a faster reader than you thought! You might discover that your comprehension is better than you thought, too. Whatever the result, you need to start somewhere. So let's get started!

A Minute Is All You Need

The two big parts of speed reading are speed, of course, and also *comprehension*. It doesn't mean much if you read quickly but don't understand. To get started, you need to have a baseline, a starting point from which you can compare your progress as you work through this book. To help you determine your current *reading speed* and comprehension, I provide you with a simple evaluation process with some timed reading exercises.

def•i•ni•tion

Reading speed is the rate at which your eyes and brain decode and understand words. Word-for-word readers have a slower reading speed than those who read more than one word at a time. **Comprehension** involves the mind perceiving and understanding ideas and concepts. When reading, this can mean absorbing very specific details or merely grasping a general concept. Personal understanding is the key.

The first timed exercise is the One-Minute Timing Exercise, coming up later in this chapter. In Chapter 2, you'll find the 3-2-1 Drill. Both have accompanying progress charts in Appendix C so you can track your results and really see the progress you're making with both speed and comprehension.

Now for what you'll read: Appendix B contains an eclectic group of seven nonfiction articles for you to practice with. Some will interest you; others won't. When evaluating your speed, try reading not just those that interest you but also those that don't. Why? Because in your "real life," you'll encounter reading material that doesn't interest you but that you have to read anyway. It's good practice to see how you interact with it.

Documenting Your Comprehension

When you were in school, your teachers probably evaluated your comprehension by having you answer questions after you'd read a chapter or lesson. The process was usually the same: you'd read the text and then answer the end-of-chapter questions or take a section test to see what you learned.

The problem with this now is that you might have come to rely on these types of evaluations to confirm your understanding of what you read. That's fine for school, but as you know, in your daily reading—magazines, newspapers, textbooks, procedural manuals, business reports, and so on—quiz questions aren't included on the last page! Without that definitive way of evaluating what you learn, you might feel uncertain about your level of comprehension. And in the real world, you have to be able to feel confident with your level of understanding.

Do you frequently understand what you read the first time, or are you used to doubting yourself and doubling back over what you read? Learning to trust your brain—believing you will understand it the first time through—is an important piece of the speed reading process. To help you with this, you'll be evaluating your own comprehension on the practice readings in this book. After your designated reading time,

> **Speed Tip** _____
>
> Learn to trust your brain. Although you may be used to going back over material you already read, double- or even triple-checking your comprehension, be reassured that your brain really does get it, if you let it.

you'll write down all the key points you understood from the reading—*without looking back* (that's cheating!). There's no one best way to write your key points—you can use bullet points or full sentences or whatever you like.

After you've written down the key points you remember, you'll evaluate your percent of comprehension on a scale of 0 (absolutely no understanding) to 100 percent (complete understanding). Your goal is to become good at securing solid comprehension numbers, because as you become more competent at gauging your own comprehension, you'll find increased confidence in speeding up your reading. Be sure to document all your reading exercise scores on the charts in Appendix C.

One-Minute Timing Exercise

In this exercise, you determine how many *words per minute* (WPM) you read. This is your starting point on the path to speed reading—and it only takes 1 minute!

Here's how it works; please read all the instructions before starting:

> **def•i•ni•tion** _____
>
> Your **words per minute** (WPM) rate is the average number of words you read in 1 minute.

1. Choose any practice article from Appendix B to read.

2. With a timing device (a clock with a second hand, a stopwatch, or another digital timer), time yourself reading silently and *normally* for exactly 1 minute. At the end of 1 minute, mark the line you're on.

3. On a separate piece of paper, write down as many key points as you can remember—*without* looking back at the reading.

4. Calculate your words per minute (WPM) by counting the number of lines you read and multiplying that number by the number of words per line listed under the title of the article. Here's the formula:

   WPM = # of lines read × # of words per line

5. At this point, gauge your percent of comprehension on a scale from 0 to 100 percent of how much you think you understood based on the key points you wrote down.

Now turn to Appendix C and document your results on the "One-Minute Timing Progress Chart."

What Your Numbers Mean

You've completed your first 1-minute timing! Congratulations! You should have two numbers in front of you: your words per minute and your percent of comprehension. But what do these numbers mean? Let's look at the speed results first.

100 to 200 Words per Minute: Slow Readers

If you read between 100 and 200 words per minute, you're considered a "talker." Talkers do one of two things when they read: they either move their lips to sound out the words they're seeing or internally hear their own voice reading to themselves word for word. This is called *subvocalization*.

Many times this speed is a result of how you learned to read. If you learned *phonetically*, you're probably used to sounding out the words, either with your lips or mentally whispering, hearing them in your head, and then comprehending them. It might have been important when you were learning how to read, but when you are a fluent reader, you no longer need to say and hear every word you're reading.

> **Speed Secret**
>
> The fastest you can read while talking word for word is 240 words per minute. Speed talkers may hit 400 words per minute, although they are an elite group. For more on how to kick the talking-while-reading habit, see Chapter 13.

def•i•ni•tion

Phonetics is a method of reading that breaks down language into its simplest components. Children learn the sounds of individual letters first and then the sounds of letters in combination and in simple words. Some know this method as the "look and say" method of reading.

Subvocalization is the learned habit of reading word for word, either mentally or physically. It is also sometimes referred to as *mental whispering*.

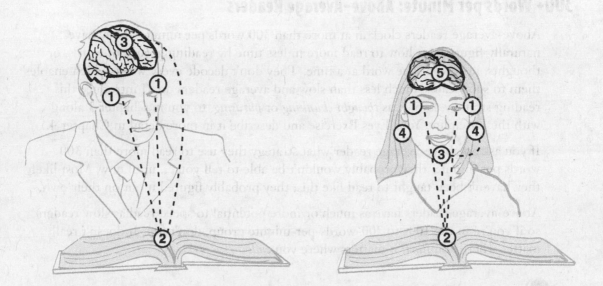

An efficient reader (left) uses his eyes and brain. An inefficient reader (right) uses her eyes and brain as well as her mouth and ears.

You may be thinking that all you have to do to read faster is to zipper your mouth and cork your ears, but unfortunately, it isn't that easy. Do know, however, that you can learn to reduce the talking just by speeding up your reading. Throughout this book, I offer specific suggestions for reducing the talking. But for now, just know that the faster you read, the less word-for-word talking you can do.

200 to 300 Words per Minute: Average Readers

If your reading speed is between 200 and 300 words per minute, you're considered an average reader. Average readers definitely do some internal talking, like the slower readers, but they also do some of what the above-average readers do (more on that in the next section).

This is the most common group for those readers who have not had any reading training since elementary school. But being "average" is not something to be ashamed of! Doctors, lawyers, economists, and other professionals read at this speed. And they have so much to read! Imagine if they could double or even triple their speed.

300+ Words per Minute: Above-Average Readers

Above-average readers clock in at more than 300 words per minute. They have naturally figured out how to read more in less time by reading groups of words, or thoughts, instead of one word at a time. They don't decode every word, which enables them to subvocalize much less than slow and average readers do. (I introduce this reading strategy, known as *thought chunking* or *phrasing*, to you in Chapter 3 along with the Discipline Your Eyes Exercise and describe it in more detail in Chapter 4.)

If you ask an above-average reader what strategy they use to read more than 300 words per minute, they probably wouldn't be able to tell you ... until now. Most likely they haven't been taught to read like this; they probably figured it out on their own.

Above-average readers have as much or more potential to speed read as slow readers, so if you're in the 100- to 200-words-per-minute group, don't fret. It doesn't really matter where you *start*; it matters where you *end*.

Speed Bump

A person needs two things to speed read successfully:

♦ A solid *sight vocabulary* (the ability to see a word and immediately understand what it is and what it means)

♦ A beginning reading speed of more than 100 words per minute

Don't expect as dramatic gains in speed as someone with a starting reading speed of more than 100 words per minute and a good sight vocabulary. Work at your own pace and comprehension level.

700+ Words per Minute: The Excellent Reader

Reading at 700 words per minute or higher is an incredible starting point. It means you already have command of the other speeds (assuming you know how to slow down!) and already get through your material quicker than most. You already know what it's like to move your eyes fast over words and generally trust your brain's ability to comprehend at this speed.

You can easily double or triple your reading speed using the ideas in this book, although some concepts, like looking for key words, might actually slow you down. You'll do well getting to know all the hand and card pacers as described in Chapter 2; they'll immediately accelerate your reading rate.

Shifting Your Reading Speed Gears

When you think of reading speeds, you might believe there are only two speeds: slow and fast. In reality, there are degrees of slow and degrees of fast. After all, speed reading is *not* about reading fast all the time; it's about …

◆ Knowing how and when to speed up and when to slow down.

◆ Reading at the speed appropriate for the material.

◆ Shifting your gears, as needed, for the conditions of the reading road.

◆ Being a flexible reader.

Think of the reading speeds like a five-speed car gear shift, with first gear being the slowest reading speed and fifth gear being overdrive. Right now, you're most likely in either first or second gear. Although you want to get into third, fourth, or fifth gear, you just don't know how … yet.

> **Speed Secret**
>
> When you do have the ability to go into high gear, you'll have more speed choices, making your reading journeys more efficient … and more fun!

The following table details the approximate words-per-minute range, and other pertinent information, for each of the five gears.

	First Gear (Very Slow)	Second Gear (Slow)	Third Gear (Medium)	Fourth Gear (Fast)	Fifth Gear (Overdrive)
Words per minute	Up to 200	150 to 300	300 to 600	600 to 800	800+
Purpose and difficulty of material	Studying; note-taking	Difficult material requiring a high level of comprehension	Average or easy material for good comprehension	Easy material; skimming get the gist of; skimming; scanning	Very easy material to skim
Type of material	Textbooks; new concepts	Technical reports	E-mail, newspapers, magazines	Newspapers, magazines, fiction books, familiar material	Newspapers, magazines, fiction books, very familiar material
Level of background knowledge	Little or none	Little or some	Some to much	Much	Varies

If, by the end of this book, you can double or triple your current reading speed while understanding this gear shift concept, you are well on the road to being a better and faster reader.

Faster Reading Means More Reading Done

In a study done by Jamestown Publishers, readers of different speeds were asked to read for 1 hour a day, 6 days a week using books that were 72,000 words long—approximately the size of a pocket novel. Here are the readers' results for 1 week:

- The slow reader (150 WPM) read ¾ of a book.

- The average reader (250 WPM) read 1¼ books.

- The above-average reader (350 WPM) read 1¾ books.

- The excellent reader (700+ WPM) read 3½ books.

Using this information, the study administrators calculated how many books the readers would read over 10 years:

- The slow reader could read 360 books.

- The average reader could read 600 books.

- The above-average reader could read 840 books.

- The excellent reader could read 1,680 (or more) books.

The reward of adding a few hundred words per minute to your current reading rate is measurably amazing!

Raising Your Reading Speed Comfort Level

We all have various comfort levels. How comfortable are you in a crowd of people? How comfortable are you on an airplane? How comfortable are you speaking in public? How comfortable do you feel driving fast? 70 miles per hour? 85? 110? What about 210 miles per hour, the speed many race car drivers travel? You might not like going that fast, but racers have learned to drive at top speeds because they've raised their comfort level.

How do you raise your reading speed comfort level? First, you need to learn how to be *uncomfortable!* I call this your *discomfort zone.* In this book, you are asked to do things you are not used to, so your comfort will be challenged. To reach higher reading speeds, you need to feel uncomfortable first, because then you know for sure you are working at learning something new.

def•i•ni•tion

> You know you're in your reading **discomfort zone** when you get an uneasy feeling when you're trying something new. Most new speed readers feel it the first few times they try to read fast and realize their comprehension isn't what it should be. This uneasiness is expected, necessary for the learning process, yet temporary. When you learn the new strategy, you reenter the comfort zone at a higher level.

Speed reading is about using reading strategies and also about having a speed reading mind-set. It means believing you *can* read faster and you *will* read faster. It means not being overly concerned about comprehension at first, but knowing that it will follow when your eyes become adept at picking up information in a new way.

If you find yourself in your discomfort zone and want to re-enter the comfort zone with faster speeds under your belt, here are a few ideas:

- *Practice, practice, practice!* Practice on *everything* you read: e-mails, magazines, books, newspapers, and all other daily reading tasks.

- *Remember the gear shift.* You don't always need to read in overdrive. Sometimes third or fourth gear is sufficient.

◆ *Teach others what you know.* When I travel, I read. And when I read, I typically use a pacing technique (described in Chapter 2) that involves using my hands or a card. Inevitably someone asks me what I am doing. When I show them, they are pleasantly surprised and thrilled, which reinforces that what I'm doing really works.

◆ *Don't compare yourself to others.* Your reading abilities are yours and yours alone. You are out to achieve your personal best, not compete in a race.

◆ *Know that you are normal.* In almost every speed reading class I teach, someone wants to know if what they're doing is "normal." My answer is always "yes!" However you interact with these strategies is normal.

Road Conditions for Success

As you approach Chapters 2, 3, and 4, you will find some basic learning conditions to help you reach the higher gears:

◆ *Be confident and have a positive attitude.* Obviously, a positive, can-do attitude supersedes a negative, can't-do one.

Speed Tip

Do you keep a wish list of books you want to read? If not, now is a good time to create that list! Include all the books you want to read but haven't had time. With this list, you'll always have an idea for something good to read.

◆ *Relax.* And I don't mean sleep! Learn to set yourself up in a place that's just comfortable enough, but not too comfortable, with a calm mind and body. (For more specific suggestions on how to set yourself up for calmness, see Chapter 6.)

◆ *Turn pages.* The faster you read, the more important the speed at which you turn pages will be (see Chapter 2).

◆ *Use your hands.* Chapter 2 is dedicated to the hand methods. Have fun experimenting with them and seeing which ones work the best for you.

Learning to Let Go

You've probably been reading the same way for a long time—since you first learned how in elementary school, most likely. How can you convince your mind that it's okay to let go of your old habits and make way for some new ones? Being able to "see" yourself reading fast in your mind's eye is a great way to get your mind primed for learning these new habits.

I think about golf superstar Tiger Woods, who readily admits to using mental visualizations to secure his success. He says: "Visualization is a major part of my shot-making … it's kind of a feeling thing that has been very effective for me during my recent swing change …. Remember the visualization thing, it makes a huge difference in your performance."

To help you implement a little of Tiger's strategy, mentally create this scene:

> Imagine yourself sitting upright at a clean desk or table with a book or magazine article in front of you. No distractions around. You are focused and concentrating on the material in front of you. Mentally answer the questions *Why am I reading this?* and *What do I need it for?* Then, place your finger on the page and pull your eyes down the page much faster than is comfortable—and have fun doing it! You are amazed at how much you still understand. The reading piles are quickly gone or at least under control. You now find time for reading because you find reading effortless and relaxing.

Now let's put the visualization exercise into real practice:

> Set yourself up at a clean desk or table with a book or magazine article in front of you. No distractions around. You are focused and concentrating on the material in front of you. You mentally answer the questions *Why am I reading this?* and *What do I need it for?* Time yourself for 1 minute as you read, pulling your finger down each page quickly to glean a few ideas but not everything. Try to advance to a new page every 5 to 10 seconds. Mark where you started and stopped. Write down what you think you read about.

Did you have fun? Did you surprise yourself at how much you were able to write down? Whatever your experience, at least you got started on seeing yourself reading in a new way!

Taking Short, Frequent Breaks

When you first take up running as a form of exercise, you typically don't (or can't!) run for long stretches without a break. You may even start to run for just 100 yards, walk for 200 yards, run for 100 yards again, and so on. Every time you run, you get a little better, and go farther without taking a break.

The same is true for speed reading. When you first start, you may only be able to go a few paragraphs and then need to or naturally slow down. You resume your speed reading efforts again after a short break or after a few lines of reading in your "normal" way. The more you practice this way, the sooner you are able to go longer stretches without needing a break.

When you're more skilled in speed reading, still take frequent 5-minute breaks every 30 to 60 minutes to give your eyes and brain a break. They need this time to assimilate all you're reading and gather energy to continue.

There is no one best way to read, just the way—or ways—that works best for you!

Reading Horizontally and Vertically

The most skilled speed readers can quickly read across lines horizontally *and* read several lines vertically in one glance. Their *peripheral vision* is very wide, and they can pick up a lot of information in a glance.

def•i•ni•tion

> **Peripheral vision** is what your eyes see outside their central area of focus. You can widen your central area of focus because of your peripheral vision.

As you begin to break out of the word-for-word habit (if this is your issue), you'll start seeing more words in a glance horizontally. As you continue to read wide horizontally, you can then work on stretching your vision vertically. The easiest material to play with is anything with narrow columns, or about six words per line, such as newspaper or magazine columns.

The Value of Comprehension

Speed reading without comprehension is called *speed looking*. To learn to speed *read*, you need to separate comprehension from speed development. This can be difficult, especially when you've been taught to read every word and if you don't understand it, go back and reread it. But in the following chapters, I encourage you to *not* read every word (see Chapters 3 and 4) and to learn to be comfortable without comprehension, *temporarily* (see Chapter 5).

Speed Tip

> Vertical peripheral vision typically doesn't take place without horizontal vision, so work on that first.

Comprehension isn't the only thing affected by speed. *The faster you read, the more you have to concentrate.* Think about it. When running, you have to focus more on where you're going than you do when you're walking. When you're driving really fast, you have to focus more on where you're going than you do when you're driving slowly. The same is true with reading. You immediately reduce daydreaming (see Chapter 13) and concentrate more the faster you go.

As a result of your improved concentration, you have a stronger chance of better comprehension. And with better understanding comes a much higher chance of retention.

> **Speed Secret**
>
> Faster reading speed leads to more concentration, which leads to more comprehension, which leads to stronger retention.

The Value of Background Knowledge

The more you already know, the easier reading is. The more vocabulary you have, the easier it is to predict the words you're reading. The more life experience you have, the easier it is to understand a wide range of reading materials and genres. This is your *background knowledge*. It's very personal to you; it's a result of all you've experienced in your life. It's extremely valuable for aiding in the increase of reading speed and securing comprehension. Think about it: if you know something about what you're reading before you begin, isn't it an easier read than if you had no idea what you were reading about?

When you read material unfamiliar to you—which so much is—you might think your comprehension would be compromised. In some cases, yes, but in most cases, you probably have some glimmer of background knowledge that, when applied, leads you to better understanding of what you're reading. This is what I call *building bridges of knowledge*. When you read about something new, you relate it to some of your existing background knowledge and stick the two together. This is how you gain more background knowledge.

def•i•ni•tion

> Your **background knowledge** is the accumulation of knowledge gained through personal experiences. The trips you take, the people you talk to, the teachers you learn from … all these and more contribute to your background knowledge. In your day-to-day life, and especially when you read, you are constantly learning new things, creating more background knowledge.

So what can you do to deliberately create more background knowledge? Here are some ideas to consider:

♦ Before reading, think about how much you already know about the topic.

◆ Preview (I call it *cheat reading*) your reading material to get some background knowledge before you jump in (see Chapter 7).

◆ Ask questions and satisfy your inborn curiosity.

◆ Listen more than you talk so you can really hear what others are saying.

◆ Travel to new places and experience a variety of transportation means such as bus, train, and airplane.

◆ Engage in stimulating conversations with others and learn from them.

◆ Build a broad vocabulary.

◆ Regularly experience new things.

◆ Read widely on topics you enjoy and dip into some areas you've not yet been exposed to.

◆ Get a copy of *The Dictionary of Cultural Literacy* and read a little every day.

Sometimes, your background knowledge may seem inadequate for new learning activities like taking a college course or getting a new job. No matter what we do, it takes some time and personal experience to get our background knowledge in an ideal state for faster reading and good comprehension.

The Least You Need to Know

◆ Calculating your baseline reading speed and comprehension is vital to knowing who you are as a reader and what possibilities lie ahead for you.

◆ Reading faster is a conscious choice, and not everything needs to be read fast or slow.

◆ When you learn how to read faster, expect to go into the discomfort zone—a feeling of unease—because you are reading differently.

◆ When you first learn to read faster, your comprehension tends to temporarily go down. This is a temporary yet necessary part of reading development.

◆ You can use visualization to help create your speed reading mind-set.

◆ The more background knowledge you have, the easier it is to read with speed and good comprehension.

Chapter

2

Winning Hands Down

In This Chapter

◆ Help from your hands

◆ The importance of column width

◆ Finger methods 101

◆ Keep your place and concentrate

◆ Turn, turn, turn the page

Pick up any speed reading book, including this one, and you'll find information on the value of using a hand or card as a guide when reading. This is, hands down, *the* best strategy for increasing your reading speed. In this chapter, I introduce you to 13 proven ways you can use your hands or a card to improve your reading speed. It's your job to figure out which one(s) work best for you.

But here's the tricky part: you've probably been reading without using your hands, so you can expect to enter your discomfort zone, albeit temporarily, when you try the methods in this chapter. But the positive results you get from using these methods, including a speed increase and stronger concentration (which in a short time leads to better comprehension), will sell you on the need to use them. And the more you use them, the more comfortable you will become. Try them all on a variety of materials and decide which one(s) are best for you!

Faster Reading at Your Fingertips

Perhaps the concept of reading with your fingers isn't as foreign to you as you might think. After all, when you look for a number in the telephone book, do you use your finger to read down the columns of names? Or when you're looking back in an article you read for some important fact, do you use your fingers to skim down the page? Many people do.

def•i•ni•tion

A **pacer** is a visual guide—your fingers, whole hand, or a card to move your eyes down and across the lines of text with the results of increased concentration and faster reading speeds.

Speed Secret

When you read, you use your eye muscles to push and pull your eyes across and back over lines. Your hand is a stronger muscle and, when added to the page, adeptly forces your eyes to move along with it.

Using your hands or a card, or any other kind of *pacer* when reading has many benefits:

♦ It forces your eyes to focus on a line or section of words.

♦ It naturally encourages concentration.

♦ It forces your eyes to move in a directed pattern across and/or down the page.

♦ It guides your eyes to keep their place and to find the next line accurately.

♦ It involves more of your body in the reading process, which keeps you alert.

♦ It capitalizes on the human phenomenon where your eyes naturally follow movement. (If you are reading at the kitchen table and a fly flew over the table, your eyes would be attracted to it. If you were sitting in a room with windows, anything that went by the window would attract your eyes and attention. So intentionally putting movement on a page will encourage your eyes to follow that movement.)

♦ Ultimately, it allows you to read with speed!

Using a pacer is *the* best way to get into high gears while reading. If you want to get into third, fourth, or fifth gears, add your hands or a card to the page!

When to Use Pacers, and When You Don't Need To

Readers new to using pacers sometimes believe they have to use the method all the time and on everything. At first, you do want to experiment with it on all your reading. The more practice you have, the quicker you'll get used to reading with a pacer and the more comfortable you'll become reading at faster speeds.

Think of a race horse and jockey. The horse comes out of the gate with a lot of energy, and the jockey uses the riding crop repeatedly to stir the horse into keeping pace with the other horses. He doesn't have to use the crop when the horse is running fast. However, when the horse's energy starts to falter, the jockey uses the crop to push the horse toward the finish line with speed.

Reading with a pacer is a similar process. You start reading using your preferred method with a lot of energy and speed. As you continue to read, you find your eyes and brain reading quickly on their own and naturally find that you don't need the pacer. Then for many reasons, such as coming upon unfamiliar material, excessive daydreaming, or various interruptions, you see your speed slipping. Now's the time to use your pacer again to get you back up to speed.

Speed Tip _____

Use pacers to help you focus, concentrate, and stay awake, especially when you have a lot to read and not much time to do it in.

Some Challenges Ahead

Try all the pacers in this chapter, even if it's only for a minute for each, so you can find the ones that work best for you. Start by experimenting with some of your own reading material—any text will do. Then move on to the articles in Appendix B.

Force yourself to read faster, and remember that it's okay to forego comprehension while you're in this learning phase. Push your fingers or card faster than you're comfortable so your eyes will get used to viewing text faster than your brain can process. *This potential loss of comprehension is temporary and will come back the same—or better!—in a short period of time with experience.*

Columns: Wide or Narrow?

Which do you think is easier to read, wide columns or narrow columns? Wide column text takes up the entire print space of the page going from the left margin to the right, making the lines you read long as well as the return sweep of your eyes back to the next line. The average number of words in a wide column, either on paper or on-screen depending on the page size, is 18 to 25 words. Research recently conducted by

def•i•ni•tion

Regression, also known as *back-skipping,* is when your eyes go back over words they've already read.

Speed Tip

When reading wide or narrow columns, use a pacer to help you keep your place and reduce regressions. You can also use other reading strategies like reading bigger words and thought chunks to keep your eyes moving fluidly across the lines (see Chapter 4).

IBM shows that readers of wide columns with long line lengths have less comprehension and *regress* more than readers of narrow columns.

Narrow column text is laid out in columns of six to eight words across, making the eyes sweep more across the lines but reducing the need to regress. The IBM research showed readers of shorter line lengths read a little faster and had better comprehension than those reading longer line lengths. Newspapers and magazines use narrow columns because they pay attention to the research and know people can read and absorb better when reading narrow columns.

In preparation for experimenting with these hand and card strategies, find some reading material that contains wide columns (long line lengths) and narrow columns (short line lengths). (Magazines typically have some of both.) Sit at a desk or table so your reading material is on a hard surface, not on your lap or suspended in the air.

Single Finger Methods

Reading with one finger is a simple way to familiarize yourself with reading with your hand, and I introduce you to five different finger methods in the following paragraphs:

- Left Pointer Pull (B)
- Right Pointer Pull (B)
- Center Pointer Pull (N)
- Z Pattern (N)
- S Pattern (N)

You'll notice the similarities between the five methods, but each one is unique and worth practicing to help you determine the best methods for you.

Left Pointer Pull (B)

Left Pointer Pull is a great method for keeping your place and for encouraging your eyes to complete their journey accurately back to the beginning of the next line.

Here's how to do it:

1. Start by pointing the index finger of either hand and curling in your remaining fingers. (Like you're giving the "We're number 1!" sign.)

2. Place your pointer finger on the left margin of the first line of text.

3. Start reading, moving your eyes to the right, and slowly move your left pointer finger down the left margin to the next line as your eyes approach the end of the first line.

4. Continue moving your pointer down the left margin. Encourage your eyes to move faster across the lines to meet your finger at the beginning of the next line.

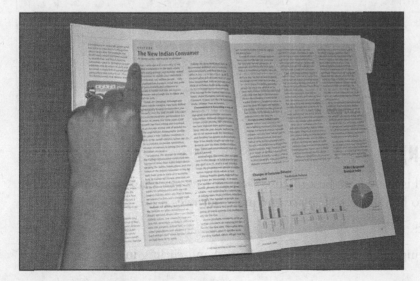

Starting finger position for the Left Pointer Pull.

Right Pointer Pull (B)

Right Pointer Pull is the exact opposite of the Left Pointer Pull. Instead of placing your pointer finger at the beginning of the line, on the left margin, you place it at the right margin. You read *to* your finger now instead of *from* your finger as before.

Here's how to do it:

1. Start by pointing the index finger of either hand and curling in your remaining fingers.

2. Place your pointer finger on the right margin of the first line of text.

3. Start reading, moving your eyes to the right, and slowly move your right pointer finger down the right margin to the next line after your eyes reach the end of the line.

4. Continue moving your pointer down the right margin. Encourage your eyes to move faster across the lines to meet your finger at the end of the line.

Starting finger position for the Right Pointer Pull.

Center Pointer Pull (N)

Center Pointer Pull is one of the best methods for narrow newspaper or magazine columns. It's used to help keep your place and pull your eyes down the text.

Here's how to do it:

1. Start by pointing the index finger of either hand and curling in your remaining fingers.

2. Place your pointer finger in the center of the column under the first line of text.

3. Start reading, moving your eyes to the right, and slowly move your pointer finger down the center as your eyes move left to right.

4. Continue moving your pointer down the center of the column. Encourage your eyes to move faster across the lines.

Speed Tip

When you have a little experience with Center Pointer Pull, try placing your hand a few lines below the line you're on to encourage you to spread your peripheral vision.

Starting finger position for the Center Pointer Pull.

Z Pattern (N)

The Z Pattern method and the S Pattern method that follows are the slowest of all the pacers, but are still good for guiding your eyes and keeping your place. Try this or the S on a newspaper or magazine with narrow columns.

Here's how to do it:

1. Start by pointing the index finger of either hand and curling in your remaining fingers.

2. Place your pointer finger on the left margin of the first line of text.

3. Move your finger across and under the first line you're reading.

Starting point of the Z Pattern pacer.

Your finger starts to draw the letter Z by moving your hand across the first line of text.

4. When you reach the end of the first line, move your finger diagonally down and back to the beginning of a line a few lines down to draw the middle part of the letter Z. As your hand draws back here, you move your eyes back and forth across the lines as quickly as you can to meet with your finger at the beginning of the line it lands on.

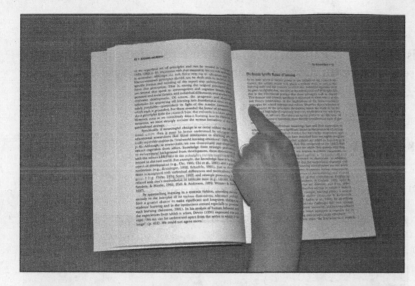

Continue drawing the letter Z by moving your finger diagonally down a few lines back to the left margin.

5. Move your finger across and under the line you're on to make the Z complete.

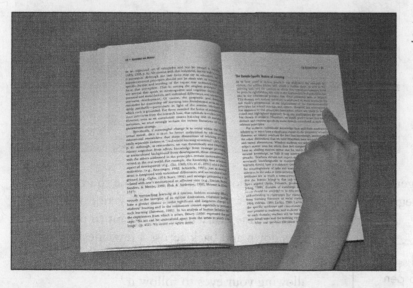

Finish your Z by moving your hand across the line of text you're on.

Continue with steps 3, 4, and 5 until you're done with your reading or don't need your pacer anymore.

S Pattern (N)

The S Pattern pacer is similar to Z Pattern, but in it you use rounded curves to move your hand. You can use S Pattern for detailed reading, although many use it for skimming.

Here's how to do it:

1. Start by pointing the index finger of either hand and curling in your remaining fingers.

2. Place your finger in the middle of the first line of text.

Starting point of the
S Pattern pacer.

3. Move your finger across the line and then down in a curve shape to eventually return to the beginning of another line a few lines down. This is not meant to underline every line; it's meant to pull your eyes down and back across a few lines at a time.

Speed Tip _____

If you want, you can use an unsharpened pencil, a pen (with the cap on), or a highlighter instead of your finger. This is especially useful if you are taking notes or highlighting while you're reading.

4. Continue moving your finger in an S Pattern, allowing your eyes to follow it.

Continue with steps 3 and 4 until you're done with your reading or don't need your pacer anymore.

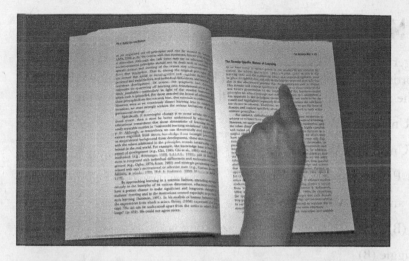

Move your finger in a curve-shape pattern down a few lines.

Continue to move your finger in an S curve-shape pattern down a few more lines.

Staying close to the center, continue moving your finger in an S curve-shape pattern.

Multiple Finger Methods

Using a multiple finger method gives you more control over your reading. You get to decide how many words to focus on at one time and how quickly you move through the text. These are the multiple finger methods we'll look at in the following sections:

- Long-Smooth Underline (W)

- Short-Smooth Underline (W)

- Double Pointer Pull (B, especially W)

- The Vulcan (N and some W)

- Point-to-Point (B)

- Open Hand Wiggle (B)

Try each one on your own material and on a 1-minute timing to see which one(s) work best for you.

Long-Smooth Underline (W)

Wide columns are more challenging to read because of the distance your eyes travel across the lines and the long jump back to the beginning of the next line. Try Long-Smooth Underline to make wide-column reading easier.

Here's how to do it:

1. Using your index finger, middle finger, and ring finger, point your fingers, pulling back your middle finger so it's equal in length to other two fingers. Curl your thumb and pinky comfortably inside your palm.

2. Rest your forearm on a desk or table, and place the reading material under your hand.

3. Place your three fingers at the beginning of the line under the line of text you're starting on, and follow your fingers across the line to the end. Quickly move your hand back to the beginning of the next line. You're not reading (stopping your eyes) on the return, so your hand should be moving very quickly here.

4. Continue moving your three fingers back and forth under the lines as quickly as you can, reading the text as you proceed. Although it might feel somewhat frantic, know that you are in control.

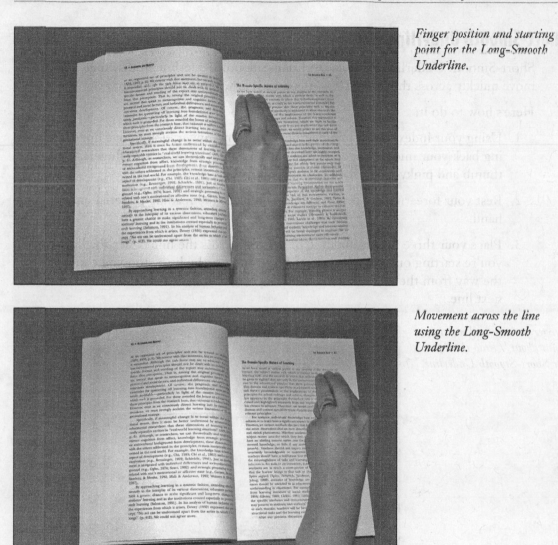

Finger position and starting point for the Long-Smooth Underline.

Movement across the line using the Long-Smooth Underline.

To help this become a very quick movement back and forth, let your forearm move your hand. If you don't, you may find your hand getting tired too soon.

Speed Tip

When using Long-Smooth Underline as a pacer, let your fingers pull your eyes along. You should sense that your eyes are being pulled along by your hand.

Short-Smooth Underline (W)

Short-Smooth Underline is similar to Long-Smooth Underline in that they both move quickly across the lines. The difference is how far across they go.

Here's how to do it:

1. Using your index finger, middle finger, and ring finger, point your fingers, pulling back your middle finger so it's equal in length to other two fingers. Curl your thumb and pinky comfortably inside your palm.

2. Rest your forearm on a desk or table, and place the reading material under your hand.

3. Place your three fingers about $1/4$ of the way across the line under the line of text you're starting on, and follow your fingers across the line, stopping about $1/4$ of the way from the end of the line. Move your hand back to the $1/4$ indent of the next line.

Finger position and starting point about $1/4$ into the line for Short-Smooth Underline.

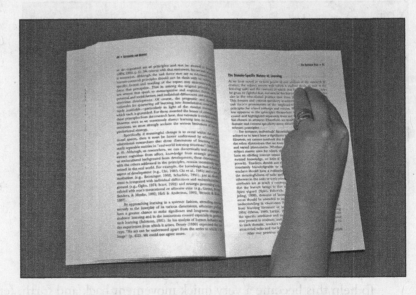

In effect, you are only underlining the middle $1/2$ of the line and your eyes are stretching left and right to read peripherally what you aren't underlining with your fingers.

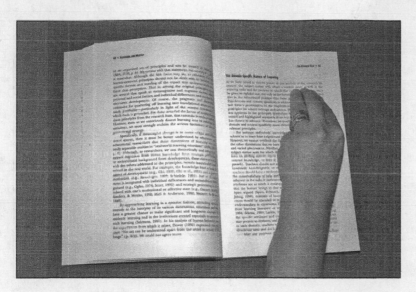

Movement across the line, stopping about $\frac{1}{4}$ from the end of the line.

4. Continue moving your three fingers back and forth under the middle $\frac{1}{2}$ of the text as quickly as you can.

Although your pace will feel a bit slower than when using Long-Smooth Underline, you may still feel somewhat frantic because you're taking in more words.

Speed Bump

If you go too slowly with either Long-Smooth Underline or Short-Smooth Underline, you'll tempt yourself to point to each word, which will slow you down big time. For the best results, keep your hand moving.

Double Pointer Pull (B, W)

Double Pointer Pull encourages a quick left-to-right eye movement going from one fingertip to the other. It helps you focus on pages with a lot of words and especially on pages with wide columns.

Here's how to do it:

1. Point your index fingers out from each hand, curling your remaining fingers in toward your palms with your thumbs tucked around your middle fingers.

2. Place your left pointer finger at the left margin of the line you're reading, and place your right pointer finger at the right margin of the same line.

Starting finger position and location for the Double Pointer Pull.

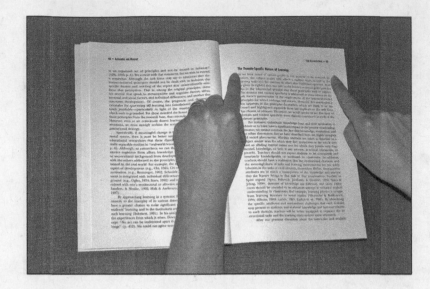

3. Move your eyes from the left to the right while you pull your fingers down the page, line by line. If you go fast enough, you'll feel as if your eyes are bouncing from fingertip to fingertip.

Fingers continue down the left and right margins while the eyes move left and right in Double Pointer Pull.

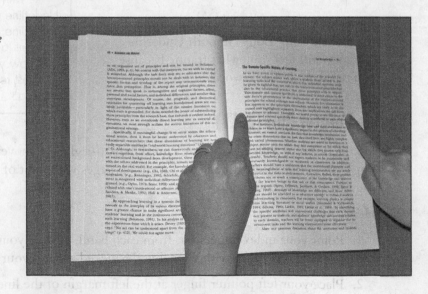

The Vulcan (N, and Some W)

I have dubbed this method the Vulcan because your hand looks like the hand position Vulcans used on *Star Trek*. It's not one I've seen mentioned in other books, but it is a method I've seen people use creatively and effectively, without formal instruction. Here's how to do it:

1. With your left hand closed in a fist, point your pinky and pointer (index) fingers only.

2. Place your pinky finger at the beginning of the first word on the left margin and your pointer finger at the end of the same line. You might need to adjust your hand position to get your fingers to line up evenly. (If you prefer to use your right hand, place your pointer finger at the beginning of the first word of the line and your pinky finger at the end of the same line.)

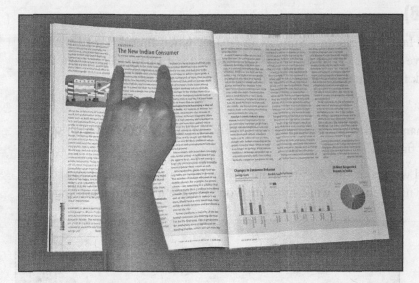

Finger position and starting point for the Vulcan.

3. Pull your fingers straight down as you move your eyes quickly left to right.

Point-to-Point (B)

Point-to-Point is a more active version of the Vulcan. You can use it on both size columns and to help you establish a reading rhythm.

Speed Tip

Be careful of your line lengths: if too wide, your fingers will be spread too wide, making it uncomfortable to read for any length of time. In this case, you can use Point-to-Point (see the following section).

Here's how to do it:

1. With your left hand closed in a fist, point your pinky and pointer (index) fingers only.

2. Touch your pinky fingertip on a word about $\frac{1}{3}$ of the way in from the left margin. Your pointer fingertip should be hanging in the air, waiting for its job, which will be to touch a word about $\frac{1}{3}$ from the end of the line. When your pointer touches down, raise up your pinky finger. (If you use your right hand, touch your pointer finger about $\frac{1}{3}$ in from the left margin. Your pinky should be hanging in the air. Then touch your pinky fingertip about $\frac{1}{3}$ from the end of the line.)

3. Read with your eyes going across the lines touching the left part of the line and then the right part, creating a tennis match–like rhythm.

Open Hand Wiggle (B)

I like to use Open Hand Wiggle on a Sunday newspaper when there's a lot I want to read and I don't have all day to read it. The only downside, if I dare call it that, is that my fingers get black from the newsprint. Nothing soap and water can't fix!

Here's how to do it:

1. Open either hand with your fingers comfortably extending outward with space between your fingers.

2. Lay your hand with your middle finger approximately in the center of the column. In effect, your middle finger will be guiding you because it's the longest finger.

Finger position and starting point for Open Hand Wiggle.

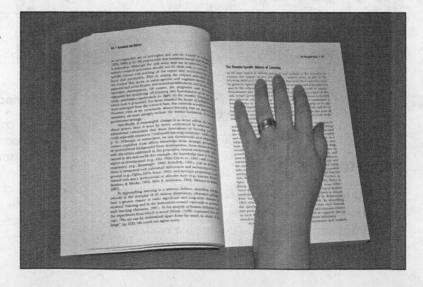

3. Wiggle your hand back and forth in an S-type motion, pulling your hand quickly down the page while your eyes read left to right. It may help to act as if you're dusting or erasing the words on the page.

Card Methods

As an alternative to reading with your hands, you can use a blank white card to speed up your reading. White (or colored) index cards without lines or the back side of a business card all work well. If the card contains writing, your eyes will be distracted, so blank is better.

Here are the card methods we'll look at:

◆ Blank Card (B)

◆ White Card Cutout (B)

Blank Card

Many people really like this method because the card's straight edge is easy to follow and they don't have to be concerned with how they're moving their fingers.

Here's how to do it:

1. Place your white card *on top of* or *over* the line you're reading. Adjust the width of the card to match the width of the column.

2. Move your eyes from left to right as you push the card down the page. The straight edge helps you develop smooth eye movements across the lines.

> **Speed Secret**
>
> Use different size blank cards depending on the column width: use a 3×5 or business card size for narrow columns, or tape two smaller cards together for wider columns. You can also use 4×8 or 5×8 blank cards.

 Speed Bump

> Do not place your blank card *under* the line you're reading. This encourages you to go back over the material, double-checking your comprehension and not trusting your brain. It also blocks the upcoming words you're yet to read. It's best to place the card *on top*, which reduces the temptation to go back and pushes you to read the text in front of you that your eyes are eager to read.

White card position and starting point for the Blank Card Method.

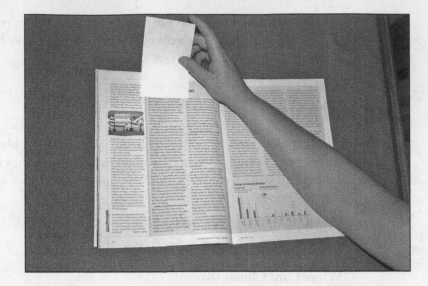

White Card Cutout (B)

I don't see many people using this method, but the people who do use it tell me about their success with it. Try it—you might like it!

Here's how to do it:

1. Have a few sizes of blank cards available or use a regular piece of blank white paper. Choose your reading material and notice the column width.

2. Fold your card or paper in half and lay the folded edge under the first line of the column. Make one pencil mark on the card where the text begins on the left and one where the text ends at the end of the column on the right.

3. Starting at one pencil point, cut the card away from the fold about the height of one line of text. Make a matching cut up on the other pencil mark. Now make a parallel cut to the fold going across to the other cut. When you open your card, you should have a window the width of the column and a few lines high.

4. Place your cutout card over your text, exposing the first few lines of text. The first line should be at the top margin of your card.

5. Move your card down as quickly as you can while moving your eyes left to right. Your eyes will have to focus on the exposed lines only. This might prove less distracting because you can't see the other words on the page.

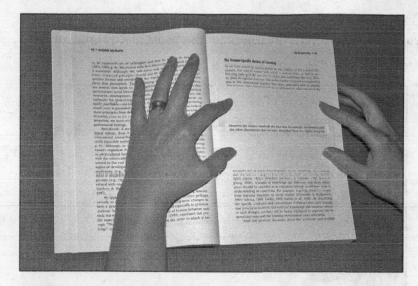

Sample card cutout placed on the page.

Fast Page Turning

While you're learning to speed read, it also helps to learn how to turn pages quickly because your speed can sometimes be limited to how fast you can turn the pages. Right-handed readers have a little more to learn, while left-handed readers will find this easily doable.

If you're reading a new book or magazine, you might want to relax the spine so the pages lay flat before you begin reading. Starting from the front of the book, run your fingers up and down the spine, pressing into the book every few pages to relax the spine.

Here's a quick process for how to turn more pages in less time:

For right-handed readers:

1. Grasp the top-right-side page of the material with your left hand. Curl your arm up and around the book at the top so your arm is above the material, and create a straight line of sorts from your elbow to your wrist.

2. Start reading quickly with your pacer. With your left hand, simultaneously grasp the next page in preparation for turning.

Speed Bump

Relax a book's spine just enough to lay the book flat for use with any of these methods. If you force it too much, you might break the spine, which wouldn't be good if you borrowed it from a friend or the library.

3. When your eyes approach the bottom of the right page and you're ready for the next page, use your left hand to turn the page and resume its place at the top of the material.

Arm and hand fast page-turning position for right-handed readers.

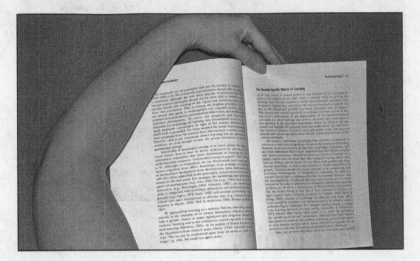

For left-handed readers:

1. Position your right hand at either the top or the bottom of the right page.

2. Start reading with your left hand.

3. When you approach the bottom of the right page, use your right hand to quickly turn the page.

And the Results Are ...

Throughout this chapter you were introduced to many possible options for speeding up your reading. You probably liked some more than others, and that's fine. The idea is to find the one(s) that works best for you. An easy way to know which might be suited to you is by timing yourself using the pacers.

One-Minute Timing

If you haven't already done a One-Minute Timing, now is the time! If you're really serious about trying them all, you can conduct a One-Minute Timing using each of the pacers, or just a few as your time and interest allow. The longest it would take is 15 minutes—13 minutes to time yourself and 2 minutes to document your results. Here you're looking more for speed than comprehension; you'll evaluate your comprehension in subsequent exercises.

Turn to Appendix B for the One-Minute Timing instructions and Appendix C for your progress chart.

3-2-1 Drill

You can also practice with the 3-2-1 Drill. This really challenges you to read quicker and get your eyes and brain to start communicating better and faster. It goes like this:

1. Choose any reading in Appendix B. Time yourself reading for 3 minutes with a pacer of your choice. Concentrate on comprehension.

2. When your time is up, mark the line you're on. How far did you go?

3. Write down the key comprehension points you remember on a separate piece of paper, *without* referring back to the reading.

4. Next, time yourself for 2 minutes reading the same material and stopping at the same place you stopped in 3 minutes. You'll have to speed up your reading! Add more key points after you're done reading.

5. To really challenge yourself, read the same material for just 1 minute, stopping at the same place you did for the 3-minute timing. Add more key points.

Keep track of your results on the "3-2-1 Speed Drill Personal Progress Chart" in Appendix C.

The 3-2-1 Drill conditions your eyes to know what it feels like to move quickly across and down the lines and your brain to get used to seeing more words faster. It will start to familiarize your brain with the speed at which you wish to read and force it to grasp comprehension in a shorter period of time.

Speed Tip _____

To tally your words per minute, multiply the number of lines you read in the article by the average number of words per line (noted at the beginning of each reading).

The Least You Need to Know

◆ Adding your hands or a pacer card to your reading helps you read faster, keep your place, and concentrate better.

◆ Being aware of the column width is important for choosing which pacer strategy is best.

◆ There are two kinds of hand methods: single finger and multiple finger; each have at least five variations for you to choose from.

◆ One of the two card methods might help you increase your reading speed.

◆ Your speed may be limited by how fast you can turn pages. Learn to turn them faster, and you will read faster.

Peripheral Vision and the Power of Prediction

In This Chapter

◆ Bigger stops and faster jumps

◆ Increase your peripheral vision

◆ Open your eyes to new possibilities

◆ Some new reading strategies

◆ Your eyes—give 'em a break

Have you ever watched someone's eyes and mouth while they were reading to themselves? Some people's eyes move slowly, stopping on every word. Some move their eyes forward a few words and then backtrack over words they just read. Still others mouth the words silently, even to the point of whispering.

Speed readers move their eyes quickly, consistently, and rhythmically across the lines, rarely backtracking and never moving their lips. They have also learned how to expand their peripheral vision to see more words at a time. After reading this chapter, you'll know how to do this, too!

What Your Eyes Do When They Read

When you read, your eyes stop, or *fixate*, on one or more words. In between each stop, they *saccade*, or jump, to the next word or words. The average reader makes 4 stops per second, which means your eyes stop every $\frac{1}{4}$ second. It also means you can only read 4 words in 1 second. Although 4 words per second might seem like a lot, trust me when I say you can do better than that!

If you learned to read by the phonics method (sounding out every word and then hearing it in your head before understanding it), it makes sense that you may still be individually decoding words while you read silently. This means you stop your eyes on one word at a time and have a *narrow eye span*. Skilled speed readers have learned to expand their peripheral vision. Their *wide eye span*, both horizontally and vertically, enables them to see more than one word at a time. And that means gaining reading speed.

def•i•ni•tion

A **fixation,** or eye *stop*, is a coordinated positioning and focusing of both eyes on a word. A **saccade,** or eye *jump*, is the series of small, jerky movements the eyes make when changing focus from one point to another. If you read word for word, you have a **narrow eye span;** you've been trained to see and process one word at a time. If you read more than one word at a time, you have a **wide eye span.** Faster readers read fast because they pick up more words in an eye stop than slower readers.

Let's look at some examples of different types of readers and where their eye stops fall. Each stop is numbered above the letter, word, or phrase. Can you figure out which kind of reader you currently are?

The *slow, word-by-word reader* has 12 individual eye stops or 3 seconds of reading time ($\frac{1}{4}$ second per stop × 12):

1	2	3	4	5	6	7	8	9	10
The	best	way	to	read	faster	is	by	expanding	your

11	12
peripheral	vision.

The *faster reader* has 5 eye stops, or 1¼ second of reading time:

1	2	3		4
The best way to	read faster is	by	expanding	your

	5		
peripheral		vision.	

The *fastest reader* has 2 eye stops, or ½ second of reading time:

1		2	
The best	way	to read faster is by expanding	your peripheral vision.

Remove Your Blinders

Your success as a speed reader depends on your ability to increase your peripheral vision, both horizontally, so you see more across a line, and eventually vertically, so you see more above and below the line you're reading.

Right now, it's like your eyes have had blinders on. Consider horse-drawn carriages in large cities that take visitors around the busy streets. The horses wear blinders on the outside of their eyes to focus their attention straight ahead and to avoid distractions. You may have used your reading "blinders" in a similar fashion to keep your focus on one word at a time and to avoid being overwhelmed by the other words around you. To become a great speed reader, you must go forth bravely into the world … without your blinders.

You can help your eyes adjust and capitalize on this newfound visual freedom with some fun exercises (I give you some later in the chapter). Your ultimate goal is to control your eyes so they move rhythmically and smoothly across and down the text. Although at first your brain will race to keep up, by frequently experimenting with the strategies in this book over a short period of time, it will come around and function clearly—and more efficiently (see Chapter 5).

The Power of Prediction

We make predictions all the time. Who's going to run for president? What's going to happen to the movie's hero or heroine? Who's going to win the big game? Predictions keep us involved and force us to think ahead. The same is true for reading: if we make predictions, we are more involved and can read faster with solid understanding.

Try reading this:

Tihs is naet:

The phaomnneil pweor of the hmuan mnid. Aoccdrnig to a rscheearch taem at Cmabrigde Uinervtisy, it deosn't mttaer in what oredr the ltteers in a wrod are; the olny iprmoetnt tihng is taht the frist and lsat ltteer be at the rghit pclae. The rset can be a total mses and you can sitll raed it wouthit porbelm. Tihs is bcuseae the huamn mnid deos not raed ervey lteter by istlef, but the wrod as a wlohe.

Are you surprised by how much of this you could read? Your brain had to predict the words based on what you know—here's where background knowledge (see Chapter 1) comes in handy!—so you could understand what you were seeing. Thankfully, when you read most other text, it doesn't look like this, making it even easier to make predictions. Trust that your brain will work hard in your favor and make accurate predictions most of the time.

Teach Your Eyes New Tricks

Let's work on your eyes! To do so, you need to first leave your brain behind ... but only temporarily. Comprehension can't be a concern, for now. Your eyes first need to mechanically learn how to pick up more information at a glance before even attempting to understand it.

In the following sections, I give you several exercises to train your eyes. Try them all and pick your favorite to play with often.

The Left-Right Exercise

Let's start with one of my favorite ones, the Left-Right Exercise. You can do this exercise almost anywhere, at any time. It works especially well using a wall because you can follow the straight-line seam created where the wall meets the ceiling.

1. Wherever you're seated, and after reading these directions, pick your head up from the book and look straight ahead.

2. Continue looking straight ahead and don't move your head.

3. Look left—but don't move your head!—and locate a spot as far as your eyes can see without straining.

4. Then move your eyes to the right—not your head!—to locate a spot the same height as the left point and as far as your eyes can see without straining.

5. Start with the left point and then, without moving your head, move your eyes to the right point. Move back to the left and then to the right, gradually going a little faster each time. Challenge yourself to go as fast as you can and as smoothly as you can for 10 round trips back and forth. Avoid blinking, but if necessary, limit it to once or twice during the 10 round-trips.

The more you do this exercise, the smoother your eye movements become and the more stretched out your eye muscles get, creating the framework for a wider eye span.

A Cut Above

Here's a neat trick: if you cut a sentence horizontally in half and tried to read it using just the top of the letters, you could easily understand it. But if you tried to read below the cut, you'd have a hard time. This is because the top of the line contains the shape of the letters you're most familiar with. The bottom doesn't.

While I was facilitating a training class for a federal government agency, I was told that all their e-mails HAD to be written in ALL capital letters. BESIDES THE FACT THAT BUSINESS E-MAIL ETIQUETTE STATES THAT WHEN YOU USE ALL CAPITAL LETTERS, YOU ARE SCREAMING, IMAGINE TRYING TO READ EVERYTHING IN CAPITAL LETTERS LIKE THIS. IT'S LIKE TRYING TO READ THE BOTTOM HALF OF THE LETTERS ALL THE TIME. When you read the tops of letters, you can follow the rounded shape of lowercase letters, which allows you to make word predictions based on what you already know. All capital letters have straight lines on the top, making it difficult to make predictions.

Can you read this?

Did you know that the typical businessperson spends an average of 2 or 3 hours per day on e-mail? Sadly, many don't plan for this time in their workday and are, therefore, forced to work more hours than needed.

Now try this:

Did you know that the typical businessperson spends an average of 2 or 3 hours per day on e-mail? Sadly, many don't plan for this time in their workday and are therefore, forced to work more hours than needed.

If you found the second example easier, all you need to do is to focus your eyes on the top of the words by fixating your eyes on the blank space between the lines. Your eyes will naturally be attracted to the top half of the words, which is easier to read and begins your quest for reading vertically.

The License Plate Game

When taking long car trips, my family and I played the "license plate game" to pass the time. We each picked a state, not the one we were in but usually one nearby, and challenged each other to find the most cars with that state's license plate.

This game is great for your eyes because it forces you to look at a speeding vehicle, quickly identify the state it is from, and then "read" aloud the letters or numbers to confirm with the other players which car you saw. If you read off the license plate incorrectly, you wouldn't get credit for that car. This fun game strengthens your ability to process pictures, colors, and letters quickly when you read. This inevitably helps you read faster.

Another version of this game can be done while you're walking down the street. Very quickly steal a look at a poster in a store window, a truck with writing on the side passing by, a menu posted outside a restaurant, or other writing you see and then immediately turn away and try to recall what you saw. Check yourself by looking at it again.

This game forces you to look quickly and make a prediction and challenges you to spread your peripheral vision to read it all. This is a foundation for increasing your reading speed.

Squeeze the Margins

Reading a newspaper column is quite different from reading an e-mail. It's not just the content that's different, but also the column width. The average newspaper column is 6 words across, while an average e-mail is anywhere from 18 to 25 words across. The eye jump from the end of one line to the beginning of the next line is much longer on an e-mail than a newspaper, which makes it hard for your eyes to find the next line accurately. Positioning your pointer finger at the beginning of the line you're reading—or using your cursor if you're reading on a computer screen—helps you keep your place. (Remember the pacer methods given Chapter 2?)

You can begin to expand your peripheral vision by squeezing the column margins of your favorite magazine or newspaper with your eyes:

1. With a pencil, mark a light line straight down the column approximately ⅓ from the left side margin and ⅓ from the right side margin. If you already have a wider eye span or want to challenge yourself, you can put your line down the center of the column.

It would seem that after the latest sell-off, financial services stocks would be a screaming "buy" for most investors.

After all, the average price-earnings ratio of such stocks stands at 11.9, down from 12.2 in April, and making it the lowest valuation of the 10 sectors that make up the Standard & Poor's 500 stock index, according to S&P of New York.

Through Oct. 19, the Russell 1000 Financial Services Index was down 8.7% year-to-date, making it the index's worst-performing sector, and the index lost 7.2% of its value for the week. Yet for many investors, the lower valuations aren't enough to compensate for what could be a multiyear slowdown of earnings.

"For me to get excited, I would need to see more of a pullback," said Cory Shipman, financial-institutions analyst with Stanford Group Co. of Houston.

He noted that many of the regional banks he follows trade at p/e's of 13.7, which is in line with the historical average for the group. This is, of course, much more attractive than the 16 times at which they were trading.

Problems at Calabasas, Calif.-based mortgage lender Countrywide Financial Corp. and other lenders took the sector downward this summer.

However, Mr. Shipman isn't convinced that banks are in a position to expand their earnings, given eroding economic conditions. He thinks that poor credit quality will continue to pull the stocks down.

"Earnings growth is going to be more difficult to achieve going forward," Mr. Shipman said. "Do these stocks deserve to trade at historically average multiples, given those prospects?"

Exacerbating matters is a concern that the number of loan defaults hasn't yet peaked. The lack of clarity on a potentially dangerous situation has many investors holding back.

"We're trying to figure out whether the [banks'] loan book is shrinking," said Sam Dedio, portfolio manager of the $11 million Julius Baer U.S. Smallcap fund, offered by Julius Baer Investment Management LLC of New York. "If it's still in shrinking mode, and the loans are coming off the books or are uncollectible, then the earnings won't be there."

Of the four Julius Baer funds that Mr. Dedio manages or co-manages, none have exposure to banks or investment banks.

Sam Stovall, chief investment strategist at S&P, cautions investors against dumping financial stocks wholesale right now.

"What we've been saying is, 'It's too late to underweight,'" he said. "We should have been more nimble

The left figure shows where the two lines can be drawn in preparation for reading by squeezing the margins. The right figure shows the single line location.

2. Read the column by stopping your eyes on the first line, and spreading your peripheral vision to see as far left and as far right as possible, then jumping your eyes over to the second line, again spreading your peripheral vision.

3. Advance to the next line of text and continue stopping your eyes two (or one) times per line while working toward expanding your peripheral vision. If you want to use a guide for your eyes, you can use the Point-to-Point pacer (see Chapter 2).

Eventually, you won't need to make the pencil mark down the column and will be able to do this more naturally. As you get proficient on narrower newspaper or magazine columns, try this on wider-columned material. You'll probably add a few more pencil lines initially and eventually take some away as your peripheral vision expands.

Use Your Hands

In Chapter 2, you were introduced to many options for reading with your fingers, hand, card, pen, or pencil. All encourage your vision to expand peripherally.

To really challenge your eyes, I suggest you consistently experiment with Long-Smooth Underline and/or Short-Smooth Underline.

Get Rhythm

Speed readers read with a rhythm. Their eyes swing easily across the lines or from a series of lines to a series of lines. Although our rhythm frequently changes when we read, keeping the rhythm constant for any stretch of time pushes your eyes to increase their peripheral vision to keep up with the rhythm. One way to experience this rhythmic reading is to read with a metronome:

1. Start reading a line of text on the "tick" and finish the line on the "tock."

2. By the time your eyes jump back to the beginning of the next line, you should be hearing the next "tick."

If you don't have a metronome, you can create the same concept by creating a recording of a knock on a table or other noninvasive sound *exactly* every few seconds for a minute and try reading with it on. You might need to increase or decrease the speed depending on how wide the columns are or how fast you're reading.

Stretch the Eyes

Moving your eyes smoothly, quickly, and accurately from one word to the next is a necessary skill for effective speed reading. It takes accurate tracking of your eyes from one word (or group of words) to the next. Try these exercises to test and expand your peripheral vision.

Part I: For the first exercise, focus your eyes on the first letter in the middle of the column (R). Stare at the R and *without* moving your eyes, see how many letters you can see to the left and to the right. (Try not to say each letter out loud or in your mind as this will slow you down!) Then move your eyes down to each line, challenging yourself to see wider each time.

Center column

^

N	W	L	R	T	J	N
S	R	W	M	F	P	L
T	D	S	P	A	R	O
L	R	T	Y	X	Y	E
P	B	N	Q	I	N	M
M	Y	C	W	D	H	A
C	Z	L	E	U	L	R
O	M	K	R	H	T	J
J	V	B	K	R	M	P
L	S	Z	P	Q	B	C
U	G	W	T	E	Z	A
S	Q	X	Z	W	M	Y

Most word-for-word readers can only see one letter (at the most) on either side when they start. With practice and awareness, it gets wider. Even just being aware of the width of your peripheral vision and your desire to expand it is a great step to making it wider.

Part II: Now start again with your eyes in the center column and quickly pull your eyes down the column, mentally noting how far you're able to see on either side. Feel free to use your index finger placed under the center column letters to guide you. Do this at least five times and see if you feel your eyes seeing more widely while focusing on the center.

The following exercise is a great introduction to my favorite eye-training exercise called Discipline Your Eyes described in the next section.

Part III: Use the following letters to get your eyes started moving in a directed pattern across the line. Start "reading" each letter on every line (recognizing the letter but not hearing it in your head) starting on the left, then the middle, then the right, returning to the beginning of the next line, just like you do when you read words. Feel the eye motion and eye stretch as you move from one letter to the next. Consider using a blank card pacer (see Chapter 2) to help keep your place. Try it at least five times and see how you can get faster and feel a wider stretch.

L	R	T
W	M	F
D	S	P
R	T	Y
B	N	Q
Y	C	W
Z	L	E
M	K	R
V	B	K
S	Z	P
G	T	W
Q	X	Z

Hopefully, you are aware of the three intentional eye stops across each line and a stretch of your peripheral vision. Play with this exercise often to remind your eyes and brain how you want to move your eyes.

Discipline Your Eyes Exercise

I have used and continue to use this exercise in my training classes, mostly because it works! It's great for warming up your eyes and brain before you read anything, and it also serves as a challenging eye-training exercise. It incorporates a speed reading strategy called *thought chunking*, which you will learn more about soon (see Chapter 4).

This exercise was originally published in 1956 in Paul Leedy's book *Reading Improvement for Adults* (McGraw-Hill). Although it's more than 50 years old, it still proves to be a simple yet incredibly powerful drill for spreading peripheral vision:

1. With your timing device (a clock with a second hand, a stopwatch, or another digital timer), time how long it takes you to read the following:

The purpose   of this drill   is to discipline

the little muscles   that move the eyes   from left to right.

Incorrect habits   of reading   have frequently caused

these muscles   to behave   in an undisciplined

and inefficient manner.   Try to make   your eyes march ahead

in three   rhythmic leaps   across the line.

Try to feel   the tiny tug   on these six

little muscles   that move each eye.   You will note

that some phrases   are short   others are longer.

This is done   intentionally.   The amount

of line width   that various people   can see differs

with the individual.   In these exercises   try to group

as one eyeful   all the words   in the unit;

look at a point   just about midway   in each word group.

At times   you will feel   as though the field

of your vision   is being stretched.   So much the better!

At other times   the phrase will be   too short.

We shall strive   for wider and wider   units as we proceed.

In that way   your eyes will grasp   more and more

at a glance.   Read this exercise   two or three times

every day   for a few days.   Try always

to cut down   on the time   that it took you

to read it   each preceding time.   You will soon get

the knack of it.   Do not let   your eyes "skid"

or "slide"   when you look   at a phrase.

Look at it	in the middle.	Give it a strong,
fleeting glance.	See it all.	in one look;
then be off	to see the next	and the next,
and so on	to the very end	of the exercise.
And now,	how long	did it take you
to read this?	Put your time	in Appendix C

It may take you as much as 2 minutes or as little as 30 seconds. Read across the lines, not down, and read for understanding, at least the first time through.

2. When you're done, turn to Appendix C and document your results on the "Discipline Your Eyes Personal Progress Chart."

How did you do? Did your eyes feel stretched? Were you able to stop your eyes just three times, or did your eyes stop more often? Did you feel any reading rhythm as your eyes progressed down the page? You may have begun to feel a reading rhythm of three stops and three jumps across the line. If not, you will with repeated reading of this exercise.

Now that you know what the exercise says and what it intends you to do, read it again, once more timing yourself. This time, read for speed, not comprehension. Then track your score on the "Discipline Your Eyes Personal Progress Chart" and come back here to continue.

You might find that you matched or bettered your first reading time because your eyes were already stretched and hopefully the words flowed better to your eyes. If you can learn what it feels like to read this way, you'll be better able to know when you're doing it on your own reading material.

The exercise has 280 words. If it takes you 1 minute to read it now, your reading speed is 280 words per minute. I suggest a time goal for this page of between 15 to 40 seconds (1,120 WPM down to 424 WPM). If you're currently around 1 minute, aim for 40 seconds. If you are at 30 seconds now, aim for 15 seconds. Have fun challenging your eyes and learning how to move faster across a line.

Rest for Tired Eyes

After all these eye exercises, your eyes might be feeling tired or strained. You may have a similar feeling if you stare too long at a computer screen. Your eyes need a well-deserved break. Try the following eye therapies to see which are the most relaxing for your eyes.

Eye Rub

When something on your body is sore, often a massage makes it feel better. Your eyes are no exception.

1. With your eyes closed, gently and rapidly stroke your top and bottom eyelids back and forth with your fingertips.

2. Continue for 5 to 10 seconds.

Your vision may be blurred immediately after the exercise, but that's okay. Just blink rapidly. The blurriness will disappear and your eyes will feel significantly refreshed.

Palming

This is my favorite because my mind, head, and neck get to take a break, too!

1. Rub your palms together quickly to warm them.

2. Close your eyes and cover them with your palms. (If you wear glasses, remove them first.)

3. Place your elbows on the desk or table in front of you and rest your face in your palms, which are still covering your eyes. Relax your neck and shoulders.

Palming position with elbows resting on a table. Your hands are covering your eyes and supporting your head and neck.

4. Experience total darkness for 20 to 30 seconds, or longer if time allows. Take long, slow, deep breaths. Relax your face, brow, and jaw. Don't squeeze your eyelids shut.

5. When you're ready, slowly let in light by spreading your fingers and then remove your hands. Now you can get back to reading!

Palming with Visualization

A variation on the Palming exercise includes an element of visualization. While on step 4, picture in great detail a relaxing and pleasant scene. Include a situation that requires your eyes to follow or track moving objects. For example, you might picture yourself on the deck of a ski chalet watching skiers slaloming down the slopes. Or envision watching a tennis match where the ball is going back and forth from one player to another. Another idea might to imagine yourself lying on the beach watching your hands as you pour a handful of sand from one hand to the other. Move on to step 5 after 30 to 60 seconds.

And the Results Are ...

Throughout this chapter your background knowledge about speed reading has increased and you've had the opportunity to play with stretching your peripheral vision and making predictions. You probably found some ideas more useful than others, and that's fine. The idea is to find the ones that work best *for you.* The best way to know which exercises might be suited to you is by timing yourself.

Choose to either do a One-Minute Timing and/or a 3-2-1 Drill in Appendix B. Consider first warming up your eyes using the Discipline Your Eyes Exercise. Use your preferred pacer method, and remember to track your scores in Appendix C.

The Least You Need to Know

◆ Your eyes stop every ¼ second to pick up information, so learning to pick up more in each ¼ second increases your reading speed.

◆ Learning to spread your peripheral vision is key to achieving faster reading rates.

◆ You can teach your eyes to see more at a glance, both horizontally and vertically.

◆ After exercising your eyes, they deserve a rest.

Chapter 4

The Eyes Have It

In This Chapter

- Eye warm-ups
- The bigger the words, the bigger the bang for your reading buck
- Meet the whole group
- Mix-and-match strategies

Which do you think is more important for speed reading, your eyes or your brain? If your eyes are fast but you have no brain comprehension, the activity is useless. If your brain comprehends everything, but your eyes move slowly, you won't be able to speed read. So to read faster, you need the cooperation of your eyes and your brain, but think of your eyes as the catalyst for your brain.

Your eyes are the gateway to your mind. If your gate is open a $\frac{1}{2}$ inch, that's what the mind processes. If your gate is open 4 inches, the mind processes that much. The goal of this book, and specifically this chapter, is to help you learn how to broaden your eye span to see more words at a time while maintaining, or improving, comprehension.

As you read through and experiment with the strategies in this chapter, try every strategy a few times before deciding whether you want to keep it or discard it. There's no one best way to read, just the way(s) you find most useful.

First Things First

Before we go too far, let's pause a moment to think about your eye health. When was the last time you had your eyes checked? Given that your eyes are so important for reading, you need to take good care of them. After all, your eyes are the input mechanism to your brain. If your eyes aren't tuned up, it will be even more challenging for you to read quickly—or read slowly or comfortably, for that matter!

The American Academy of Ophthalmology recommends most adults get regular eye exams (see the following table) or when you feel your vision has changed enough to make reading difficult. If you wear glasses, you may need an update to your prescription. If you've never worn glasses (lucky you!), as you get past the age of 40, your visual acuity may be affected and you may need reading glasses to see the words on a page clearly.

Suggested Frequency of Eye Exams for Adults*

Age	Frequency
Under 40	Every 5 to 10 years
40 to 54	Every 1 to 3 years
55 to 64	Every 1 or 2 years
65 and older	Every 6 to 12 months

* Based on the American Academy of Ophthalmology Guidelines. This is assuming no preexisting conditions or risk factors exist. More frequent exams are recommended if risk factors are present.

Speed Secret

The good news about getting a pair of glasses for reading is that you can see your reading material clearer. The bad news is that you may need another pair of glasses specifically for reading on a computer screen. Reading on screen requires a distance of approximately 18 to 30 inches; when you're reading on paper, the distance from your eyes to the page is typically less.

Get Ready to Run

In Chapter 3, you experimented with several ways to increase your peripheral vision and see more words at a glance. That's good exercise for your eyes, because your eyes are like any other muscles in your body: when not in use, they become a little rusty.

The more you use them, the more fluid they become. I don't know of any runner who doesn't warm up his or her legs before heading out on a run. Nor should anyone head out to read, either on paper or on screen, without warming up his or her eyes first.

Now, I'm not talking about 10-minute sweaty warm-ups; I'm talking about a cool 30 to 60 seconds—that's all! The Left-Right Exercise (see Chapter 3) is the easiest one to start with; the Discipline Your Eyes Exercise is also good (see Chapter 3).

Speed Tip

Copy the Discipline Your Eyes Exercise and place it near everything you read. Put a copy on or near your work area, next to your computer screen, and in your reading piles to remind you to warm up your eyes!

Focus on the Bigger Words

If you're a word-for-word reader or feel you have to read every word to understand, you're reading in first gear. You might like the comfort of first gear, but it's not going to get you where you want to go. You want and need to read faster.

Reading faster means reducing the number of times your eye needs to stop on the page for your brain to comprehend what you're reading. Reading the bigger words, the *key words*, is one way to accomplish this.

Reading the key words accomplishes several things:

def•i•ni•tion

The bigger words you read are also called the **key words**. Key words are typically three letters long or longer and carry the most meaning in a sentence.

- ◆ It speeds up your reading.

- ◆ It reduces your subvocalization, or mental or physical talking.

- ◆ It encourages you to naturally spread your peripheral vision.

- ◆ It ensures comprehension because the bigger words typically carry more meaning.

- ◆ It improves focus and concentration because you're looking for the bigger words.

Reading key words will be uncomfortable at first because you're not used to it, but as you practice more, your eyes and your brain will adjust.

Meet the Key Words

Read the following paragraph several times. As you read, focus your eyes *only* on the bold, bigger words. (Note that sometimes a smaller word is included because it's at the beginning of a sentence or a valuable action word.) Be aware of your peripheral vision, and see if you can spread it as you look at the bold words.

> **If** you are **really serious about getting** your **finances** under **control, then** you **need** to **first know** your **spending habits. Start** by **reviewing** your **checkbook register. Then** for **1 month, write** down *everything* you **spend money** on, **from** the **coffee lattes** to **fast-food meals** to **groceries** and **other necessities. Include** how **much** you **spent** and **how** you **paid** for it—**know** that **checks** and **credit** and **debit cards** are **trackable** while **cash expenditures** are **not. After** the **month, review** and **add** up your **expenses. You might** be **shocked** at **how much** you **spent** on **bottled water** from the **quickie mart! Learn** from **this** and **make** the **necessary adjustments.**

Speed Bump

There are no right or wrong key words, but if you read too many words, you'll waste your time. If you read too few, you'll have trouble understanding. Play around with this method until you feel good at it.

How do your eyes feel? Were you able to just stop your eyes on the bold words? Could you understand what the paragraph was about without "reading" every single word? Now look at the words that aren't bold. Not very important, huh?

This paragraph contains 106 words, 66 of which are identified as key words. If you think of this as a typical example, you can safely assume that about 50 percent of the words on a page are significant for comprehension while the remaining 50 percent are not. By getting good at locating the bigger words on your own, you can just about double your reading speed immediately!

Try reading the following paragraph looking for and stopping your eyes *only* on the bigger words. Work at spreading your peripheral vision. This time, you choose the key words. Do it several times until you feel your eyes are moving smoothly.

> Do you know anyone who is not busy these days? We are all busy doing lots of things that we hope will get us ahead at work, manage our families, and/or develop our skills. But how many of us consciously make time to spend with friends on a regular basis? With so much of our lives caught up with getting things done and our modes of communication being done via e-mail and voicemail, I can easily see how we neglect our friends. More than that, we have neglected our own need for quality human interaction. In several articles I read

recently, the authors suggest that a person can reduce stress by simply making time for more face-to-face communications and other real-life interactions. It can even add years to your life.

How did you do with this paragraph? Did you find the exercise possible, or were you worried about finding the "right" words? Were you aware of the different movements your eyes made? Do you think you were talking less?

You might be thinking that reading faster means skipping words. It might feel this way, yes, but if the other smaller words weren't there, you'd have a pretty hard time understanding what you read. By reading the key words, you're incorporating more words into a glance, using your peripheral vision and focusing on the bigger words so you can move your eyes forward faster. And you're not hearing those words in your head, but the words and their meanings are registering in your brain.

> **Speed Secret**
>
> Reading just the key words does *not* mean skipping words. The smaller words are incorporated with the larger words each time your eyes stop and pick up a key word.

Play with the Bigger Words

Let's see how this works on a One-Minute Timing. With an article from Appendix B, or starting where you left off during your last One-Minute Timing, time yourself reading for 1 minute looking *only* for the bigger, key words. Challenge yourself to go as quickly as you can. Recognize that your comprehension may temporarily suffer; don't be preoccupied with it at this point. Remember to write your results on the "One-Minute Timing Progress Chart" in Appendix C.

What do you think about this new reading method? Do you like it? Do you think you could get used to it with more experience? Play with it on easier reading materials first, like e-mail, newspapers, magazines, and light novels. Then move on to the more challenging or technical material when you feel comfortable with the strategy.

 Speed Tip

When you do any timed exercise in this book, always compare your newest score with your oldest, or first, One-Minute Timing. This is how to best gauge your true progress.

And be reassured that not every strategy in this book will work for you, so if this one doesn't do it, there are more! Keep trying them all to find the right combination for you.

Grab a Chunk and Go

When you learned to read, you learned one word at a time. But every sentence is not only made up of individual words but also groups of words that form a thought. You can read much faster and with good comprehension when you practice *thought chunking*.

def•i•ni•tion

Thought chunking is a reading strategy in which you learn to look for the groups of words that form thoughts in a sentence.

If you look at the way the words are put together in each group, you'll find a chunk of meaning, making it easier to read and understand at a glance. (A great example of this is the Discipline Your Eyes Exercise you learned in Chapter 3. Turn back and review that exercise if you want to.)

Meet the Chunks

To practice, take a look at the following paragraph. It's the same one you read looking at the bigger words in the previous "Meet the Key Words" section, but now it's separated into chunks with slash marks. Read and digest each slash mark–separated thought as quickly as you can and then move on to the next. Feel how your eyes need and like to move ahead.

If you are really serious/about getting your finances/under control,/then you need/to first know/your spending habits./ Start by reviewing/your checkbook register./ Then for 1 month,/write down *everything*/you spend money on,/from the coffee lattes/to fast-food meals/to groceries and other necessities./ Include how much you spent/and how you paid for it/—know that checks/and credit and debit cards/are trackable/while cash expenditures/are not./ After the month,/ review/and add up/your expenses./ You might be shocked/at how much you spent/on bottled water/from the quickie mart!/ Learn from this/and make the necessary adjustments./

Speed Tip

The size of the thought chunks doesn't matter, as long as each chunk is a thought and makes sense to you. If you group too many words together, you'll waste your time; if you group too few, you'll have trouble understanding.

Using the first sentence as an example, there are 20 words broken into 6 chunks of meaning. Think about your brain: would it rather process 20 individual words or 6 thought chunks? The 6 thoughts are much easier!

Try reading the following paragraph, looking for where one thought ends and another begins. Again, work at spreading your peripheral vision. Try reading the paragraph several times until you feel your eyes moving smoothly.

Do you know anyone who is not busy these days? We are all busy doing lots of things that we hope will get us ahead at work, manage our families, and/or develop our skills. But how many of us consciously make time to spend with friends on a regular basis? With so much of our lives caught up with getting things done and our modes of communication being done via e-mail and voicemail, I can easily see how we neglect our friends. More than that, we have neglected our own need for quality human interaction. In several articles I read recently, the authors suggest that a person can reduce stress by simply making time for more face-to-face communications and other real-life interactions. It can even add years to your life.

So how was this strategy for you? Easier or more challenging than reading the key words? Were you aware of your eye movements? Learning to move your eyes from thought chunk to thought chunk forces your eyes to move in directed strides across the lines instead of the lock-step, word-for-word reading.

You might have found your head bobbing up and down as you reached the end of a chunk or heard a little sing-song *la-la, la-la, la-la* in your head. These are quite natural, and once you get used to the strategy, your head will likely stay still. If you have a sense of rhythm when you're reading, but it isn't sing-song, then you are doing it correctly and you will read noticeably faster.

> **Speed Secret**
>
> Some people find they're more concerned with getting the concept of phrasing right instead of just trying the exercise without worrying about accuracy. As with key words, there is no right or wrong thought chunks—as long as each chunk makes sense!

Play with the Chunks

Let's see how this works on a One-Minute Timing. With an article from Appendix B, or starting where you left off during your last One-Minute Timing, time yourself reading for 1 minute looking *only* for the thought chunks. Challenge yourself to go as quickly as you can. Remember that comprehension may temporarily suffer; don't be preoccupied with it at this point. Remember to write your results on the "One-Minute Timing Progress Chart" in Appendix C.

> **Speed Tip**
>
> Reading in thought chunks works best on material with wide columns. Some newspapers and magazines columns are very narrow, making it challenging, but not impossible, to read using this strategy. E-mail and other online text is usually shown in wide columns, so try this method on those materials.

How do you like this method? Is it one you could see yourself using in the future? Try it on easy readings (e-mail, newspapers, magazines, etc.) before deciding to keep it or move on to the next method.

The Power of Combination

As you learn these tools for reading faster and more efficiently, you might feel capable of implementing only one at a time. Or you might want to combine a couple. The more comfortable you are with one method, the easier it is to work with other methods to create a more powerful reading strategy.

In addition to increasing your peripheral vision, which enables you to read more in less time, one of the best reasons to get proficient at any of these methods is you naturally concentrate better! In our world of constant interruption and distraction, we could all use more strategies to help us concentrate.

Remember that you can use these strategies for on-screen reading tasks as well. (For more about reading on screen, see Chapter 12.)

And the Results Are ...

When you start using any new reading strategy, three things can happen to your reading speed:

◆ It can speed up.

◆ It can stay the same.

◆ It can slow down.

If, right off the bat, you find your speed increasing, stick with that method and get good at it. It comes naturally to you, and you are in a good place ready to make it yours.

If your speed stays the same (within 25 words of your first timing), you may be overly concerned with your comprehension and not ready to let it go. (Remember, you need to train your eyes to pick up the information *first* before asking your brain to understand it.) You may also be having some initial difficulty picking out the bigger words or thought chunks—that's normal! With a little more practice, you should find this gets much easier.

If your speed goes down (more than 25 words less than your first timing), a couple things might be at play. You might rightfully be preoccupied with quickly locating the "right" bigger words (*Is this a big word or is that a big word? I'm not sure …*) or thinking about getting the thought chunks (*Is this a chunk? I'm not sure …*). This mechanical process of learning a new strategy is quite natural and normal. Be reassured that when your eyes adjust to locating this information, your speed will increase with your reading confidence.

Or you might definitely not be ready to let go of comprehension. You've been reading with the quest of comprehension ever since you learned how to read. Now, you're being asked to "read" without concern for comprehension (at first). It is a challenging thing to do, but know you *can* do it!

The best thing you can do is *trust your brain!* It's quite capable of processing more information at a glance if you allow it to.

Speed Tip _____

These reading tools are not skills. Skills are built over time by repetitively using the tools. Experiment every day on the reading material you have at work, for school, or for pleasure.

The Least You Need to Know

- The eyes are the window to your brain, so they need to read with acuity. Take good care of your eyes.

- Reading the bigger, key words can help reduce mental talking while helping you read faster—with comprehension.

- Quickly locating the thought chunks while reading immediately improves your comprehension. Speed also comes with practice.

- Combining key words and thought chunks is a very powerful method for reading with speed *and* comprehension.

5

Working on Comprehension

In This Chapter

- ◆ Trust your brain!
- ◆ Comprehension issues
- ◆ Practice makes better
- ◆ Experience is key
- ◆ Speed and comprehension

Have you ever read something, no matter the speed, and still not understood it? At times, even the most confident reader struggles with comprehension, so it's not surprising that comprehension is the biggest concern of most new speed readers. After all, what's reading without comprehension? If you're only looking at the words and not understanding what you read, then you are *speed looking*, not *speed reading!*

So how can you ensure comprehension when reading at any speed? That's what this chapter is all about.

Learn to Trust Your Brain

The brain is a marvelous, wondrous part of the human body. It's the control center of everything you think and do. And it's headquarters for reading comprehension.

def•i•ni•tion

Speed looking is the name for what you are doing when you read quickly to the bottom of a page and have no idea what you just read. It does not complete the act of reading, because your brain wasn't engaged.

In school, you probably had reading sections or units with comprehension questions at the end to test what you learned from the material. Your teachers used this as a way to gauge what you retained from the reading, but more things were at play than that. These read-and-question lessons actually helped prepare you for the real world of reading with comprehension *without* the questions. Unfortunately, many people doubt their brains and have created bad reading habits like rereading unnecessarily or out of habit, or reading word for word. This makes them feel lulled into believing they need to read it all and, thus, must understand it all. It doesn't necessarily work that way. These habits, when done in excess, do not serve you in the long run.

Think about your level of comprehension of the last chapter in this book or an article you recently read. What percentage of the material did you think you understood? Take a moment to assess your comprehension and assign a percentage between 0 (absolutely no understanding) and 100 percent (complete understanding). Chances are you didn't move on to this chapter or go to another article unless you had at least 70 percent comprehension or felt like you got enough from it, were satisfied, and moved on.

If you feel unsure of your comprehension, *trust your brain!* Think about what it's done for you up until now. It's helped you get through school, do your work every day, and learn how to do myriad other things. You have the ability to understand what you read, the first time, thanks to your brain. Rest assured it will help you time and time again when you decide to call upon it and trust the result.

Opening the Window

It's natural that you want to feel comfortable with what you understand when you read. So when you first learn to read faster, you might immediately become uncomfortable because your eyes and brain have to learn to communicate differently. You go into your discomfort zone (see Chapter 1). Know that this is temporary and with repeated experience with the methods, your brain *will* catch on again—sometimes better than it did before!

When you started reading this book, your eyes fed back to your brain a certain amount of information. If you're a word-for-word reader, it was one word at a time.

Using the analogy of a window to represent your eyes, your "window" or eyes were open about, say, 1 inch. Your brain sat behind the window feeling very comfortable with the 1-inch "breeze" of information coming to it.

When you start learning to read faster, your window opens wider to, let's say, 4 inches. Now, your eyes and brain have to make new connections; your eyes need to learn how to pick up more information at a glance and your brain needs to process a larger load. Your eyes are doing their job by dutifully picking up more information. What's your brain doing? It's freaking out! It's not used to all you're feeding it, and doesn't feel comfortable or confident in understanding it. But if you continue to insist that your window be open 4 inches, in a short period of time, your brain will get used to it. How long depends on how much you experiment with the speed strategies. The more you experiment, the sooner you'll feel confident about your comprehension again.

So your eyes need to become proficient at their task first before the brain can become proficient at its task. You need to unlearn your old word-for-word habit and relearn a more efficient and effective way of feeding information back to your brain.

> ### Speed Secret
>
> When learning to feed more information back to the brain, you will probably enter the discomfort zone (see Chapter 1), although with continued practice, you will emerge at a faster speed with good comprehension. After you are comfortable with your new speed level you push your eyes again to take in more words faster, you will again enter the discomfort zone and again emerge at an even higher rate with good comprehension. So to build up your reading speed and comprehension levels, use this process again and again.

The Power of Attention

This might seem obvious, but it's worth mentioning: in order to understand what you read, you must pay attention to it! This means you've secured a location appropriate for reading (see Chapter 6), you've established your "why" or reason for reading (see Chapter 6), and your eyes and brain are ready to receive. If the material warrants a cheat read (see Chapter 7), you would do that before jumping in.

This approach is an active one, unlike someone who sits in his comfy beanbag chair with the radio blasting, opening the material to the page he's to start on and simply floating his eyes across the words, often several times, hoping something will stick. He's not ready to receive, let alone understand. Be ready to receive, and comprehension can follow!

Practice on the Easy Material

By just reading this book, you won't become a speed reader. However, if you read this book *and* play around with the strategies, you have a much higher probability of becoming a speed reader.

To make it easier, choose practice reading materials that are familiar and easy to understand, such as your favorite magazines, newspapers, or easy novels. Don't take your new strategy and try to use it on your most challenging or technical material if you aren't yet able to use it on your easier material. If you have background knowledge, you'll have a much better chance of understanding what you read when reading at a faster rate.

> **Speed Tip**
>
> When are you going to have time to practice speed reading? Today. Right now. This minute. After all, you read every day—e-mails, newspapers, reports, websites, and so on. Practice and experiment on your regular workload. No need to make a separate time to practice!

Remember, comprehension is temporarily compromised while your eyes are learning how to pick up more information. You don't want to hyperchallenge your brain with difficult content as well!

To drive this point home, let's assume you know how to drive an automatic transmission car. You're a good driver and comfortable behind the wheel. On a vacation or business trip, you visit a new city, San Francisco, California—the city of 40-plus hills—and rent a car to get around. The only car the rental company has is a stick shift (not your first choice) and on top of that, you're not familiar with the area. You now have another foot pedal (the clutch) and a stick shift that needs to be shifted up and down in addition to what you're used to doing with the gas and brake pedal and the steering wheel!

It's not that you don't know how to drive; it's that you don't know how to drive *this* car. Driving this new car is quite challenging, and you have to be mentally focused on every move you make. You're definitely not as comfortable behind the wheel of the stick-shift car as your own automatic. Talking on your cell phone or drinking coffee while driving is not even an option … at first.

This is just like learning to speed read: you know how to read, but your reading machine now has more things to consider—where your hands are going, how your eyes are moving, and where your eyes are stopping to pick up information. Again, this is quite a challenging task and you have to mentally focus on every move you make. You're definitely not as comfortable reading this way as your old way.

But the more you drive that stick shift car, or use faster reading strategies, the more comfortable you will feel. You realize that the hills, or technical or difficult material, are a real challenge and you wish you started to drive on the flatlands of Iowa!

So play with the strategies. Practice on everything you read, and stay away from the hard stuff until you've mastered the easy stuff. You'll find some techniques easier than others. It's that simple!

Fear of the Word *Not*

When people learn to speed read, one of their legitimate concerns is what about the word *not*. This small word can dramatically change the meaning of a sentence and its paragraph. It can alter your understanding of an entire article.

People say they really need to read slowly in order to find the word *not*. Who says that reading slowly will ensure you finding that little word? Slow readers do miss it. Here are your choices:

♦ You can read everything slowly in fear of the word *not*.

♦ You can read faster, trusting that your eyes and brain will find it. If it doesn't initially see it, your brain will tell you to go back and double-check your understanding because something that you are reading doesn't make sense.

♦ You can read faster and train yourself to look for the word *not*.

The second two choices will enable you to overcome fear of this little word and at the same time, encourage you to trust your brain. Which choice are you deciding upon?

> **Speed Secret**
>
> In addition to the word *not*, many readers are concerned about missing a person's name or spend a lot of time paying attention to numbers. If you don't need to know the name or number, then don't worry about it! Get what you need and move on.

Expand Your Vocabulary

It's virtually impossible to read with understanding without knowing what the words mean. This is why having a broad vocabulary is so important for learning to read faster. Remember the discussion on background knowledge in Chapter 1? The more background knowledge you have, the faster you can read and the more you will understand.

With nearly half a million words in an average English dictionary, it's quite a daunting task to read and study every one of them! So how can you expand your vocabulary? You have several options, in order of *least* useful to *most* useful:

Read and study a dictionary. Although you might think this can help, memorizing words out of context doesn't build background knowledge. You may never come across that word or don't know when you will. If you're lucky, you might recognize a word you studied, but you'll need to look it up several times until it becomes part of your background knowledge … not very efficient or effective in the long term.

When you're reading, look up words you don't know. This is more targeted to getting the information you need *now*. But if you don't see the word again or use it within a few hours, you'll need to look it up when you do come across it.

Sound out unfamiliar words. Sometimes you can determine the meaning of the word because it looks or sounds like a word you already know.

Determine the meaning of the word in the context of the sentence. A dictionary definition isn't necessary all the time. Many times, you can figure the word meaning well enough from the rest of the sentence, paragraph, or page.

Learn the parts of words. Many words in the English language are made of other words derived from Latin and Greek. For example, *pre-* means "before." What other words do you know that start with *pre-?* Here's a sampling:

Speed Tip

To help learn lots of new words, create flash cards with the word on one side and the definition on the other. If possible, include a sentence example of how to use it. Or keep a separate notebook with the words you look up so you can review them. If you want to organize the words, write them in an address book to keep them in alphabetical order. Repetition is a key to learning!

prepubescent   before puberty

preview   anything that serves as an introduction (before) of something still to come.

preface   an introductory statement (it comes before the statement)

prefabricate   to manufacture before shipping and building

preference   one choice before another

preheat   to heat an oven before cooking

prepare   to make ready before an event

Can you think of others? Now's a good time to look up *pre-* in a dictionary to shed light on other words you might not have thought about.

The next time you come across a word you don't know, try using the clues already in front of you before going to the dictionary. Growing your sight vocabulary will help you read faster—with improved comprehension.

Speed Tip

To learn more about word parts, go to your favorite search engine and search for "word parts." You'll yield many lists with their meanings. You may be surprised by how many you already know!

Broaden Your Experiences

Think about this: you're reading the Sunday paper and come across an article about the Sistine Chapel in Rome, Italy. Would you read it? Chances are higher that you would if you'd been there, studied it in school, or were planning to go there. If you'd never traveled there nor had any interest in going, you probably wouldn't read the article.

If you read the article, how fast or slow might you read it? How good might your concentration be? How well do you think you'd understand what you read? And how well might you remember the information?

If you have been to the Sistine Chapel, Rome, or Italy, you might read the article faster than someone who has never been. Your concentration would be strong and your comprehension solid. And depending on what you might use the information for, such as an upcoming trip or sharing with a friend, you have better chances of remembering it longer. This is just one example of the type of life experience that can help you read faster with good comprehension.

The most effective (speed) readers I know have a breadth of life experience, either through reading or personal experience. They read varied material in a wide range of topics, which provides them a deeper understanding about life experiences through the author's eyes, and also about the world they live in. Many of them enjoy traveling, which enhances their background knowledge in so many areas.

Speed Secret

When was the last time you read something unfamiliar or took a day trip to a place you've never been? These activities, besides being fun, build your background knowledge, which helps make comprehension while reading easier!

Here's something you can do right away to broaden your life experience: walk into your local library or bookstore and wander over to a section you don't normally frequent. If you're a die-hard sports lover, try the mystery section. If you're a history buff, try the technology section. You don't have to get or read a book in these other areas, but by just picking up a book and reading the front and back cover, the table of contents, and a few pages of the text, you can learn a lot and expand your knowledge (see Chapter 10 for more information on shaking hands with a book).

Learn to Control Your Speed

The purpose of this book is to teach you how to speed read. However, it's just as important to understand that reading doesn't need to be—nor should be—fast all the time! You need to learn to gauge your speed using the appropriate gear for the task so you walk away with the greatest comprehension.

Your Environment and Your Reading

Let's return to our car analogy: imagine you're driving to work on the highway during the height of rush hour. Can you go the posted speed limit? Can you drive at a constant speed, or will you need to vary your speed according to the traffic pattern? What's preventing or enabling you to get to work on time? In addition to the mass of other cars, you may come upon a construction zone, an accident, or other drivers rubber-necking to see someone pulled over changing a tire, which then forces you to slow down. If it's a sunny day, you may be able to go faster than if it's raining. And if you listen to traffic reports before leaving home, you might be able to detour to avoid a major backup.

Speed Tip

If you need to review the speed appropriate for various types of content, revisit Chapter 1's "Shifting Your Reading Speed Gears" section.

Now imagine you're going to work *after* rush hour one day. How might your drive be different? Can you travel faster now? Will you be able to go the posted speed limit or even faster? What's now preventing or enabling you to get to work in a timely fashion? Chances are much greater that you'll be able to go faster at more constant speeds.

Let's relate this to reading. When you read, are some times better or more productive and efficient for you than others? Are some places more effective for reading that encourage higher levels of concentration? Are you aware of your most productive times of day—and do you read then? How do you approach unfamiliar or technical material? These are just some of the conditions you need to first be aware of, and then make adjustments for, to make the best use of your reading time and energy.

Becoming aware of and personally applying *your* ideal conditions enables you to adjust your reading speed to get you where you want to go efficiently—with an appropriate speed for the task *and* good comprehension.

Speeding Up and Slowing Down

Using the following table with one reader's sample responses, review some of the things that can help you speed up your reading and things that cause you to slow down. Keep in mind that the ultimate goal for reading is to *understand*. Would your responses be the same or different? Can you now see why there's no one "right" reading speed? There are too many conditions to constantly consider!

Take into Consideration	Things That Help Me Speed Up	Things That Cause Me to Slow Down
My purpose	If my purpose is for just getting the gist	If my purpose is to read for details
My responsibility	To be able to discuss casually	To be able to present to colleagues
Eye-movement strategy	Reading thought chunks	Not reading thought chunks
Pacer	Using a hand or card method	Not using a hand or card method
Cheat reading	Cheat reading	Not cheat reading
Vocabulary	Easy/familiar vocabulary	Difficult/unfamiliar vocabulary
Interest	Interested	Not interested*
Noise	Quiet, free of distractions	Lots of interruptions/TV/people talking around me
Light	Gentle	Too bright or dim
Temperature	Comfortable	Too hot or cold
Background knowledge	Some to a lot	Little or none
Familiarity	Familiar	Unfamiliar
Time of day	Best in the early morning	Worst in evening after 8 P.M.

continues

continued

Take into Consideration	Things That Help Me Speed Up	Things That Cause Me to Slow Down
Sleepiness	Well rested	Tired*
Print size	12 point	Smaller than 10 point or larger than 14 point
Time	Pressed for time	Have plenty of time
Column width	Narrow	Wide
Author's style	Easy to engage	Difficult to understand
Comfort level	Comfortable enough	Too comfortable or uncomfortable
Physical condition	Well rested; exercised that morning; not hungry	Excessively tired; hungry; feeling ill
Other?		

* If you aren't interested or if you're tired, you'll probably read slowly; however, with the speed reading strategies and other speed-up factors, you can speed up your reading.

Hopefully, you now realize how much control you have over your reading speed—a lot! Being aware of and being flexible with these factors as well as the possible reading gears will make your reading much more efficient and effective—and that includes comprehension!

What About Technical Material?

Just what does *technical material* mean? Although you might consider something that's difficult for you to read as being technical material, it may not be. Think of technical material as nonfiction material with unfamiliar vocabulary or completely new information. You may have quite a bit of background knowledge about this material, making it just plain challenging, but not technical. In all my years, I've never heard anyone say they read a technical novel! If anything, the writer challenges us to think differently via complex characters. So when I talk about technical material, I'm talking about nonfiction.

def•i•ni•tion

Technical material is writing that includes vocabulary specific to a particular field, profession, or trade.

Theoretically, you could consider medical journals, articles about the economy, and legal documents as "technical" material. However, if you're a doctor, the medical journal is nowhere near as technical as it would be to a plumber. If you're an economist, the economic article wouldn't be as technical as it would be to a doctor. And the legal document isn't as technical to a lawyer as it would be to her client!

In addition to unfamiliar vocabulary or a lack of background knowledge, other qualifiers used to identify technical material include the way the material is presented and structured. Sometimes the way material looks can lead you to believe it's technical or at least tedious to read:

- *Textbooks* are filled with tons of facts and figures as well as unfamiliar content and vocabulary.

- *Small print books* with smaller than 12-point font look technical, or at least challenging.

- Some *fonts* are easier to read than others. If you're challenged by a font, you might consider your material technical.

- If the piece's *line spacing* is compressed without any white space between the lines, it might appear technical for some.

- If the *column width* is wide across a page, it will appear more technical than if the columns were more narrow.

- If you open a book and there's *all text*—no pictures, bullet points, bold or italics, illustrations, etc.—some consider that technical.

In Chapter 10, you learn more about how to read and study technical material.

And the Results Are ...

Throughout this chapter you've learned more about the relationship between speed reading and comprehension. If anything, I hope you understand that many factors are involved in reading comprehension—some of which you have direct control over.

Now's the time to check in on your reading progress. Do either a One-Minute Timing or a 3-2-1 Drill (or both!) in Appendix B. This time, add in the step of writing the key comprehension points on a separate piece of paper for your One-Minute Timing. (You already do with the 3-2-1 Drill.) If you are trying to gauge your comprehension, this is a great way of doing it! And do consider warming up your eyes using the Discipline Your Eyes Exercise. Use your preferred pacer method, and be sure to track your score in Appendix C.

The Least You Need to Know

- ◆ Your brain is capable of more than what you give it credit for—trust it!

- ◆ Your eyes and brain need to learn to communicate differently in order to read faster.

- ◆ Comprehension temporarily dips as the eyes learn to feed more information back to the brain.

- ◆ Broadening your life experiences helps your reading comprehension abilities.

- ◆ You ultimately have control over your reading speed so you can maximize comprehension.

- ◆ What's technical to one reader might not be technical to another.

Part 2

Get In, Get Out, and Don't Go Back

In Part 1, you learned how your eyes and brain can communicate differently to read significantly faster with comprehension. In addition to these physical speed techniques, the best readers use additional strategies to be even more effective and efficient.

Reading certainly involves moving your eyes across and down the lines of text, but it also involves thinking and awareness of the writing pattern by the brain. Knowing how your material is structured helps you find the important information quickly and move on. Employing the strategies presented in Part 2 will greatly enhance your ability to quickly get through your reading demands.

Get In, Get Out, and Don't Go Back

In Part 1, you learned how your eyes and brain communicate differ and to read significantly faster with comprehension. In addition to these physical speed techniques, the best readers use additional strategies that even the efficient and efficient.

Reading certainly involves moving your eyes across and down the page often, but it also involves thinking ahead an awareness of the writing pattern by the brain. Knowing how your material is structured helps you find the important information quickly, and move on. Techniques that integrate present in Part 2 will greatly enhance your ability to quickly get through your reading material.

Chapter 6

Getting Ready to Get In

In This Chapter

- Looking at *why*
- What's the best time?
- Finding your space
- Speed reading and the mind and body
- Determining the best strategy for you

Have you ever heard the saying, "Preparation is the key to success"? In the case of speed reading, this is definitely true! You can learn all the speed reading strategies in the world, but if you aren't finding time to read or setting yourself up for concentration success, you're missing vital parts of the speed reading formula.

In this chapter, we look at the importance of setting yourself up for good concentration and how it affects your ability to read fast with good comprehension. How you "get in" to your reading is key for predicting how well you will read.

When Multi-Tasking Doesn't Work

Do you feel you have good concentration while you read? If you do, great! If you don't, you're not alone!

In his book *Crazy Busy*, Edward Hallowell, M.D., talks about strategies for coping in "a world gone *ADD*." It seems that since the mid-1990s, people have become compulsive multi-taskers (or even triple- or quadruple-taskers!) because of a desire or need to keep up with and respond to the many things that come at us every day—the phone calls, the e-mails, our colleagues, the media, and so on. According to Hallowell, "If none of what you are doing requires your full attention, it's fine to multitask, even though you may make mistakes, miss important points, be impolite, or fail to produce your best work."

Multi-tasking might be fine for some activities, but not for reading. Reading—either speed reading or "regular" reading—is a *mono*-focus activity. You need full concentration to look at words and understand them. You need full concentration if you want to use any speed reading strategies and if you hope for solid comprehension or retention. The good news is that, when performed in the right mental and physical environments, speed reading strategies encourage mono-focusing and force you to concentrate on what you're reading.

def•i•ni•tion

ADD is the medical diagnosis for *attention deficit disorder*. Common symptoms include inattention, hyperactivity, and impulsivity. It could be diagnosed in an inattentive daydreamer or someone who just can't keep still. There are cognitive and observation evaluations available by medical professionals who can diagnose this condition.

Evaluating Your Current Reading Habits

It takes conscious effort to set up your space, your body, and your mind for one and *only* one activity, especially when that activity is work—and reading is work! It's not like watching television, where you can sit lazily and passively and be entertained without much, if any, effort on your part.

Over your reading years, you've probably created habits—some effective, some not so effective. Your effective habits enable you to read with concentration. Your ineffective habits distract you from concentrating while you're reading. To see how effective or ineffective your current reading habits are, complete the following reading habits evaluation.

Reading Habits Self-Evaluation

To encourage you to think about your reading habits, respond to each of the following statements with either Y (*yes, always*), S (*sometimes*), or N (*no, never*):

Reading and Time Management:

1. I am good at finding time for reading. _____

2. I resist the temptation to pick up the phone while reading. _____

3. I resist the temptation to check my voicemail while reading. _____

4. I resist the temptation to check e-mail the moment it arrives. _____

5. I always carry reading material with me. _____

6. I listen to audiotapes/CDs for personal or professional development. _____

7. When I come across usable information, I immediately make note of it, either on the material, flag it with a sticky note, or write it down in a notebook. _____

8. When I am interrupted by my mental to-do list, I write it down and return to reading. _____

Reading Awareness:

9. I am aware of the eye movements used in the reading process. _____

10. My eyes "stop" on the more important words in text. _____

11. I understand the relationship between background knowledge and reading comprehension. _____

12. I read in a quiet, distraction-free environment. _____

13. I generally read without listening to music (with lyrics). _____

14. I do not read while the television is on. _____

15. I generally read work or study material at a desk or table. _____

16. I have good lighting where I read. _____

17. I am aware of and try to take care of mental and physical distractions before I read. _____

18. I am generally relaxed when I have a lot of reading to do.   _____

19. I am aware of my reading speed and shift it depending on what I am reading for and what I already know.   _____

20. I enjoy reading.   _____

Reading Strategies:

21. I know how and am able to …

    ♦ Reduce daydreaming when I read.   _____

    ♦ Avoid going back over material I already read.   _____

    ♦ Avoid mentally whispering while reading.   _____

    ♦ Stop moving my lips while reading.   _____

22. My personal reading pile consists of quality material I have chosen to receive and read.   _____

23. I know how to deliberately skim reading material, looking for the writer's outline before reading it line by line.   _____

24. I can find the writer's outline in most nonfiction reading material.   _____

25. I can quickly locate specific, useable information.   _____

26. I use my hands, a pen, or a white card to help me read faster.   _____

27. I continually question the author's point of view.   _____

28. I know how to reduce my to-read stack.   _____

Now, count your number of Y's, S's and N's. Write your totals here:

Y's   _____

S's   _____

N's   _____

The more Y's you have, the better. Anything you mark as N or S are areas to work on.

Make a date with yourself in 6 to 8 weeks to respond to this evaluation again and see if anything has changed. Hopefully, you'll see more Y's than S's and N's!

Remembering the *Why*

The most important and useful question you can ask yourself before you start reading anything is "Why am I reading this?" This simple yet powerful question helps focus your mind on the reason(s) why you're spending your time and energy reading what's in front of you.

So why do you read? There are myriad possible reasons:

- Find a new idea
- Identify a practical solution to a problem
- Forecast trends
- Understand a concept
- Revisit something you already know about
- Share with colleagues
- Increase your knowledge base
- Find information you need for your job
- Keep current
- Help get ahead in your career
- Earn a promotion
- Ask smarter questions
- Prevent faulty thinking
- Become better at something
- Understand political points of view
- Do research
- Build your vocabulary
- Make better decisions
- Improve your parenting skills
- Enjoy reading more

Speed Tip

Some people rephrase the why question, asking, "What is my purpose?" or "What is my motivation?" Any of these work.

Keeping your reason why in mind when you read helps you determine where to spend your reading time. If you're reading to understand political points of view and you come upon material about the history of a political party, you might want to read it. However, if you find a section about social scandals in government, you might decide it's not worth your time. Always ask yourself why.

Carving Out Time to Read

If reading really is a mono-focus activity, then finding time for it can be quite challenging. How often do you have time to "just" read? Some people plan their reading time, while others think they'll read when they have some "free time."

Really, there's no such thing as free time. When you have a day or evening with nothing planned, you always find things to do, usually activities you've wanted to do but haven't had the time—until now. Reading may be one of those activities. If you wait to read until you have free time, you'll always be frustrated with your reading workload. If you can plan some reading time on a regular basis, however, your reading workload will be more under control and reading will become a more enjoyable activity.

Speed Tip _____

You have to consciously make time for the important things. If reading is one of your "important things," you'll find time for it. I sometimes plan to go to bed an hour earlier so I can have some time to read a novel or magazine. If I'm working on a new training program and have a lot of research reading to do, I make several appointments with myself during the workday to get that reading done. Sometimes I get up an hour early to get caught up on my reading. I also limit my TV time. When there's a will to read, there's always a way!

What Can You Read Right Now?

When you do find yourself with moments of free time, ask yourself this simple question:

What can I read right now?

Asking this one question encourages you to think more frequently about fitting in more reading into your days. You might be surprised at when you can work in some reading time.

Finding More Reading Time

Sometimes extra reading time just happens. It's when you least expect to have the time but find yourself with a few minutes with nothing to do. Consider these possibilities to work in some reading:

- ◆ Read during your wait time at doctor's offices and other appointments.
- ◆ Read during your kids' sports practices or play rehearsals (you really need to watch the games!).
- ◆ Arrive early for classes or appointments and use that time to read.
- ◆ Arrive early for work or stay late and read during this "extra" time.
- ◆ Get up an hour earlier to read.
- ◆ Read over breakfast or lunch.
- ◆ Cut your TV time to make more reading time.

Speed Tip _____

According to the A.C. Nielsen Co., the average American watches more than 4 hours of TV each day. That adds up to 28 hours a week, or 2 months of nonstop TV-watching per year! In a 65-year life, that's 9 years glued to the tube! If you reduce your TV watching to even 3 hours per day, you'll buy yourself 7 extra hours of "free time" per week you can spend on reading.

- ◆ Reduce your web-surfing time to make more reading time.
- ◆ Read during your bus or train commute.
- ◆ Read during the last 10 minutes it takes for dinner to finish cooking.
- ◆ Read more during work hours.

To make the most of these moments of reading time, remember to carry reading material with you everywhere you go. Put some in your briefcase, purse, or car so it will be there when you have the time.

Speed Tip _____

Read at work? Won't you get in trouble for that? Not necessarily. Reading work-related materials at work helps you keep current with your profession's trends, find nuggets of information that make your job easier, or teach you something new. You can even subscribe to your business reading online. (For ideas on how to read faster online, see Chapter 12.)

Reading When You're Tired

Ask anyone you know if they're well rested, and most likely they'll laugh in response. What about you? Are you well rested? Okay, stop laughing for a minute and think about this: how are you supposed to read with concentration and understanding if you're constantly tired? Without enough sleep, we tend to be cranky, our judgment is impaired, and our learning abilities are compromised—definitely not the time to expect good comprehension when reading!

Speed Secret
The average person requires 8 hours of sleep per night, and most people have a pretty good idea about how many hours of sleep they need to be their best every day. To help ensure that you get your necessary amount of sleep, it helps to establish a set bedtime for yourself—just like you might do for your children.

But what do you do if you're tired when you finally find that elusive time to read? Maybe you're one of the many people who seem to be tired all the time or you save your reading for the end of the day after everything else is done. If you're using reading to lull you into sleep during these times, you'll probably only read a few pages before you fall asleep. If, on the other hand, like many businesspeople and students, you're reading for work or study, being tired and trying to read is a combination that just won't work.

What to do? You can plan your reading time at your peak time(s) of day. If you're a morning person, read in the morning when you're fresh. If you're a night owl, make time when you feel the most alert.

If you're a morning person and have reading to do late at night, a short, 30-minute power nap might be the recharge you need. Or you could go to sleep and get up early to do your reading. Either way, you'll get more done in less time with better concentration and comprehension.

If you have to read when you're tired and sleeping is not an immediate option, here are a few ideas to help you be as alert as possible:

◆ Plan short, frequent breaks every 15 to 30 minutes.

◆ Drink ice-cold liquids.

◆ Do jumping jacks or stretch on breaks. Movement increases the blood and oxygen flow to the brain.

◆ Eat smart study snacks. Protein (like a cheese stick or hard-boiled egg), fruit, and veggies are good choices. This encourages a more balanced blood sugar level, which keeps your energy high.

♦ Avoid caffeinated beverages, foods made from white processed sugar (including high-fructose corn syrup), or white flour carbohydrates (like pizza and pasta). These foods and drinks cause your blood sugar levels to spike and plummet, making you more tired in the long run.

♦ Drink plenty of water.

Finding the Best Place(s) to Read

Think about where you read. What distracts you there? A ringing phone or dinging e-mail? Other people? Your own thoughts? You can't read with concentration in an environment where overwhelming external or internal distractions exist.

Let's look at some factors that are most conducive, and some that aren't, for enhancing reading concentration. You may not agree with all of these, and that's okay. The following list is generalized to get you thinking about how these factors affect you and your ability to concentrate when you read. Note that a *positive* factor helps your reading speed, concentration, and comprehension, while a *negative* factor tends to hinder all three areas.

State of Mind/State of Being:

Positive Factors	*Negative Factors*
interested	not interested
peak time of day	tired time of day
relaxed	stressed
time pressured	not time pressured
well rested	tired
not hungry	hungry
feeling well	feeling ill

Distractions:

Positive Factors	*Negative Factors*
not preoccupied	preoccupied
no mental to-do list	pressing mental to-do list

music without words	music with words
no e-mail dinging	e-mail dinging
no one interrupting	others interrupting
phone to voicemail	phone ringing
no television	television on

Location:

Positive Factors	*Negative Factors*
at a desk	on a couch
at a table	in a recliner
at the library	on a bed
uncluttered space	cluttered space

Type of Reading:

Positive Factors	*Negative Factors*
familiar content	unfamiliar content
column width you prefer	column width you don't prefer
12-point font	10-point font or smaller
good-quality copy	poor-quality copy

External Environment:

Positive Factors	*Negative Factors*
comfortable	too hot or too cool
well lit	dimly lit
quiet	noisy

If you make it a point to be aware of these things as you set yourself up for reading, you're sure to make smart choices. Your increased concentration will be the prize!

For Businesspeople

As a self-employed business professional, I find reading in my home office hard to do. I read e-mail and other work documents there, but I find it difficult to concentrate on professional materials that I read for information. I'm so used to getting things done at my desk that when I read there, I'm constantly thinking of other things I could be doing. My phone is tempting, as is e-mail. To solve this problem, and so I can read with concentration, I move to a clean table in another room, either in the kitchen or dining room. If you work with others in an office building, consider moving yourself to an empty conference room, the cafeteria during off hours, or an empty office—and, ideally, tell no one where you're going.

If you're tied to your desk because you have to be there to answer the phone or for some other reason, find someone who could cover for you or swap phone coverage for a half-hour, so you can get some quiet, distraction-free reading time. If you have a door, close it. If you don't have a door, try being creative with signs behind your chair saying something like "Working on a pressing project. Come back at 2:30 P.M." One participant in a workshop says she uses police tape to gate off her cubicle to get some quiet time! Another swears by the use of earplugs to drown out her noisy neighbors' conversations. Think creatively, put your ideas into action, and you'll be getting your reading done in no time.

> **Speed Tip** _____
>
> Before reading, try my arm-swing test to clear the physical distractions away from under your reading material. Place your elbow (either one) on your desk or table. Lay your forearm down across the front of your body with your palm facing you. Anchoring your elbow, slowly push the back of your hand and forearm away from your body, creating a semi-circle of space in front of you. Clear away anything your hand or forearm touches, leaving a clear space for your reading material (and note paper, if applicable).

For College Students

When I work with college students and ask them where they think is the best place to read and study on campus, they inevitably respond with their dorm room, the lounge in the dorm basement, or the library.

In fact, these aren't the best places on a college campus. The dorm room is the most distracting because a bed, the telephone, e-mail, other people, music, and possibly a TV are all nearby, waiting to distract you. The dorm lounge might have comfortable couches that call to you to take a nap, a TV, and other people around to distract you. The library sounds like a good place, but depending on the school and the study area setup, it can be a very busy social place with comfy couches in a usually too-warm environment. Again, not conducive for alert reading or studying.

Speed Tip

If you don't feel comfortable being in an empty classroom by yourself at night, ask a friend to join you. You work in one corner of the room while he or she works in another. Make a plan to meet for short breaks at scheduled times.

So where *is* the best place for a college student to read on campus? An empty classroom! It's the one place the body and mind know they need to work. The chairs aren't too comfy, and there's always a clean desk to work on. The lighting is typically adequate, and there are no distractions like in the dorm or library. Study cubicles are next best bet. They usually can be found all over campus. Find the ones most off the beaten path for best concentration results.

Calming the Body and Mind

Have you ever tried to read in a rush? As a student, have you ever realized, 10 minutes before class, that you were a chapter behind in your reading and frantically tried to catch up? At work, have you ever remembered, in a panic, that 60-page report you were supposed to read for a meeting that's starting in just 30 minutes? In either case, you probably "sped read" what you could but found that you were doing more speed *looking* than speed *reading*. You probably didn't get much out of it.

If this happened to you today, though, you could relax, knowing you have at your fingertips many proven speed reading strategies so you can get through more material with more comprehension. Let's look at some things to help prepare your mind and body for reading.

The Effects of Music

For most regular reading you do, listening to music can greatly enhance your reading speed and your comprehension. But not just any music helps; classical music *without words* works the best. Jazz, hip hop, rock 'n' roll, and other music genres have words and distracting rhythms that aren't appropriate for reading and learning.

For optimal learning, Dr. Georgi Lozanov, the father of *accelerated learning*, suggests listening to slow baroque music, played quietly in the background. He specifically sites composers like Bach, Handel, Correli, and Telemann. New Age piano or guitar also works well. And don't forget about Mozart.

Why classical music? The rhythm of classical music matches your heartbeat at rest, which is 60 beats per minute. When listening to this kind of music, your heartbeat slows down, causing your body to relax and be ready for maximum learning. Listening to this kind of music when reading reduces mental stress and anxiety, activates the body for learning, and improves memory or awareness.

def•i•ni•tion

Accelerated learning is a teaching approach designed to make learning happen faster. By taking a course based on an accelerated learning course design—which incorporates learning styles with interactivity, colors, music, frequent review, and more—you will find learning easier and more fun.

Speed Secret

The brain is composed of two hemispheres, the left and right. Processing words is mostly a left-brain activity, one that is logical and sequential. By adding music, you add more of the right side of the brain, which is more creative and expressive, so you're learning with both sides of your brain, or whole-brain learning. Whole-brain learning makes the brain more active in the learning process, which enables you to read with enhanced concentration, comprehension, and retention.

At times, a few minutes of stimulating music that quickens the heartbeat and awakens the imagination can also be useful. Marches and upbeat songs work well. In my workshops, I have recently used Chubby Checker's "The Twist," the Macarena party dance, and KT Tunstall's rhythmic "Suddenly I See" to energize a group.

Keep Your Eyes on the Prize

Just as you shouldn't listen to music with words while you read, you shouldn't have a television on while reading, either. With television, you not only have the words, but you also have the visual distraction on the screen. Remember, concentration requires monofocusing, and watching TV while reading is multi-tasking.

Other visual distractions can include people walking past your door, goings-on outside your window, pictures on the wall in front of you, or photos of friends and family on your desk. If any of these frequently distract you, be creative and look for ways to not be distracted by them.

If you have visual distractions but think you can't do anything about them, try these possible solutions:

♦ Keep one wall of your desk/office clear of photos and distractions so you can turn around to that side of your desk to read.

♦ Close the window blinds or angle them up so all you can see is the sky, not the goings-on on the ground.

♦ Close your door and put a "Please do not disturb—reading" sign out.

♦ If you're reading on a screen, remove anything taped to the periphery of your screen (like Post-it notes, photos, etc.) and any distractions in your visual field (like personal photos, clipped pictures, notes, etc.).

♦ Position your eyes away from a television screen or any movement in front of you. (You may need earplugs to block out the sound, too!)

Tune Out the Mental Distractions

You've set up your physical environment perfectly so no distractions will keep you from your reading. You're ready to read—except for the fact that you're hungry, you have a headache, you're hot or cold, or you have to use the restroom. Taking care of your physiological needs before you sit down to read can greatly improve your chances of reading with good concentration. Otherwise, you're going to half concentrate on your reading and still think about your stomach, your headache, your temperature, etc.

Learning to keep your mind relaxed will help keep your mental distractions at bay while reading. In addition to taking care of your physical needs and listening to appropriate music, try taking a series of long, slow, deep breaths in preparation for reading and during reading breaks. This helps relax your body and mind and sets it up for more focus and concentration.

Time and Page Goals

If your reading is a study or work activity, then setting time and page goals helps you stay on track. With a time goal, you decide how long you want to read, without interruption, until you take a break.

A page goal is a little more flexible. You can monitor either the time it takes you to read your material or how far you want to be in your reading by your first break. By placing a bookmark or Post-it note at the place you want to get to in the time you chose, it might motivate you to keep going and stay focused.

Both strategies are especially effective for reading that you aren't very interested in but are required to read. It forces you to get it done, and quickly.

Take Frequent Short Breaks

There's nothing valiant about sitting in one place and reading for hours on end without a break. Your body doesn't appreciate it, and your brain certainly won't work at top capacity this way.

A short break—3 to 5 minutes maximum— can rejuvenate your body and stimulate your brain. Generally speaking, it's better to take a short break at least every hour when the reading material is somewhat familiar to you, or every 20 to 30 minutes when the reading material is unfamiliar.

Speed Tip

There's evidence proving that most people remember the first things they read and the last things they read more than middle things. So if you take a short break every 20 to 30 minutes, you'll remember two firsts and two lasts versus only one first and one last if you took a break every hour.

So what can you do on a short break? Here are a few ideas:

◆ Get a drink

◆ Use the restroom

◆ Do some aerobic exercise like jumping jacks or run around the block

◆ Splash cold water on your face or take a very quick shower

◆ Stretch your body

◆ Listen to a song that motivates you to move

◆ Change the laundry from the washer to the dryer

But remember these are short breaks just to rest your brain a little. You want a respite but not a distraction, so *don't* do the following:

◆ Watch T.V

◆ Check e-mail (unless you're looking for one specific communication)

- Make a phone call

- Surf the web

- Start a conversation, especially with someone you don't see often

- IM (instant message)

These activities draw your attention away from your reading for much longer than 3 to 5 minutes. Save these as rewards for finishing your work!

The Library

If you want motivation to read within a certain time frame, borrowing a book from your public library is just the ticket. When you check out a book from a library, you agree to return the book by its due date. Most times it's 30 days, but sometimes it's 14. There's your motivation for making time to read and read fast!

Many libraries—public, corporate, and school—have state networks to find almost any book or magazine you want. Using library services prevents book clutter in your home (because you can't keep it), and the best part is, if you don't like the book you checked out, you can always return it and get another one—no charge!

Start with the End in Mind

When faced with a reading task, most people don't know how long it will take. They just buckle down and start reading. If, instead, you set page goals with time frames attached, you'll read with more concentration and purpose and complete the reading in less time.

Let's say it's 7 P.M. and you have to read a 30-page chapter. Most people would have no real idea how long that would take, but you can figure it out by one of a few options:

- Read one page and see how long it takes you. Let's say for simplicity's sake it took 1 minute. Based on that, your chapter will take about 30 minutes to read. If you try to read faster and get each page down to 30 to 45 seconds, it would take you less time to complete the chapter.

- Read the chapter for 10 minutes and see how many pages you got through. Multiply that number by 6 (there are six 10-minute periods in an hour) to figure out approximately how long it will take to read the chapter.

◆ Set your own page goals by creating 4
long strips of paper, each about 2 inches
long, out of an 8½×11 piece of white
paper. Write one each of these numbers
on top of each strip of paper: 5, 10, 15, 20.
Before starting to read, place the 5 strip
in the material where you want to be in
5 minutes. Then place the 10 strip where
you want to be in 10 minutes, and so on.
See how close or far you are from your
goal at these times.

Speed Secret
Great American thinker and philosopher Earl Nightingale said, "If you spend one extra hour each day in the study of your chosen field, you'll be a national expert in five years or less." What do you want to be an expert in?

Decide on *Your* Strategy

If you follow the advice in this chapter, you are on the way to setting yourself up for
reading success by knowing *why* you are reading, securing a distraction-free environment, calming your body and mind, and setting time and page goals. The last piece of
the concentration puzzle, and probably the most important one, is to decide on what
speed strategy you want to use.

If you've read all the previous chapters, you know about how to read using a pacer
(your hands or a card), reading key words, and reading thought chunks. You understand how to spread your peripheral vision to read more in a glance. And you have
an understanding about what helps keep your comprehension when you're trying out
new speed strategies. Experiment with any or all of these strategies to keep your focus
and concentration—and of course, speed!

And the Results Are ...

If you're the kind of person who believes you'll always get distracted while you read, I
wish I could have you in one of my training programs.

After spending the morning teaching you all the speed strategies, in the late afternoon,
I give a scanning exercise that has a set, 3-minute time limit and a goal to see if you
can quickly and accurately locate the information requested by a series of specific questions. I start the exercise with my stopwatch and then everyone focuses on the task.

During the test, I intentionally rip—and I mean *rip!*—a piece of paper off the flip-
chart pad in the front of the room, tear it into little pieces, crumple up each piece,

and throw them on the floor. Believe me, it's not a quiet activity! I then take an empty chair from either the front or back of the room and drag it to the opposite end of the room. I then place it on top of an empty table. If drinks are available in the room, I loudly pour a cup of coffee or pop open a soda can. At this point, I stop intentionally making noise and wait to stop the exercise.

My first question to the class is not "How did you do on the exercise?" but rather "Who can tell me what I was doing during the exercise?" The looks I get are incredulous. "What do you mean what you were doing? I have no idea!"

I then tell them what I did and show them the torn and crumpled paper, point to the chair on the table, and show them the poured coffee or soda. They can't believe it. They didn't hear a thing! They were reading with a reason *why* (to find the answers to the questions) and they had a set time frame and strategies to use. They were sitting upright at a desk and ready to perform their task. These are the same ingredients required to read in a noisy place without being distracted.

> **Speed Tip**
>
> Some participants get quite competitive when doing this exercise. It's clear that this sense of competition drives some readers to work quickly and in a focused manner. If you have that competitive streak, find ways to create it in your own reading load.

So your task now is to do a One-Minute Timing (or if you like, a 3-2-1 Drill) to check your speed and comprehension found in Appendix B. Remember to document your progress in Appendix C. See how well you can set yourself up for reading success using the information in this chapter. Good luck!

The Least You Need to Know

◆ Reading with concentration means *mono*-tasking, not *multi*-tasking.

◆ Answering the question "Why am I reading?" is the first step in getting the focus necessary for any reading task.

◆ Not much reading gets done unless you can find time—or *make* time—to do it!

◆ Some places are more conducive than others to read. For businesspeople, it may be away from their desk. For college students, it may be an empty classroom.

◆ Calming the body and mind includes reducing visual and mental distractions.

◆ Setting time and page goals—competing with yourself—keeps you on track to get your reading done with the most concentration and the least amount of time.

7

Getting In

In This Chapter

- ◆ Are you right-brain or left-brain dominant?
- ◆ Giving you the *what for*
- ◆ The view from the top
- ◆ Nonfiction reading made easy(er!)
- ◆ Getting in to technical material

When you realize that more than 18,000 titles of magazines are published in the United States every year, the concept of reading *everything* takes on a new meaning! If you did want to read it all, you'd be reading about 50 magazines a day, many of which would be of no interest to you. Instead, it's important—and time-saving—to read only things of value to you.

In this chapter, I first want to help you decide whether or not you should even get into a piece of reading material and when you do, how best to approach it. In Chapter 14, I show you specifically how you can create a personally valuable reading workload. (If this type of planning is what slows down your reading, you might want to read Chapters 7 and 14 consecutively.)

Nonfiction, Fiction, and Your Brain

If you ask people what they like to read, some will say "I like a good novel," while others will say "I like to read for information." This tells you the former prefer *fiction* while the latter prefer *nonfiction*.

def•i•ni•tion

Works of **fiction** consist primarily of literature whose content is produced by the imagination and is not necessarily based on fact; novels and short stories fall in this category. **Nonfiction** gives facts and information; newspapers or magazines are examples of nonfiction. Most business reading is considered nonfiction. Books can be either.

But there's more at work here than reading for a story or plot or reading for facts. Believe it or not, how you *think* reflects what you prefer to read.

Reading and Your Dominant Brain

Roger Sperry, a pioneer in conducting behavioral investigations of the brain's two hemispheres, concluded many things based on his work. One of his conclusions is that everyone is either *right-brain* or *left-brain dominant*. Everyone has some ability from both sides of their brain, however, Roger Sperry thinks that everyone has a dominant, or stronger, side.

Left-brain dominant people are considered efficient. They like being organized and show a high regard to time. They enjoy learning details and want one correct answer. They crave routines and are good at making decisions. Many left-brain dominant readers prefer to read more nonfiction than fiction.

Right-brain dominant people tend to be disorganized (maybe even messy) and pay little attention to time. They like to see the big picture of concepts before getting into the details and want to see several possible answers to a question. They enjoy the concept of play and are considered somewhat impulsive. Many right-brain dominant readers prefer to read fiction.

The following list contains more characteristics of both sides of the brain. Compare the two sides and see which side sounds more like you.

Right-Brain Characteristics	Left-Brain Characteristics
Spatial thinking	Logical thinking
Brainstorming	Making decisions
Nonverbal communication	Verbal communication
Creativity	Calculation
More emotional	Less emotional
Strong imagination	Some imagination
Global reasoning	Analytical reasoning
High intuition	Low intuition
Creative thinking	Critical thinking

Fiction Versus Nonfiction

When you were young and just learning how to read, you probably started with fiction. For most people, fiction is easier to read because it engages the brain visually (your mind's eye pictures what you're reading), auditorily (you hear what the characters say in your head), and kinesthetically (you mentally experience what the characters experience). It's like your own movie playing in your head while you read.

Nonfiction can be more challenging. Many students who initially loved to read soon find less pleasure in reading sometime around middle school, when textbooks—*nonfiction* textbooks—become the primary learning material. Textbooks and other nonfiction don't engage the brain visually (although pictures might appear in the book), auditorily, or kinesthetically. Instead, they engage your brain digitally, providing data and information. This is one of the main reasons reading nonfiction is more challenging than fiction.

> **Speed Secret**
>
> Fiction and nonfiction are different types of reading material that require different approaches. Understanding how to apply the strategies to the different materials makes you a more flexible and skilled reader.

Remember *Why* and Add *What For*

In Chapter 2, I introduced you to the concept of identifying the reason why you're reading so you'll know, before you begin, what you want to get from the reading material. Answering *why* directs your reading by helping you look for specific information. *Why* are you reading this? Not having a good enough answer to your why question tells you that you should find something else to read that does!

Now let's add another idea to the *why*: "*What* might I need the information for?" The following table lists some sample article titles, reasons for reading them, and how they might be used.

Article	*Why* Read It?	*What* Need For?
"The New India: Customer Service American Style"	To understand why we're turning to other countries for our services	For correcting faulty thinking; be informed and have more to talk about at work or with friends
"The Greening of America"	To see what's being talked about in our environment	For what role I might play in helping my family or company be more environmentally friendly
"Retirement Plans: Save Yourself"	To learn more about what's recommended for retirement	For possibly finding a new savings strategy or confirming that my savings are in the right place
"Eat Yourself Thin"	To see if I know this already or if there's something new	For finding that magic bullet for losing weight

Speed Tip

Not all parts of a book have equal value to your *why* and *what for* questions. You can fast-forward or skip when reading a book if the material isn't worth your full time and attention.

There are many more reasons for reading, like being informed in meetings, being up to date for predicting trends, or finding a new strategy to better manage your employees (or your kids!). What reasons can you come up with for why you read?

Knowing your reasons for reading engages your brain and definitely puts you on the track to faster reading.

Getting a Bird's-Eye View

It's time to do a timed practice to build your speed reading skills. Although I include this here, you can always do a timed practice whenever you want. You don't have to wait for me to suggest it!

Note: nonfiction is more challenging to read, so the next few sections deal specifically with this type of reading material. Find a nonfiction book or magazine to keep handy for use in this chapter. You could even use this book if nothing else is easily available to you.

Pretend you have a nonfiction book on time management in front of you. You've never seen it before but are interested in reading it. You chose the material because a friend recommended it (your *why*) and you want to find some ways to manage your time better (your *what for*). You think you're ready to read. But wait! You're not quite ready yet!

It's just like visiting a new town you've never been to before but are interested in visiting. You're in the town because a friend said it was quaint (your *why*) and you want to take photos of the more interesting sites (your *what for*). You could start walking in the town, street by street, hoping to come upon something good to take a picture of, or you could go up in a helicopter to get a bird's-eye view of the town, quickly finding some neat old buildings and town landmarks to photograph.

Obviously, you're not going to take a real helicopter ride, but if you did, you could see the entire town in much less time than it would take you to walk it. And when the copter lands, you'd know exactly which direction to head to get the photos you want. A big time-saver!

If you were to just start reading when you were "ready," you might start reading from the beginning, word for word (like walking street by street). Or instead, you could hypothetically go up in your helicopter to get a bird's-eye view of the material, looking for valuable information based on your reason why and what you are reading for.

So what should you look for when you're up in your hypothetical helicopter? Here are the biggies:

Copyright date   This lets you know how current, or not, the material is. It puts the information into historical context.

Table of contents   This gives you the outline of the book/magazine and what topics you might want to read about.

About the author   This information tells you about his or her expertise, where he or she is coming from based on their experiences, and what you might expect to find in the material.

llustrations or photos   A picture is worth a thousand words, especially if it has a caption, and quickly provides clues to the reading content.

Quotes and *information placed in the margin*   This material usually reflects something valuable.

Speed Secret

Using this bird's-eye view approach to your reading material is a lot like putting together a jigsaw puzzle. Looking for this easily identifiable information first is like looking for the corner pieces and straight edges of the puzzle.

Not all these areas are present in everything you read, but see which apply to your sample material. After reading about the areas, take a few minutes to flip through your material to locate these areas.

This quick overview helps you decide where you want to go in the reading and where to spend your time, if at all. This deliberate and general view is explained in greater detail in Chapter 10.

Where's the Meat?

Speed reading involves using your eyes and brain to process words more rapidly. In addition, speed reading means being able to find the most important information quickly. I call the most important information the "meat," and consider the other explanation and details the "potatoes and veggies." When speed reading, you should look for the meat first and leave the potatoes and veggies for later.

In elementary school, when you first learned to read, it made sense to read from the beginning of the chapter or article to the end. Now, as an adult, if you continue to read this way, you might be wasting a lot of time reading information you have no need for. This may come as a surprise to you but reading is *not* a linear activity! You don't have to read from the beginning to the end to say you read something. You do, however, need to find and read what's most important—the meat.

So where do you find the meat? Think back to high school, where you (hopefully) were taught how to write essays. Before writing the essay, you had to do some research, come up with a thesis statement, and create an organizational structure called an *outline.* You were also taught that every essay contained three parts: an introduction, a body, and a conclusion. Most published nonfiction material you read follows this basic three-part outline structure.

Why should you be interested in this? *Because every piece of published nonfiction has an outline*—and the most important details are in the outline—so it's in your best interest to find it before you read!

I affectionately call the process of finding the writer's outline *cheat reading*. I use this term because many times, depending on your *why* and *what for*, you don't need to read more than the outline to get the information you need. It's also used to introduce you to the writer's structure and flow so you can better understand the point when the material is technical or unfamiliar.

It's Okay to Cheat Read!

If cheat reading means finding the meat, or the author's outline, you need to know where to look for it. Start with these areas:

- Title
- Introduction
- Subheadings
- First sentence of every paragraph
- Conclusion

def•i•ni•tion

An **outline** is an ordered list of the essential features or main aspects of something discussed, usually organized in headings and subheadings.

Speed Bump

Most published nonfiction has been edited, which makes it easier to find the writer's outline. When reading unedited documents and e-mails written by your colleagues and other nonpublished writing, it might be more challenging to pinpoint the outline.

Unlike fiction, the *title* in nonfiction generally reflects the subject or theme of the material.

The *introduction* points you in the direction the author wants to lead you. An introduction may consist of just the first paragraph or several paragraphs, or if there is a subheading, the introduction usually ends at the first subheading. Once you know where the material is headed, you can move on. (Yes, I am giving you permission to not read it all!)

The *subheadings* are the legs of the outline. They provide the ordered structure where the writer's central ideas are found. When you come upon a subhead, you know you have entered a new subtopic area.

The *first, or topic, sentence of every paragraph* is so important it warrants its own section. Read the following "Focus on the Firsts" section to see why!

The *conclusion*, typically the last paragraph or two, summarizes the ideas presented.

For a very broad overview of your material, you can read the title, the introductory paragraph(s), the subheadings, and the conclusion. But if you want a lot more substance in your reading, read the first sentences of paragraphs.

Focus on the Firsts

The first sentence of every paragraph, or the *topic sentence*, is *the* most important part of cheat reading. You may know this already, but it's worth repeating:

> The main idea of almost every nonfiction, published paragraph is found in the first sentence of the paragraph.

By reading just the first sentence of every paragraph in the order written, you'll find the meat of the writer's outline.

def•i•ni•tion

The first sentence of a paragraph, where the author wrote the main idea, is called the **topic sentence.**

So if you want to get the main ideas quickly without wasting time, read the title and the first few paragraphs of introduction, and then *stop* reading all the rest of the words. Read *just* the first sentence of a paragraph, get the idea, and move on to the first sentence in the next paragraph. Continue doing this until you feel you've read enough based on your *why* and *what for*, or until you reach the last few paragraphs. Be sure to read the last few paragraphs fully because they typically serve as the conclusion of a nonfiction piece.

Reading firsts helps you …

- ◆ Find and retain the answers to your *what for* question.

- ◆ Familiarize yourself with the writer's structure so you can choose which paragraphs to read in more detail.

- ◆ Quickly weed out uninteresting or uninformative material.

- ◆ Build a mental framework that makes it easier to remember.

- ◆ Save time—perhaps the most important reason of all!

Speed Tip

If you can't find the main idea in the first sentence, you can try a couple other places. Some authors like to put their main ideas in the last sentence. Rarely will you find it buried in the middle. Sometimes, the first sentence of a paragraph is more fluff than information. In such cases, it's okay to move on to the second sentence. But remember, you only want to read into the paragraph just enough to get the main idea and then get out!

Where to Look for Other Clues

Some other clues can indicate what's important in a piece of writing. When looking for the writer's outline, also look for these (some of which I briefly mentioned earlier):

◆ Pictures, illustrations, graphs, or charts

◆ Captions

◆ Anything pulled out in a margin or box

◆ Bold or italic print

◆ Bulleted and numbered lists

◆ Length of the article

Pictures, illustrations, graphs, or charts are visual representations of the author's ideas. Many times, these help solidify your understanding of a concept written about in the text. Speed read by reading the pictures!

Captions are text descriptions of the pictures that clarify what you're looking at. Sometimes a picture with a caption is all you need to understand what's being described in the text.

Depending on the material you're reading, you might find things placed *in the margin* such as an important quote from the article or a definition of a term discussed. These are pulled out of the text because the information has been deemed useful and important.

Bold and italic print draw your eyes to important information. In academic textbooks, a bold word indicates a new vocabulary word and italics shows a point of emphasis. In other nonfiction, bold may be something the author wants to draw your attention to and italics may show an important description or point of emphasis. Both are worth noting when cheat reading.

Bulleted and *numbered lists* are examples from a main point. Earlier in this section, for example, the bulleted list gives you the "outline" or overview of where to look for other clues in the writer's outline. In this case, each paragraph that follows explains each point.

Looking at the *length of the article* is useful for time management purposes. If you have 10 minutes to read and you want to read a 17-page article, you might decide to cheat read it first so you can get through more of it in the time you have. Or if you have a 30-page textbook chapter, you might want to break it down into smaller sections, making it easier to follow the writer's outline.

So how can you best use all this information for your reading needs? Perhaps just knowing that the main ideas of paragraphs are typically located in the first sentences (or two) empowers you to focus your attention there. Or perhaps understanding that the introduction and conclusion should provide you with where the reading intends to go and where it ends up will help you get what you need quickly. Using this cheat reading process as a guide, not a strict procedure, helps you identify the most important ideas, quickly!

Speed Tip _____

When pressed for time, sometimes you're better off doing a first sentence cheat read than reading everything really, really fast. For example, you have a document with 20 paragraphs. You could read the first sentences of all 20 paragraphs in the same amount of time you could read just the first 20 sentences. You'd understand more and have a better overview of the main points of the entire article rather than just the first 20 sentences.

Cheat Reading Made Easy

Here's an easy exercise in cheat reading. After reading these directions, be prepared to time yourself for 2 minutes.

1. Using your chosen nonfiction magazine or book, turn to the table of contents and locate an article or chapter you'd like to read.

2. When you start timing, read the first paragraph or two of the introduction in its entirety. Remember to practice with your favorite speed reading strategies!

3. Then *stop* reading everything and focus your attention on just the first sentence of the next paragraph down, then skip to the next first sentence of the next paragraph down, and continue on. Remember, you are *only* looking for the writer's outline, not all the details.

4. Look around for other clues such as pictures, captions, bold, or italics.

5. If you reach the end of the material before the 2 minutes are up, read the last concluding paragraph in its entirety.

6. At the end of the 2 minutes, close the reading material and on a separate piece of paper, write a summary of what you just read. Spend at least 2 minutes doing this. You can write in either bullet points or sentences.

Did you find the writer's outline? From my experience, it's there about 95 percent of the time on edited material. As for the other 5 percent, that's usually either poor writing or poor editing. You'll come across this at some point, but more often than not you'll find the outline.

Did you get farther in the 2 minutes than if you read every word? Did you get a general understanding of the article? Hopefully you did because you were reading the writer's outline.

What you didn't get were the details, or the explanation, of the writer's main ideas. The meat you find when cheat reading consists of about 50 percent of the content, while the remaining 50 percent consists of details and explanation.

> **Speed Tip**
>
> When cheat reading in the future, you can figure out how much time you might want to spend on a chapter or an article by multiplying the number of pages by 15 seconds per page. You may cheat read in less time or more, depending on your speed reading strategies and the number of words on a page, but 15 seconds is a good starting point for calculating your time.

By learning how to locate the writer's outline, you can accomplish any or all of the following:

♦ Weed out unimportant or not useful material, quickly!

♦ Find the important information, quickly!

♦ Be introduced to difficult, technical, or unfamiliar material by first cheat reading the writer's outline and then allowing you to feel more comfortable approaching the details.

- ◆ Pick and choose the area(s) you want to spend your reading time on.

- ◆ Create stronger long-term retention through repetition. Cheat reading first and then reading in more detail provides you with the built-in repetition needed to build strong retention. (See Chapter 9 for more on reading and memory issues.)

- ◆ Quickly review something you read a while ago, revisiting the main ideas without rereading it all.

Speed Tip

When I teach high school and college students, I suggest that instead of rereading the chapters before exams, they cheat read the chapter, solidifying what they do know while looking for material they don't know and need to focus on. This allows them to study and still get sleep before the exam.

I credit cheat reading for allowing me to stay current with the magazines I regularly read. Even if I had the luxury of time to slowly pour over every word in the material, I still wouldn't because this strategy provides me the immediate gratification of getting the information I need in less time. That enables me to read more … and there's always more! I also use cheat reading for reading newspaper articles and nonfiction books. I tell you how in Chapter 10.

Cheat Reading Fiction

Cheat reading is a strategy used solely for nonfiction because there's a predictable structure inherent in that type of writing. Fiction has a very different structure and, therefore, needs to be read differently. That's the beauty of fiction!

There are certainly things to consider when reading fiction, such as identifying the basic elements, analyzing its literary characteristics, and tracking the characters. Chapter 10 dives into fiction in more detail.

Approaching Technical Material

I've noticed a strange but common occurrence with many people I've taught to speed read: they start reading something technical or unfamiliar and begin "studying" it. This only makes their brain work harder than necessary. *Study reading* is done at a very slow speed and typically entails reading word for word in an effort to memorize.

I've seen these same people struggle with technical material because they have little to no understanding about what they're reading. How can you remember something when you haven't even figured out what the material is about? No wonder technical material isn't fun to read.

Take my advice: *don't read to remember; read to understand.* Creating usable memory requires having some general understanding. Once you understand, you have a much better chance of remembering.

When you approach material you consider technical, do you immediately think *This is going to be hard?* Don't think that! Instead, remember what you've learned thus far and approach technical material, or any completely new information, with smart reading strategies. Try cheat reading, reading the bigger words or thought chunks, or using a hand or card pacer method. Each of these techniques, when skillfully combined, make a difficult reading task into a less challenging, more efficient one.

def•i•ni•tion

Study reading is anything you read and learn from that you need or want to use later on. For students, it's usually for tests and papers. For businesspeople, it's typically for sharing at meetings, writing reports, and giving presentations. Some people just like to learn new things so they spend time study reading what they're interested in.

And the Results Are ...

If you read through this chapter without trying to actually cheat read, that's considered cheating! Knowing about the concept is different than personally experiencing it. Try it now, it only takes 4 minutes to do—2 minutes to locate the writer's outline and 2 minutes to write down your keepers. If you already did the exercise, consider doing it again on other material. The more experience you have doing this, the more comfortable you'll become making it a regular habit.

The Least You Need to Know

- Nonfiction is more challenging to read than fiction.

- Before reading anything, ask yourself why you are reading *and* what are you reading for.

- Get an overview of nonfiction to help you know where you want to spend your time.

- The most important information in nonfiction is located in the first sentence of every paragraph.

- Cheat reading enables you to get through more reading in less time.

- When approaching technical material, read to understand first and then read to remember.

Chapter 8

Getting Out

In This Chapter

◆ What's your exit strategy?

◆ Look for the golden nuggets of information

◆ Think and question while you read

◆ Watch for turn signals

◆ Remember this is a marathon, not a 50-yard dash

As you learned in Chapter 7, reading any piece of nonfiction straight from word one to the very last word is typically not the most efficient or effective strategy. (For fiction, however, it *is* the best strategy, as you'll see in Chapter 10.) By taking advantage of cheat reading, including reading first sentences, the "getting in" part is pretty easy (see Chapter 7 if you need a refresher). Now your decision is whether it's time to "get out," or if you need to go back and read some more information. After all, why read everything all the time if you don't have to?

What do I mean by "getting out"? I mean knowing when you've found all the information you need from your reading. When you have, you can and should get out and move on to something else. In this chapter, I offer several reasons why you might want to "get out" of the reading, and give you options how to do it.

Skimming, Scanning, and Skipping

One obvious way to get out quickly is to use any speed reading strategy that puts you into the higher-speed gears. In addition to those you've already been introduced to in earlier chapters, two more overdrive gears are called *skimming* and *scanning*. Many people think skimming and scanning are the same thing, but they're not. Their purposes are actually quite different.

Skimming: A Quick Filter

Skimming is looking for general or main ideas. For example, when you read a newspaper, your eyes typically skim the headlines looking for a general article of interest. You might also skim a chapter or report to get a general understanding of what it's about. You probably also skim the menu of a restaurant you've never been to before to see what they offer.

Speed Secret

Consider cheat reading "deliberate" skimming. *Deliberate skimming* is intentionally looking for the writer's outline and getting a general overview by following the text in the order the author intended. *Haphazard skimming*, on the other hand, has no rhyme or reason as to where your eyes go, providing you with bits and pieces of disjointed information. Deliberate skimming is more effective and efficient than haphazard.

Skimming should be used when …

♦ You're being introduced to a new topic area.

♦ You need to review material you've previously read.

♦ You already have a lot of background knowledge about the topic.

♦ You want to understand the big picture, or main ideas, first before delving into the details.

♦ You want to get the essence without all the details.

♦ You have a lot to read and only a small amount of time.

For the average speed reader, an effective skimming rate ranges from 800 to 1,200 words per minute. Edward Fry, the author of *How to Skim* (Cambridge University Press, 1963), believes that skimming can be done effectively at this speed with 50 percent comprehension. From my experience performing skimming drills in my classes, people aren't too comfortable with 50 percent and aim for more at this speed.

Your hands are very helpful for skimming as they quickly pull your eyes down the page looking for general ideas. Some of the most useful skimming hand strategies from Chapter 2 include the following:

- ◆ Z Pattern
- ◆ S Pattern
- ◆ Point-to-Point
- ◆ Open Hand Wiggle

Here's a quick skimming exercise for you to try:

1. Choose one of the shorter articles from Appendix B you haven't read yet.

2. Take only 2 minutes to deliberately skim the article.

3. Use your preferred skimming hand method and follow the format in Chapter 7 for cheat reading.

4. Write down what you think the article is about on a separate piece of paper.

5. Calculate your words per minute by dividing the number of words in the article by two.

How did you do? Is skimming a method you're comfortable with? Remember, this skimming strategy is meant for when you only need the main ideas.

Scanning Is for Finding the Right Answer

Scanning is looking for something specific. Your eyes scan a newspaper looking for the specific baseball scores from the previous night. You scan the financial pages looking for a specific stock and its current market price. You scan when looking for someone's name in a telephone directory. (Can you imagine trying to skim a telephone directory looking for one specific name? You might never find it!)

Your hands are also helpful for scanning as they help keep your place as you go down the page. It's almost as if when your hand drags down the page looking for just one thing, your mind says *no … no … no … no …* and then *yes!* when you finally land on what you're looking for.

Some the most useful scanning hand strategies from Chapter 2 include the following:

◆ Left Pointer Pull

◆ Center Pointer pull

◆ Double Pointer Pull

◆ Blank Card Method

Try this scanning exercise:

Using your preferred scanning hand method, turn to the "Tattoo Pioneer: Shanghai Kate Hellenbrand" article in Appendix B and count the number of times you see the word *tattoo* or any other word with *tattoo* in it (e.g., *tattooed*). And yes, the word in the title counts! (The correct answer is provided at the end of this chapter.)

How did you do? Are you comfortable with scanning? Remember, this scanning strategy is meant for when you are looking for specifics, not main ideas.

Speed Reading Partners: Skimming and Scanning

You probably use skimming and scanning together often without realizing it. For example, you use both strategies when looking at a web page you've never seen before, first figuring out generally what it's all about (skimming) and then looking for some piece of specific information (scanning). Restaurant menus are also good places to use both strategies. You first skim for the kinds of food offered and then scan for the food you're most interested in. Legal contracts should be skimmed first to see what main topic areas are included and then scanned to find the details specific to the contractual agreement. Textbook chapters can be skimmed to find the writer's outline and main ideas and then scanned to get the answers to the questions at the end of the reading.

Speed Tip

Many people think they're skimming material when actually they're scanning, and vice versa. This confusion is natural, but I hope this section clarifies the word usage: *skimming* is looking for general ideas; *scanning* is looking for specifics.

Skipping: Always an Option

Depending on your reason why and what you're reading for, after a quick skim, you might find that you don't need or want to continue reading. As you're reading, you might realize that you already know what you're reading and decide to skip that section. Sometimes you might just find you're not interested. I hereby give you permission to skip anything you're reading for these reasons!

When you learn to use your eyes, brain, and hands effectively with these strategies, you'll be able to breeze through a lot of information quickly and accurately. So the next time you open a newspaper, magazine, text, or other material, think about breezing through it by skimming, scanning, or skipping, according to your reasons why and what for.

Finding the Golden Nuggets

American filmmaker and novelist Nora Ephron once said, "I always read the last page of a book first so that if I die before I finish I'll know how it turned out." Although I don't recommend routinely ruining a good story, Ephron's thinking is smart in that she wants to get the good stuff—fast!

What Ephron calls "good stuff," I call golden nuggets. Golden nuggets are those bits and pieces that, when you read, make you think *Ah-ha!* or *Wow, what a great idea!* or *Gee, that's interesting.* Sometimes you find just the thing to help you smooth over a rough relationship with your spouse or help you feel confident asking for a raise. You may find a room design that's perfect for your new apartment or a workflow process worth sharing with your team. The good stuff is there; you just have to find it!

The true science of "getting out" entails quickly finding your golden nuggets. You already have many fabulous strategies to help you do this:

♦ Knowing your reason why and what you are reading for

♦ Cheat reading

♦ Using hand and card pacers

♦ Skimming and scanning (or skipping!)

Looking for golden nuggets saves you time and keeps you alert while reading. Remember Chapter 6, where I introduced you to the idea of setting time and page goals? Keeping in mind your desire to find golden nuggets helps you reach your time and page goals.

Speed Secret
Someone once told me that when you read, you're getting the collective knowledge of someone else's universe. What a privilege this is! If you think of reading as an opportunity to benefit from someone else's perspective and life experiences, and if you can find their golden nuggets, you are that much richer. The great ideas and thoughts you glean from reading help you navigate life in ways you probably couldn't have done on your own.

Thinking and Questioning While You Read

"Woman gives birth to 300-pound baby!"

"Aliens found working at meat-processing plant!"

You've probably seen headlines such as these on tabloid covers while waiting in the supermarket line. How do you react to them? Maybe your face starts to screw up, your eyebrows scrunch together, and your eyes narrow. You may even grunt, shake your head in disbelief or amazement, and/or smirk. Maybe you just roll your eyes and move on. Whatever your reaction, you're probably also thinking, whether you realize it or not, could this be true?! *Don't believe everything you read!*

> **Speed Secret**
>
> Reading is an event of thinking cued by text, according to college professor Dr. Joe Vaughan. There is no right or wrong thinking, just a personal interpretation of what you read.

All readers should have this healthy skepticism. In essence, being skeptical means you stop reading and begin thinking about what you already know about the subject based on your background knowledge and beliefs. As you read, you mentally ask yourself, or the author, questions to help you decide what you want to believe and how you want to react.

This mental questioning is essential for truly effective reading. You might ask questions like these:

♦ What is the author's background, and what gives him or her the experience to write about this?

♦ What are the writer's motives for writing this?

♦ How old is this information? When was it written?

♦ Is this truly a fact or an opinion—a personal conclusion based on the author's experience?

♦ How does this match up with my knowledge or experience?

♦ What do I want to believe?

By constantly thinking about what you're reading, why the author wrote it, and how you're reacting to it will keep you mentally involved and active in your reading process. Those who read without this mental questioning lose out on the best of what reading has to offer.

Everyone Has an Opinion

If you ask 10 people who perform the same job to read the same piece of material, you could come up with 10 varying interpretations of the same information. This is because people's beliefs are created from their base of background knowledge, and everyone's background knowledge is unique. This is one likely reason why readers who participate in book clubs get into heated discussions about the meaning of what they're reading. It doesn't mean you are right and others are wrong. Everyone is entitled to his or her own opinion.

Connecting with an Author

Have you ever made contact via phone, letter, or e-mail with an author whose writing you are either very interested in and/or take issue with? I don't recommend you do this with *every* author you read, but making that connection is a great way to solidify your comprehension, retention, and interest in the subject matter.

If the author responds, that communication also adds to your background knowledge, which helps you better read and understand future material on similar subjects.

The next time you're reading something you have a visceral response to, ask your brain a few questions and/or engage with the author. It helps you feel more confident in your ability to comprehend your material and trust your brain.

Summarize with Tellbacks

On the road to getting out, you can perform a powerful comprehension exercise called *tellbacks*. When you do a tellback, you solidify the information you read into a personalized summary and gauge your level of comprehension. Tellbacks can be quite helpful and build your confidence so you know whether you're ready to get out of your reading or if you need to stay in longer.

Do tellbacks as soon as you finish reading. You can come up with bullet points or retell the author's outline. You can say your summary to yourself, another person, your cat or dog, your mirror, etc. You can write down your thoughts, say them out loud, or record them on a tape/digital recorder to have for later review, if needed. You may feel awkward the first few times you do tellbacks,

def·i·ni·tion

A **tellback** is a verbal or written summary of something you read. In effect, the comprehension part of the One-Minute Timing exercise and the 3-2-1 Drill, when you write down or say the points you remember, include tellbacks.

but the more you do them, the more effective and efficient your brain will become at assimilating and consolidating the information you read. Your solid comprehension will enhance your retention and build reading confidence and competence for quickly getting out.

Follow the Signal Words

In every type of material you read, there are *signal words*—just like a car's turn signals—that help you anticipate a change in direction or what's coming next. If you become aware of them and intentionally look for them, signal words prove to be incredibly useful for directing where you go when reading.

def•i•ni•tion

A **signal word** is like a reading road sign: it indicates where you are or where you are headed. In reading material, signal words are conjunctions or words that join phrases, sentences, or paragraphs.

Speed Tip

Signal words are particularly useful for note-taking because they provide strong clues as to what's important to write down.

Your car's turn signals indicate whether you're turning left or right. Signal words offer a few other directional choices:

- Additional information
- Sequence or order
- Reasoning and explanation
- Reversing thought
- Example/illustration
- Summary or conclusion

Review the following list of signal words under each type of direction. You're probably familiar with most of these words already. Being aware of them helps you understand where the author intends the reading to take you.

Additional Information

also	furthermore
and	in addition
another	likewise
besides	moreover

Sequence or Order

because	in order that
finally	next
first, second, third, …	one, two, three, …

Reasoning and Explanation

the reason for	then
because	since

Reversing Thought

although	nevertheless
but	on the contrary
conversely	on the other hand
however	unlike
instead	yet

Example/Illustration

for example	in other words
for instance	such as

Summary or Conclusion

consequently	therefore
in conclusion	thus
in summary	

When you see one of these signal words, you may decide you need to pay more attention to a certain passage or that you don't need to read more at all and can get out.

Spot the Organizational Pattern

When we talk to others, we most often relate events in the order they occur so our listeners can follow our thoughts and don't become confused. In writing, authors

def•i•ni•tion

An **organizational pattern** is the author's plan of action for getting his or her thoughts across. If you can identify it in your reading, you will be able to anticipate the order in which the material will be presented.

present their ideas in *organizational patterns* so the reader will understand and follow along. If you can identify the organizational pattern, you'll follow the author's thoughts better and more efficiently, increasing your chances of getting out sooner.

Study the following list of some of the more common organizational patterns, from the easiest to identify or most common to the least common.

Organizational Pattern	Description	Example
Chronological order	Describes the order the events occurred	First, second, third
Description/explanation	Lists characteristics features, and examples	Smells like a fish; big, round and squishy; three reasons for saving money
Cause and effect	Describes the reason(s) why and the result(s)	The *Titanic* hit an iceberg, and the ship sank.
Process order	Describes how to do something	Owners manuals and cookbooks
Compare and contrast	Looks at similarities and differences	Evaluating different business models, comparative religion courses, home loan types, etc.
Classification	Arranges information into categories	Inexpensive office supplies; fast cars; low-fat food
Problem to solution	Presents a problem, including its cause, and then offers its solutions and details	High levels of pollution and possible solutions
Climactic order	Builds ideas from least to most important	Most movie scripts and fiction books

And the Results Are ...

Most times, you can get out fast using skimming, scanning, or skipping strategies. Sometimes you may choose to stay with the reading for the long haul, reading it all because your reason why or what for reasons dictate. Maybe you have a test and have no choice but read it all. Or maybe you're just plain interested in what you're reading! Whatever the reason, use the speed reading strategies that you've found work best for you so you'll get out quicker. The best way to know which are best suited for you is by experimenting with them and timing yourself.

Choose to either do a One-Minute Timing exercise or a 3-2-1 Drill in Appendix B. Consider warming up your eyes using the Discipline Your Eyes Exercise from Chapter 3. And be sure to document your time on the appropriate time chart in Appendix C. Use your preferred speed reading methods—remember the pacers, too! Track your scores.

The Least You Need to Know

◆ Getting out means using effective reading strategies to make intelligent decisions about when you find what you need from your reading.

◆ Skimming, scanning, and skipping are three options for quickly understanding the main ideas, finding specifics, or skipping it all together.

◆ Golden nuggets are the good stuff you find when reading.

◆ Always be a little skeptical of the author's motives or content by thinking and asking questions.

◆ Tellbacks are comprehension summaries that help you build reading confidence and competence.

◆ Locating the author's signal words and following the writing's organizational patterns gets you out quicker, with good comprehension.

Scanning exercise answer: The number of times the word *tattoo* or any version of it appears in the "Tattoo Pioneer" article is 49.

9

Don't Go Back

In This Chapter

◆ What "don't go back" means

◆ A look at memory

◆ What makes us forget

◆ Documenting your keepers

You got in Chapter 7 and got out in Chapter 8. Now, how do you not go back? We can look at this concept in two ways: (1) you seek to understand enough of what you're reading and have embedded it into your memory banks so you feel satisfied and have no need to go back to it, or (2) if you need to go back—for a test or project, for example—you've already identified the important parts and only have to do a quick review.

Speed reading is really about two things: increasing your words per minute and reducing your time spent on reading materials. By using a combination of understanding how your memory works and employing targeted note-taking strategies, you'll find your need to go back limited, which saves you time. And when you do go back, it will be for a specific reason.

How Your Memory Works

Some people have impeccable memories and can remember the tiniest details from years ago. Other people can hardly remember what they had for breakfast when they get to lunchtime. We're all human, and humans have *memory* issues. And here's the kicker: the human brain is *programmed* to forget! In order for it to remember, you have to actively pursue the information to harness it for future use.

In a nutshell, to create a memory, your brain goes through three processes:

♦ Acquisition

♦ Retention

♦ Retrieval

All three phases happen all the time without your conscious knowledge. But becoming conscious of the process and making it intentional can greatly enhance your memory.

def•i•ni•tion

Memory is the mind's ability to retain learned information and knowledge of past events and experiences, coupled with the ability to retrieve that information and knowledge. It could be a short-term memory, which ranges from 5 to 8 seconds to 1 day or 2, to long-term memory, which is what comprises our background knowledge.

Grab Hold of Information

Acquisition is the first memory stage, when your brain is exposed to and absorbs information. To absorb information, you need to …

def•i•ni•tion

Acquisition can be defined as the ability to come into possession of a skill or knowledge.

Pay attention! Nothing goes into your brain unless you pay attention. (When you use speed reading strategies, you're *forced* to pay attention.)

Think about the future, or more specifically, when you'll need the information again. If you have this in mind *and* have a system for remembering or finding it again, you're more apt to absorb it now.

Attach personal meaning to the information. Although everything you read is registered in your brain, only those things you attach personal meaning to will be easily remembered.

Engage in collaborative learning. You'll absorb and remember information better when you talk about it with others.

Make the information your own. If you want to remember a definition, it's easier to remember if you put it into your own words.

Preserve What You Find

Retention is the second memory phase, during which you keep the absorbed information in your head. If you haven't absorbed the information in the first place, you can't expect to retain it! In order to achieve retention, you need to …

Create order. When you were young and first learned the alphabet, you probably repeated the letters in order so you could remember all 26 letters. Order is easily found in cheat reading; you find the writer's outline, an organizational scheme your brain can easily follow.

def•i•ni•tion

> **Retention** is your ability to recall or recognize what has been learned or experienced.

Associate the information with something you already know. Remember the discussion of the importance of background knowledge earlier in the book? When you already know something about something, it makes it easier to add something new!

Use repetition over time. This is probably the most useful way to retain information. Students who cram for exams by repeatedly memorizing information over a short time frame, usually a day or night, are *not* doing this correctly. Although they might remember enough information for the exam the next day, they don't retain the material much longer than that, which means they have to restudy for the final exam. If instead, students reviewed the information a little each night for a week or more before the exam, they would have retained the information longer and stronger for future use.

Think about repetition this way: say you meet your friend Joshua for lunch once every 6 months or so. You talk about each others' families, work, and hobbies. You enjoy the conversation and are happy to know him. You return home that evening and summarize for your spouse what you and Joshua talked about, providing just the highlights and omitting the nitty-gritty details that aren't important to the summary or that you don't remember. Three months later you run into a mutual friend and you tell them you had lunch with Joshua. You search your brain for any information you can provide about what you talked about over lunch, and most likely, what you remembered is drastically reduced compared to the night you talked with your spouse. You probably remembered those things that were most important to you—his child got into his or her college of choice (but you don't remember which college it was), Joshua ran his first marathon (but you don't recall his finish time), and he changed jobs (but to where you don't remember!). You remember the essence of the lunch conversation but not all the details. You may even remember where you met but not what you ate.

Now let's say after your lunch with Joshua, you meet up with him again on the baseball field for your sons' baseball practice. This provides you with more frequent exposure to Joshua and the opportunity to follow up on your lunch conversation. You revisit the information and learn that Joshua's daughter got into the University of Vermont; he is now training for another marathon and wants to beat his first time of 3 hours, 10 minutes; and he now works as a financial analyst at an insurance company. Because you had experienced repetition with Joshua over time, your memory is now solidified.

If you want to remember something you read, find a way to review the material again shortly after reading it, talk to someone about it, or be exposed to related information soon after. However you can arrange for doing the repetition will be time well spent for retaining what you read.

Teach others. To remember anything, you must first understand it. And to teach anything, you need to first understand it. So finding ways to teach others what you're reading about helps you retain the information.

Speed Tip

Remember tellbacks from Chapter 8? Performing brief auditory summaries of what you read solidifies your understanding and enhances your retention.

Speed Secret

When creating folders in your paper or on-screen filing system, think about what category the information goes in and combine categories so you have larger categories. The less segmentation your brain has to endure, the better it remembers.

Combine similar information into groups. Thought chunking (see Chapter 4) is a perfect example of this. Instead of reading one word at a time, you can read groups of words that form a thought in the same amount of time, creating more meaning for your brain. Your brain likes to process meaningful groups of thoughts and information instead of one word at a time.

Find the emotion. It's a fact: we have stronger memories for things we experience that elicit a strong emotion, either positive or negative. People who have won a competition, experienced their own wedding day, or had a spectacular meal in a five-star restaurant can tell you in excruciating detail about that event. The same is true for those who went through a nasty divorce, got a flat tire on the highway in a strange city at the dead of night without a flashlight, or failed the last course they needed to graduate. All elicit emotions that regular day-to-day life doesn't.

Works of fiction are often rife with emotions and can, therefore, connect to your memory more readily. Nonfiction often doesn't carry this inherent emotional quality, so you must create connections between the material you're reading and your own emotions to help the information stick in your memory.

Write it down. This is useful for the retention and retrieval stages of memory. Let's say you want to remember to call your best friend on her birthday. It's 2 weeks away, and you make a mental note that you want to make this call. Maybe a week later, now 7 days before her birthday, the thought resurfaces and again you make another mental note about the birthday phone call. Now it's 3 days before, and again the thought resurfaces. You tuck it away in your head and expect it to come up on the day you want.

Unfortunately, unless something happens specifically on that day to remind you of your friend or you hear someone singing "Happy Birthday," most likely you'll forget to make the call on the exact day. You'll probably recall the memory the next day or two later.

If you wrote down the thought and stuck it in a place you would see or be reminded of more frequently, such as on your calendar, or your to-do list for that day, or on a sticky note posted by your phone, your chances of remembering are greatly increased.

In my house, when we run out of a food item, we immediately write it down on the weekly shopping list. If we don't, there's a very high probability we'll forget we needed to replace the item and would only remember when we looked for the item again, typically after we went food shopping for the week!

What does this have to do with remembering what you read? You guessed it—write down what you want to remember! And put it in a place you will see again and review it.

Salvage the Memory

Retrieval is the final memory stage, when you take out the information you've stored in your long-term memory. It's been suggested that long-term memory is permanent, that nothing is forgotten; only the means of retrieving it is lost.

I am a native English speaker who studied Spanish for more than 10 years and even had the privilege of spending a summer in Madrid, Spain, speaking with native speakers. I used to write 10-page papers in Spanish and read Spanish novels with

def•i•ni•tion

Retrieval is your ability to bring stored information into consciousness. It's like a (search and) recovery mission for your brain.

comprehension. Fast-forward 25 years. Today, I know I have long-term memory for the language, but because I haven't had the opportunity to use it in my daily (weekly, monthly, or yearly!) life, my Spanish became rusty. I know it's all stored in long-term memory and I feel confident that if I took another Spanish course, read another Spanish novel (with a Spanish-English dictionary next to me), or spent some time in a Spanish-speaking environment, most of what I learned would come back to my conscious memory.

So how do we retrieve memories? Here are a few thoughts:

Go back in time. Cue your brain by mentally going back to the time or place you were reading. This may trigger a clearer memory.

Get in the mood. Try to re-create the same emotional state you were in during the acquisition phase.

Use all your senses. If you can re-create the experience as you remembered it, it will be easier for you to retrieve the material stored in your memory.

Look back at what you've written down. When you write down things you want to remember, remembering to look at what you wrote is important!

Speed Tip

When reading, taking short, frequent breaks helps your retrieval because you have more firsts and lasts than middles.

Remember that meaningful material is stored more accurately. You'll remember things that have personal importance for you, so find something that matters in what you read so you can remember it better.

Capitalize on the firsts and lasts. This is where we remember firsts and lasts more than we do middles. If I asked you to go to the store to shop for 10 items, and I told you what the items were but you didn't write them down, you'd probably remember the first 2 or 3 items and last 2 or 3 items. You'd mostly forget the ones in the middle.

Factors for Forgetting

You can't expect to remember everything you read and recall it at will at any time. *Forgetting* is part of being human. Forgetting isn't usually permanent unless you didn't acquire the memory in the first place. It may be a temporary failure of retrieval where the memory is momentarily unavailable and accessible later. You've probably experienced this, when some bit of information is on the "tip of the tongue" but you just can't recall it right now. You eventually will remember it, but maybe not when you want to. For me, it usually comes up hours or days later out of the blue.

What causes us to forget things we read?
Here are a few common conditions:

♦ A lack of attention while reading

♦ Interference or distraction while reading

♦ Lack of interest or motivation to
  remember

♦ Not understanding what you read in
  the first place

♦ Not enough background knowledge

♦ Not enough repetition over time

♦ Not enough sleep (You need sleep to recharge your mental battery.)

♦ Stress

def•i•ni•tion

Forgetting refers to the loss of a memory. Often, the failure to retrieve a memory reflects not "forgetting" or loss per se, but the fact that the memory was not stored well in the first place.

If any of these factors exist, the possibility of not going back increases—or simply said, the need to go back increases.

Speed Tip

Scientists at Stanford University have discovered that the brain forgets trivial information so it can more easily store and retrieve important information. Forgetting not
only helps the brain conserve energy, it also improves short-term memory and recall
of important details. So the next time you berate yourself for not remembering something, remember that forgetting sometimes helps you remember!

The Ebbinghaus Curve of Forgetting

Hermann Ebbinghaus (1850–1909) was a German psychologist who pioneered an
experimental study of memory and discovered the forgetting curve and the learning
curve. He studied memories by teaching himself lists of nonsense words and then
studying his retention of these lists over periods of hours to days. What he found is
documented on the Forgetting Curve, whereby …

A   Most forgetting occurs very soon after learning and continues with no
     review or rehearsal.

B   When meaningful material is used and exposure is repeated, the forgetting curve is not so steep.

C   With more review and rehearsal, the forgetting becomes less.

D   With even more review and rehearsal, memory becomes solidified.

The Forgetting Curve shows that humans tend to halve their memory of newly learned knowledge in a matter of days or weeks unless they consciously review the learned material.

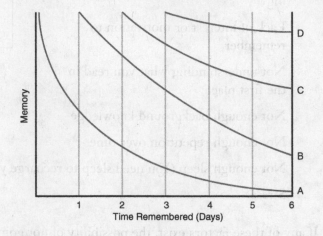

Ask anyone 60 or older about memory, and most people will admit theirs doesn't seem to be as sharp as it used to be. As early as our 20s, we begin to lose brain cells a few at a time and our bodies begin to slow down production of the chemicals our brains need to work. As we age, this makes it harder to recall stored information.

> **Speed Secret**
>
> Your distant memories aren't usually affected by aging, but your recent memory may be. For example, you may forget names of people you've recently met or even what you did last weekend. For reading, this means you may have trouble remembering what you just read! These are (unfortunately) normal changes.

When you're young, using repetition to learn things is quite possible. However, as you age, this no longer works. Instead, to remember, you need to capitalize on your background knowledge and make more associations from what you're reading to what you already know.

Here are a few more things that might help anyone at any age remember better:

- Write things down.

- Follow a set routine.

- Keep a detailed calendar with all your appointments and special events.

- Put frequently used items, like car keys and umbrellas, in the same place every time.

- Repeat a person's name when you meet new people. Also make some mental connection about their physical features to someone or something you already know.

- Mentally go through the alphabet to help trigger the memory of a word you're trying to remember.

The better you remember, the less often you'll need to go back.

Help the Best Stand Out

At times, reading something once—or cheat reading it first and then reading in detail—is not enough. Students frequently need to return to their reading material to review information for tests. Businesspeople need to return to previously read documents to retrieve information for meetings or reports. Chefs return to cookbooks to reference recipes. Expectant moms frequently return to pregnancy books to see if what they're experiencing is normal and to find out what's coming next.

So the idea of getting out needs to include how to locate the useable information again. The whole idea is to avoid rereading everything again and to have your *keepers* stand out.

def•i•ni•tion

A **keeper** is a new idea, typically some piece of information, you want to remember. Keepers should always be written down, looked at again, and/or used for future reference.

Writing on/in the Material

From kindergarten all the way to high school, many students use books issued by the school system, and students are instructed to *not* write in them. This makes sense for the school system because it can reuse the books for many years, saving tons of money. After high school, however, most formal learning courses require you to purchase a textbook or another workbook, some of which are designed for you to write in. Some people feel funny writing in books because they've never done it or for some other reason they can't bring themselves to write in their material.

Whether you like to write in your material or not, I encourage you to think about doing it. Marking your material is like marking your memory, which creates a visual association for your memory to anchor to. You might remember that you wrote something about that in the margin, on the right-hand side, in blue ink, the three key points … *oh yeah, now I remember!*"

> **Speed Tip** _____
>
> You can write in any reading material you purchase for your own private use, but *only* if you think you'll need to look at it again to find your keepers. If you don't think you'll need to go back, don't waste your time writing notes, highlighting, or creating marginalia (more on this in later sections). Remember why you're reading and decide whether taking any form of notes is necessary.

Use Color

Highlighting key ideas is very effective in helping make your keepers stand out. It doesn't matter what color highlighter you use; what matters is how much you highlight. Look at any college student's textbook, and you might see lots of highlighting, sometimes with more than one color, of information the student thinks is important. Because most of the information students read is new to them, they tend to highlight way too much, thinking everything is important.

> **Speed Tip** _____
>
> Did you know they make erasable highlighters these days? When you accidentally mark a wrong passage or want to change your mind, you can just erase the highlight.

Follow this rule of thumb when it comes to highlighting: if you find you are highlighting more than 25 percent of any page, then you probably need to take more complete notes on a separate piece of paper. More than 25 percent highlighting means the material is unfamiliar or technical for you and you need a better method than coloring it to learn it.

Here are a few other highlighting guidelines to keep in mind:

◆ Read an entire paragraph or page before highlighting anything; otherwise, you may highlight more than you need.

◆ Highlight *only* if you know you'll need to go back to review the information again. Otherwise, you are wasting your time.

◆ Highlight *only* key words or thought chunks, not full sentences.

Writing in the Margin

Another way to mark your keepers is to make personal notes in the margin. There is no right or wrong way to make margin notes. Some like to create a title of sorts next to important paragraphs, while others are happy to write cryptic keywords or phrases that only they understand.

Levenger, a catalog company that specializes in "serious tools for readers," has created its own "Helpful Marks for Readers for Masterly Marginalia," which I've reprinted here. Levenger is the only formal source I've found that provides more creative and interesting options than what I have for readers.

Speed Tip

If the margin of your reading material isn't wide enough for the notes you want to write, use Post-it notes to extend the page width.

Mark	Meaning
⬯	interesting
⬯ (hatched)	memorize this
ʔʔ ʔʔ	repeated information
⟶	causes, leads to
⟷	both cause and effect
∴	therefore
¶	paragraph
cf.	compare
w/	with
w/o	without
vs.	versus, against
def.	definition

continues

continued

Mark	Meaning
i.e.	that is
ca.	circa
re	in reference to, concerning
vo.	vocabulary word to look up
≠	not equal
≈	approximately equal
△	difference
⊢⊣	between
Rx	treatment, reaction
XR	cross-reference
← pg#	see page
vy	very
e.g.	for example
[≡]	important message (underline and brackets around passage)

Re-Creating the Structure

In graduate school, I took a psychology class, which was a new experience for me. The concepts and content were quite foreign, and we always had a chapter to read. If I used my highlighter, I'd have very yellow pages, between the new vocabulary and the details I thought were all important. I'd end up rereading almost everything when I reviewed for the test.

Instead of highlighting, I decided to cheat read the chapter first—in effect re-creating the author's outline. This gave me the big-picture ideas that were to be covered in more detail inside the paragraphs. I then used that structure to write my notes.

I'm partial to taking Full Notes, a method based on the Cornell Method of Note-Taking, originated by Walter Pauk, a professor at Cornell University. When using this method, in a nutshell, you divide your paper into two parts by drawing a vertical line down the page about 3 inches from the left edge of the paper. The left side is for main ideas, and the right side is for the details and explanations. The idea is to be able to cover up the right side notes and use the left side concepts to trigger the memory of what you wrote on the right. The following figure shows a sample way to write Full Notes.

Speed Tip

If you have a large amount of reading to do, say a 30-page textbook chapter or a 10-page contract, split it up into mini-readings or sections. You're more apt to follow the author's outline better if you break up unfamiliar material into smaller chunks.

Main Ideas	Details
← 3 inches →	
Subheading	*Details*
Vocabulary word	*Definition*
Person's name	*Who they were*
Date	*What happened*
Formula	*How it works/what it means*
Cause	*Effect*
Event	*What happened/significance*

Another way to document your structure is to create a *mind map*. Mind maps, developed by Tony Buzan, a leading authority on learning techniques, are an effective method of note-taking and useful for generating ideas by associations.

def·i·ni·tion

A **mind map** is a hand-drawn diagram used to represent the ideas in a reading and arranged around a central topic. It's used as a study aid to see a writing's structure.

To make a mind map, start in the center of a blank piece of paper with the title or main idea of the reading, and branch ideas outward in all directions, producing an organized keyword structure.

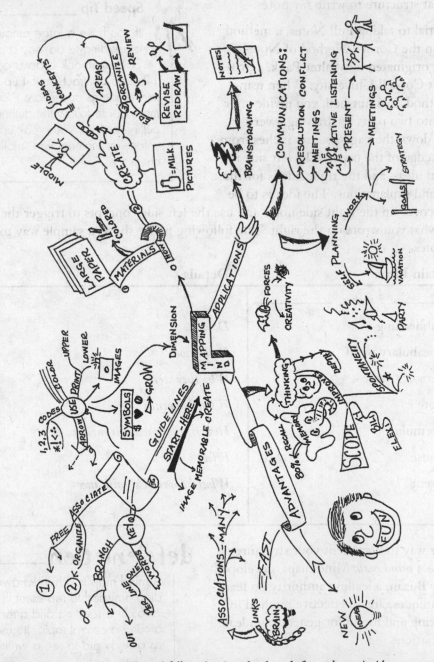

On a mind map, begin in the middle and follow the thought threads from the main ideas out to the details.

One more way to re-create the structure: when you're finished reading a book or an article, write an abstract of the material to summarize the main idea(s). You can write it on the material itself, on a large sticky note attached to the material, or a large index card, or you can type it into a document, whatever works best for you.

For most reading tasks, cheat reading is enough, but when more understanding and memory building is required, you have a few other options.

Taking Notes Outside the Material

Sometimes I pull out great keepers and consolidate them in one place in a book, usually on a blank page at the front or back of the book, so I can review just my keepers without flipping through all the other pages. Often I include the page number where an idea is located in case I want to read more about it later.

This is a *huge* timesaver when you want to review an article's or a book's contents in a targeted way. It sure beats rereading it all!

Speed Tip

If you think you're going to take a lot of notes from a piece of material, you might want to purchase a copy so you can write in it and have it on your shelf for reference whenever you want.

Post-Its, Dog Ears, and Tear Outs

If you often write in your material but borrowed something from the library or a friend, take notes on a separate piece of paper instead of writing in the borrowed material. I have a friend who, when reading a library book, writes her notes on Post-its and attaches them to the page the material is found on. When she's done reading and has to return the book, she removes the notes and resticks them onto notebook paper in the same order they appeared in the book, sometimes referencing the page number in case she needs to go back to it. Each piece of paper has the name of the book written on the top, and all the pages are numbered. She then files the pages away in a folder based on the content.

Sticky notes can also be used as flags or index markers on magazines and books so you can quickly locate usable information.

The oldest method for "marking" keeper material is via dog-earring, or turning down

Speed Tip

Consider purchasing a set of multicolored Post-it flags. You can write a few words on these and place them on the edge of important pages for easier referencing.

the corner of a keeper page. If you practice this strategy, you may have found that many times the ears perk up all by themselves, making it impossible to find that elusive page or the ears aren't big enough to find again.

Instead of dog-earring, try clipping or tearing out. This makes sense for magazines or newspapers when you find a keeper and don't need to save the remaining material. The key with these is to organize them in such a way that you'll be able to find what you need later. (See Chapter 14, where I discuss the LATCH method.)

Of course, if you've borrowed the material, don't rip out the pages! Use one of the other methods outlined in this chapter.

Taking Notes on Fiction

Reading and tracking characters names, events, and symbolisms in works of fiction can be quite challenging, especially if there are a large number of characters. One way to keep track of it all is to create note cards or separate pieces of paper for each character. On these notes, add the following:

- Description of who they are
- Who they're related to
- What happens to them
- Any significant quotes
- What role they play in the plot
- Any symbolisms

And the Results Are ...

Throughout this chapter, you've learned more about how memories are acquired, retained, and recalled and what options you have for documenting your keepers for later review.

It's now time to check in on your reading progress. Choose to either do a One-Minute Timing or a 3-2-1 Drill found in Appendix B. Consider first warming up your eyes using the Discipline Your Eyes Exercise in Chapter 3. While you read, use your preferred pacer method. Be sure to record your progress on the appropriate charts in Appendix C. When you've finished tracking your scores, try your hand at highlighting

or margin noting what you just read. If you're really feeling ambitious, try documenting the author's outline using Full Notes. Remember to put the main ideas on the left
and details on the right.

The Least You Need to Know

♦ Get in, get out, now don't go back—unless you have to!

♦ Building a memory requires three steps: acquisition, retention, and retrieval.
Being aware of them helps build stronger memories.

♦ Forgetting is a natural part of remembering.

♦ Repetition over time is the best way to retain a memory.

♦ There are many ways to document your keepers so you can easily save time
when you go to reference the information later.

10

Speed Reading Books and Magazines

In This Chapter

♦ Things to think about before reading

♦ Reading magazines and nonfiction books

♦ Finding the structure of your reading

♦ Why fiction should be approached differently

Do you read your favorite magazine the same way you read a technical report? Do you approach a novel the same way you would a textbook? Hopefully, you already naturally use different strategies to deal with each type of material.

In this chapter, I focus on some common kinds of reading materials and provide methods and suggestions for how to best approach each.

Before You Read Anything ...

When approaching any reading material, you need to consider a few important issues. Although I've talked about them in other parts of the book, let's review them here:

- Type of material
- Your level of background knowledge
- Your reason why and what for
- Your reading speed

Reading material takes many forms: nonfiction books, magazines, newspapers, academic textbooks, fiction books, standardized test passages, cookbooks, computer manuals, and on and on! If it can be written, it will be printed and read. Each type requires some individual strategies to make reading faster and more effective. In this chapter, I cover some of the more common reading materials, namely nonfiction books and magazines.

Imagine the sports buff who reads many different types of materials but only reads about one subject—sports. While reading the daily sports section of the newspaper, several monthly sports magazines, and an occasional sports biography, he might appear to be an avid reader, but in effect, he has narrowed his focus to just one topic.

Truly efficient and effective readers read widely on a variety of topics as well as materials that enhance their base of background knowledge. And you know the value of background knowledge is priceless, right? The more you have, the easier it is to read faster with good comprehension. It also enables you to read varied materials with greater ease.

Speed Secret
By reading widely, you have more interesting things to discuss when with your friends and colleagues. Try to remember this when you come across some seemingly daunting material. It might not be as intimidating as you previously thought.

No matter the type of material you read, having your purpose in mind, or the reason why you're reading, enables you to get what you want from the material and focuses your attention on meeting your needs. So if you're quickly reading the morning paper, you might only do a skim because getting the general or main topics is sufficient for your purpose. If you're reading for academic learning purposes, you might read using a highlighter, focusing your attention on areas you might be tested on. Having a purpose narrows your focus, no matter the material.

If you read every piece of material using the same reading speed, you're doing yourself an injustice. You either waste your time or expend more mental energy than you need to. People who are technically trained—accountants, engineers, researchers, and the like—have been conditioned to read slowly because most of the information they read is very detail rich or seemingly unfamiliar. This doesn't mean that they should read their favorite magazine the same way they read a professional document, but many do.

Remember, you have a proverbial reading stick shift, and you can learn how to use all the gears and know when you can shift into and out of them at will.

> **Speed Tip**
>
> If you've been reading this book straight through from the beginning, you might want to return to Chapter 1 to quickly refresh your memory about the reading gears. Remember: repetition is a powerful key for learning!

Nonfiction Book Chapters and Magazine Articles

For any problem you have, you probably can find one, if not many, nonfiction books claiming to offer the solution. And for any interest or hobby, you can probably find a magazine dedicated to it. Nonfiction book chapters and magazine articles are in many ways the easiest materials to read, for a few reasons.

For one thing, they've been professionally published, which means an editor has reviewed the materials and made changes so the text is as easy as possible to read with good understanding. The editor often also checks to be sure the author's main ideas are located in the first sentence or two of the paragraph. Compare that to documents you receive from co-workers and friends, who may not be well-trained writers and free-write more than anything. Those can be hard to read!

Also nonfiction book chapters and magazines are written in outline form. When writing, a nonfiction author typically starts with an outline and then fleshes it out. Whether you identify the outline or not, this type of writing makes the finished piece more easily understandable for the reader.

And most nonfiction books and magazines offer a table of contents, or outline. This tool is invaluable for quickly locating the articles or chapters of interest while weeding out those you don't need.

Similar but Different

In addition to similarities between nonfiction book chapters and magazine articles, some differences are worth noting. These differences, as outlined in the following table, are important when choosing the kind of reading material you want to speed read and spend your time on.

Nonfiction Book Chapters Versus Magazine Articles

	Magazine Articles	Nonfiction Book Chapters
Time frame to produce	About 1 month	A year or more
Current/up to date	Yes, as fresh as the week or day before	Minimally 1 month, usually longer; depends on the copyright date
Pictures	Many and colorful	Few and little to no color
Contents	Covers a few points on many topics	Goes into depth on one topic
Advertisements	Too many!	None
Column width	Narrow	Wider
Other material	Sidebar articles	Glossary, references, footnotes, etc.

General Reading Strategies

Both nonfiction book chapters and magazine articles are presented similarly, so it makes sense that you approach them similarly. Here are a few suggestions:

1. Look over the table of contents. Do this slowly for the book; you can go quicker for the magazine articles. Keep in mind that this is the outline of the reading material. In addition, for the nonfiction book, consider speed reading the preface or other preliminary information.

2. Highlight or circle the articles or chapters of interest.

3. Choose which topic you want to read first and turn to it in the material. You don't have to go in order!

4. Cheat read the article or chapter using any of your favorite faster-reading strategies.

5. Decide whether you need to read in more detail. If so, go back, looking for the detail you missed. If not, get out and move on to the next article or chapter of interest based on your highlighted table of contents.

Don't feel obligated to read the entire magazine or book. Remember your reason why you're reading, and read only what fits your needs.

My Method for Speed Reading Nonfiction Books

Over the years, I've developed my own method for reading nonfiction books. It basically gives the reader permission to not read all the material and read only what's of most value. Here it is; feel free to adapt it to suit your needs:

1. When choosing a book to read, I look at the font the book is printed in and the width of the columns. If either is too small or unappealing, I immediately put it back on the shelf. My eyes don't need to suffer when I read!

Speed Tip

Some publishers say that a book is simply one great chapter with a dozen other filler chapters. If this is true, then your job is to try to find the one great chapter. If you find it, read it first—it's like eating dessert first!

2. I look over the cover matter. Remember the old adage, "You can't judge a book by its cover"? Well, publishers hope their covers *will* sell their books so they make them as attractive and colorful as possible. I'm often skeptical about the quotes others provide about their impressions of the book; after all, have you ever seen a quote on a book cover like, "This is the worst book I ever read, don't buy it!"? If the book appears to meet my interests, I continue. If not, I don't. There are plenty of other books out there to choose from.

3. I skim the front matter, including copyright date (how old is the information?), author biography (is he or she qualified?), and any introductory material (why was the book written, and how is it set up?).

4. I turn to any page in the book and read a paragraph or two. If I like the author's writing style, I continue. If not, I seriously consider not reading it. My time is too valuable to waste on poor writing.

5. I look over the table of contents. I like an easy-to-read, somewhat detailed table of contents. If it's comprehensible and laid out well, I keep going. If not, I consider not continuing. I read only as much as I need.

Speed Secret

Attention all travelers! Many airlines offer interesting audio options as part of the in-flight entertainment on longer domestic or international flights. You may also get your own personal entertainment television screen located on the back of the seat in front of you to choose a program of interest. Ask about this the next time you fly.

6. If I have read or cheat read the chapters of interest and several other chapters are yet untouched, I leave them untouched. Just because the author wrote it doesn't mean I have to read it. As long as my reasons *why* and *what for* are met, I can confidently close the book and place it on my shelf and say "I have read you." I feel good about the time and energy I have spent. I am done.

Shake Hands with Your Textbooks

College students pay a lot of money for their textbooks, and most have no idea what's in them—except for what the professor asks them to read. Imagine that there are answers to the chapter questions in the back of the book but you never knew it. Imagine you were using a textbook in computer science class that had a copyright date of 5 or more years ago. Something tells me you wouldn't be learning about blogs or any other recent computer-related developments.

I encourage students to shake hands with their textbooks—greet them as a friend—before starting the class. After all, you two will be spending lots of time together! It takes just a few minutes and can make learning from the reading material a whole lot easier. All it entails is looking at a few things to see what information and resources are included:

◆ Look for the copyright date. This is usually found just before or after the title page and tells you how old or recent the material is.

◆ Read the front matter, including the preface, the author biography, information on how to read this book, and anything else you find interesting.

◆ Review the table of contents to see what's covered and the order it's presented.

◆ Look at any appendixes. Does the book feature answers to questions or supplemental information useful to know about? Does it include charts and graphs or tables? Be aware of the resources available in the text.

◆ Note if the book includes a glossary, index, and/or bibliography.

◆ Note also if any digital resources are available with the textbook. Does the book come with a CD? Is there an associated website with supplemental information, test banks, etc.?

If you take a little time at the beginning of the semester to get to know your text(s), you can feel comfortable when you're reading and studying the book(s) later.

Structures Found in Nonfiction Books

Knowing how the information in your book is structured helps with your reading speed and especially comprehension. Books can be structured in many ways. The following table lists some common examples.

Common Structures Found in Nonfiction Books

Structure	Description	Examples	How to Identify	Reading Strategy
Hierarchy	Information is sequential in nature; pieces are built on what has come previously	Languages, math, biology	When you see language such as "First, you must read about points in order to understand lines"	Must be read in order
Grids	Information can be compared and contrasted	Comparative religion or parts psychology, sociology; used when making a large purchase to see what products have to offer	When you see repeated headings or language like "Let's compare the approaches of two different theorists"	Can be read out of order; start with position of strength or what you already know the most about

Structure	Description	Examples	How to Identify	Reading Strategy
Chronology	Any time-based information	History, biography, etc.	When you see language like "In 1492"	Typically should be read in order but can be structure in a grid pattern for note-taking purposes; can be studied out of order
Static/dynamic	Information that presents a process or something working; the static portion includes the parts of a system; the dynamic presents the system as it's working	Anatomy (static) and physiology (dynamic)	When you see language like "In order to understand the process of change. Let's look first at a case study from …"	Read dynamic sections first; use static sections as reference

Speed Reading Study Material

Study material is usually academic or business in nature. Speed reading when studying is possible as long as you know you should keep your reading speed contained in the lower gears (between 200 and 600 words per minute) for most learning tasks.

Let's assume you've already read the material once, maybe took some notes on it, and are now reviewing for a test. Here are some tried-and-true study strategies to help you get the most out of your study time:

- Be sure you understand the material *before* studying it.

- Study a little each day to capitalize on the repetition-over-time concept.

- Read the chapter summary to refresh your memory about the chapter contents.

- Review any vocabulary words and their definitions.

- Review the questions at end of the chapter or make predictions about what questions might be asked on the test.

- Break the chapter into smaller sections.

- Cheat read, performing tellbacks specifically reciting the main points and supporting details.

- Pay attention and intend to remember what you're studying!

Speed Reading Technical Material

I covered how to speed read technical material in Chapter 5's "What About Technical Material?" section and Chapter 7's "Approaching Technical Material" section, so be sure to turn back there if you need a refresher. In addition to that information, let's go over a few more tips on how to best read technical material.

First, and probably most important, understand that technical material is often written in a linear fashion—perfect for cheat reading. It makes the material easy to take notes from and easy to refer to again.

Here are some other smart considerations:

- Read more in the field to familiarize yourself with the acronyms, vocabulary, and topic jargon.

- Break the reading into smaller parts.

- Take short, frequent breaks (remember you will remember firsts and lasts more than middles!).

- Be sure you're sitting up at a cleared-off desk or table with minimal distractions.

- If have a lot to digest, read for a maximum of 2 hours (giving yourself short, frequent breaks) and then power nap for 20 minutes, if you can, to give your brain time to assimilate the new knowledge.

- Perform frequent tellbacks. (Remember tellbacks from Chapter 8?)

Speed Secret

What about speed reading newspapers? See Chapter 14 for more information on reading these.

♦ Use an underlining hand movement like Long-Smooth Underline or Short-Smooth Underline (see Chapter 2) instead of a faster one.

♦ Anticipate your reading speed to be between 400 to 1,000 words per minute, maximum, when using speed strategies on technical material.

Speed Reading Fiction

For many, reading fiction seems easier than reading nonfiction. And rightfully so. Reading a story is much easier for the brain to follow than nonfiction because it can "see" the setting, "hear" the characters, and "feel" the emotions, just like real life. At times, there's nothing more pleasurable than getting caught up in a good book. With the frenetic pace of day-to-day life, you get to slow down and shift your brain into another world. Great mental therapy at a paperback price!

There are, however, several challenges to reading fiction. But once you're aware of and adept at dealing with them, they can make your pleasure reading experiences even more satisfying.

Choose the Right Book for You

Has a friend ever given you a book, saying it was the best book he or she ever read ... but you can't stand it? Have you ever started a book, found it not engaging, but refused to start another one until you suffered through that one? Both situations can be made easier by a little fiction previewing and attitude checking.

Fiction does not have an outline like nonfiction, but you can check out a few things to determine if it will be a good read or not:

♦ *Font*   Is the print too large or small? Find a book your eyes like.

♦ *Author's style*   After reading any few paragraphs inside the book, do you like the author's style? If not, you may be frustrated and your comprehension challenged.

♦ *Length*   Is the book too long or short for the time frame you have to read?

♦ *Subject*   Are you really interested in murder mysteries or just reading it because your friend recommended it? Reading widely is good to do; suffering is not.

♦ *Perspective*   If the book doesn't grab you after the first few chapters, consider letting it go.

Keep Track of the Characters

Probably the most challenging part of any story is keeping track of the characters, especially if there are a lot of them or you only get to read a little every few weeks. To reduce your frustration and enhance your character memory, consider taking notes.

Your notes could be as simple as writing the characters' names on an index card with who they are and their relations to others. It could be more involved (especially for school assignments or when reading literature), like designat-

> **Speed Secret**
>
> Some people say they're glad they stuck it out and read a book they weren't all that interested in, but many more endure feelings of guilt and inadequacy for not being able to get into it. Move on; there are *many* more books in the world meant for you to read—enjoyably!

ing a piece of paper or large index card to each character. As they are introduced in the story, write their name on top. Write descriptions about the character, including their relationship to other characters. Include examples of what they say, what they do, what other characters say about them, and what the author says about them.

Be Aware of the Basic Elements of Fiction

You can expect to find certain elements in every short story, novel, or play. By knowing they exist, you can look for them as you read. If you're a student reading literature, you might want to take notes when you come across these areas because they are typically the ones you'll be asked to know about for a test:

- ◆ *Title*   A clue pointing you toward the theme of the story.

- ◆ *Setting*   The time and place.

- ◆ *Point of view*   Spoken either in the first person (a character serves as the narrator) or third person (a narrator outside the story).

> **Speed Tip** _____
>
> The next time you watch a movie, see if you can identify the elements of fiction in the story. Once you recognize them, you'll be more tuned to seeing them again and again.

- ◆ *Conflicts (part of the plot)*   Problems that change the belief systems or lives of characters involved.

- ◆ *Climax and resolution (part of the plot)*   The moment in the story when the character makes a decision that leads to the ultimate resolution of the conflict.

- ◆ *Ending*   The final words of a story.

Use Speed Techniques

When some people learn the tools for reading faster, they get concerned that they'll be forced to read fiction fast. Just because you know the strategies doesn't mean you are locked into using them *all the time!*

Remember that *you* have the controls over what speed you read. If you like to savor the writer's descriptive style, you might want to slow down. If you're an action seeker, you can use key words or thought chunks to quickly read over the description and then slow down when you get to the dialogue. You decide how fast or slow you go.

Choose the Best Place to Read

There are no hard-and-fast rules about where to read fiction, but because most people read fiction for pleasure, not for school or work, they pick a comfy place and settle in. Remember to bring along something to drink (if allowable; some libraries and other places don't allow food or drink) so you don't have to get up for a while! And enjoy!

If you happen to read mostly nonfiction, experiment with reading a novel once in awhile. Your brain will thank you!

And the Results Are ...

Now's the time to check in on your reading progress. Do either a One-Minute Timing or a 3-2-1 Drill found in Appendix B. Remember to warm up your eyes using the Discipline Your Eyes Exercise in Chapter 3. While you read, use your preferred pacer method. Be sure to record your progress on the appropriate charts in Appendix C.

The Least You Need to Know

♦ Before reading anything, consider your reason why, your reading speed, your level of background knowledge, and the type of material.

♦ Nonfiction books are similar yet different from magazines. Magazines are like reading mini-book chapters.

♦ When reading nonfiction books, read the valuable stuff and leave the rest.

♦ Fiction doesn't have the nonfiction outline, requiring you to be able to identify the basic elements of fiction to provide its structure.

Part 3

Tuning Up
Your Speed

In Part 3, I present some valuable information about how to tune up your reading speed. I've approached this topic in several ways. The first is to look at what you can speed read and what you can't, reminding you that once you know how to speed read, you always have a choice. Next we venture into the world of on-screen reading, adapting the paper speed reading strategies you already learned for reading better and faster on-screen. And finally, I take a deeper look at the three not-so-helpful reading habits everyone has and give you tips for reducing your reliance on them.

Tuning Up
Your Speed

In Part 4, I present some valuable information about how to tune up your reading speed. I suppose that this topic has several uses. The first is to look at what you can speed-read and what you can't, equipping you so that once you know how to speed-read, you always have a choice. Even venture into the world of on-screen reading, adapting the paper-speed reading strategies you already learned for reading better and faster on-screen. And finally I take a deeper look at the three not-so-helpful threading habits everyone has, and give you tips for reducing your chance on them.

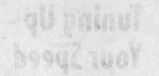

Chapter 11

What to Speed Read ...
and What *Not* To

In This Chapter

◆ Do I have to read everything fast?

◆ Choose your own reading speed

◆ The best materials to speed read

◆ Shakespeare and speed reading don't mix

◆ Experience is your best teacher

Believe it or not, not everything should be sped read. Just because you have the ability to go into the higher gears doesn't mean you should all the time, on every bit of material you pick up. Sure, some materials do lend themselves to faster reading strategies, but many do not. But how do you know when to kick it into high gear and when to slow things down?

In this chapter, I offer some thoughts about when to speed read and when to take it a little slower.

Common Misperceptions About Speed Reading

If I've been asked once, I've been asked hundreds of times: "If I learn to speed read, will I have to read my novels fast (because I really don't want to)?" Likewise, I get this a lot: "If I learn to speed read, won't I lose understanding of my business reading (because I don't want that to happen)?" I understand these concerns, but let's look at the realities.

Just because you learn how to speed read, doesn't mean you'll automatically speed read *everything*. You probably know how to run, but you don't run everywhere, do you? Most likely you walk much more often than you run. The same is true for speed reading. When you know *how* to speed read, chances are you'll also know *when* to speed read. Trust me, you won't be uncontrollably forced to read everything fast, from now on and forever!

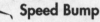

Speed Bump

Some people believe that drinking lots of coffee or eating tons of sugar or chocolate will "rev up" your brain to read faster. It might work to keep you alert for a short period of time, but it's not recommended as a speed reading strategy!

The same is true for the person who thinks he won't understand his business reading and refuses to use his speed reading strategies on that material. A big part of speed reading—if you haven't picked up on this by now—is reading fast encourages concentration which *creates comprehension*. Anyone can read fast, but reading fast and understanding what you read are the main components of speed reading (see Chapter 5).

And for the people who say they'll never speed read their novels because they love to savor every word: who says you have to read novels fast?

Speed Up or Slow Down, It's Your Choice

In Chapter 1, I talked about the reading gears and how most people are stuck in first or second gear because they just don't know how to get into third, fourth, or fifth gear. I think it's appropriate to revisit this idea now and remind you that you *always* have the choice of how fast, or slow, you want to read. When you choose to use speed reading strategies, you have more focus on your reason *why* and where your eyes and brain are going, which fosters deeper concentration, which in turn garners comprehension.

Think of your speed reading strategies like tools on a carpenter's tool belt: you'll use some of the tools frequently and others not often at all, but they're always there for you to choose from. And the more you use a tool, the better you'll be at using it. But be reassured you don't have to use any of them if you so choose.

When I taught speed reading classes that met for multiple sessions over a period of several weeks, students had time to experience what allows them to speed up and what slows them down. Toward the end of the last session, I asked them to document their experiences, listing in two columns the things that speed them up and the things that slow them down. Following is one speed reader's list.

> **Speed Secret**
>
> Reading is a conscious process; you have to make a conscious and concerted effort to create speed. Your reading speed doesn't go into high gear by itself.

Prompt	Things That Help Me Speed Up	Things That Slow Me Down
Reason *why*	If my purpose is for getting the gist	If my purpose is to read for details
What for (use for what)	To be able to discuss casually	To be able to present to colleagues
Eye movement strategy	Reading key words	Not reading key words
Pacer	White card method	Not using a pacer
Cheat reading	Cheat reading	Not cheat reading
Author's style	Easy to engage with	Difficult to understand
Vocabulary	Easy or familiar vocabulary	Difficult or unfamiliar vocabulary
Background knowledge	Some to a lot	Little or none
Familiarity	Familiar	Unfamiliar
Interest level	Interested	Not interested*
Print size	12-point	Smaller than 10-point or larger than 14-point
Column width	Narrow	Wide
Time to read	Pressed for time	Have plenty of time
Time of day	Best early morning	Worse in evening after 8 P.M.
Noise	Quiet	A lot of interruptions, TV, or people talking around me
Light	Gentle light	Too bright or dim
Temperature	Comfortable	Too hot or cold

continues

continued

Prompt	Things That Help Me Speed Up	Things That Slow Me Down
Comfort level	Comfortable enough	Too comfortable or uncomfortable
Sleepiness	Well rested	Tired*
Physical condition	Well rested; exercised that morning; not hungry	Excessively tired; hungry; feeling ill

* If I'm not interested or tired, I slow down; however, with the reading tools and other speed-up factors, I intentionally speed up my reading.

If you compare the speed-up side to the slow-down side, the responses are mostly opposites of each other. So if you aren't happy with the reading results you're getting, try doing the opposite!

What to Speed Read

Some of the best material to practice your speed reading strategies on can be found at any newsstand. Between newspapers, magazines, and light novels, you have a plethora of material to choose from.

> **Speed Tip**
>
> To find material to practice your speed reading strategies on, go to a store or library that carries newsstand-type material. Purchase or borrow at least five pieces of reading material where you can "play" with your strategies. Because you're using these for speed reading practice, you don't have to be as concerned with getting complete comprehension.

The column width in these types of material tends to be narrow, which many speed readers find helpful for locating key words and using many of the pacers. And pictures or other graphics are usually included, which makes it easier to understand. (The adage "a picture's worth a thousand words" is most often true!) Newsstand material is typically printed in 11- or 12-point font, which is easier to read. And the spacing between lines is helpful for those who tend to read the tops of lines (see Chapter 3).

Although you might not have a need to use your highlighter on this type of material, you'll want to tear out articles for later review or use sticky notes to mark useful pages.

Overall, have fun! It can be really enjoyable to experience reading in a whole new way, even if you aren't comfortable with your strategies yet.

What *Not* to Speed Read

You can read many kinds of material quickly, but some types of reading material shouldn't be read quickly, for a few reasons:

- The words themselves aren't easy to read.
- Your reason *why* prohibits it.
- You need to appreciate the author's style.
- You need to really think about what you're reading.
- You are editing, not reading.

Let's look at some types of writing you should take your time with.

Shakespeare Slows Everyone Down

William Shakespeare was a prolific poet and playwright who wrote in Old English style. Because of his turns of phrase and antiquated writing style, reading Shakespeare can be quite challenging, even in the lower gears.

Reading the Bard in the high gears is not recommended and can be quite challenging if you want to understand his writing. Take your time with Shakespeare, and other similar forms of writing, if you want to get the most out of it.

> **Speed Secret**
>
> Shakespeare wrote, "Knowledge is the wing wherewith we fly to heaven." And what better way to get more knowledge than through reading?

Thou Shalt Not Speed Read (the Bible)

The Bible is the most purchased and most read book of our time. Like Shakespeare, the Bible should not be read in the higher gears. Every passage contains thought-provoking concepts that would be lost by reading too fast.

Similarly, most other philosophical writing needs to be read more slowly.

Speed Read Poetry? Alas, It Is Not to Be

Poetry showcases the beauty of language and how distinctive thoughts can be expressed in unique and rhythmic ways. Therefore, poetry is not recommended for speed reading. Poetry should be read and digested slowly, with each word being heard or pronounced, often repeatedly.

Speed Secret

When you study something such as poetry, meaning you need to commit some information to memory, then speed reading isn't the way to go. Studying typically slows your reading speed down to first or second gear so you can mentally repeat the information or create a summary of what you know. That slow speed is very appropriate! Students need to learn how to first understand what they read—and they can do this using speed reading strategies—*before* they slow down their reading speed to study it (see Chapter 5).

"Speed Read Dialogue?" She Asked. "Surely Not!"

Dialogue is a natural speed reducer. When you read dialogue, you want to hear what the characters are saying to each other, word for word in your head and in the tone of voice described. This word-for-word reading naturally slows you down.

The next time you're reading a novel, try to be aware of how your reading flows during the descriptive paragraphs and how you automatically slow down over dialogue.

Although most readers should probably read Shakespeare, the Bible, poetry, study material, and dialogue at a slower speed, I do believe that a trained speed reader can possibly read these materials in second or third gear, if they choose. First gear is always a possibility, but even a little faster is better for concentration and comprehension.

On the Fence: Technical Material

Now we come to a somewhat gray area: technical material. In a nutshell, technical material is any material you consider difficult or unfamiliar based on your background knowledge. So what you might label "technical material" might not be "technical" to another reader.

Approach technical material with the speed reading strategies that work best for you—or not—to make it less intimidating and easier to read (see Chapters 5, 6, and 10).

Your Experience Dictates

As you've read through this book and performed the timed exercises, you've most likely come across situations where you notice a change in your reading speed. Maybe a wide column width slowed you down. Maybe reading an unfamiliar word caused you to stop and reflect. Or maybe the names in the reading caused you to slow down to take notice. Alternately, you might have found that reading about something you have interest in makes your reading speed naturally faster or one author's writing style is better than another for practicing speed reading strategies.

Being aware of who you are as a reader and how you interact with the text are important ingredients for mastering speed reading. This includes knowing what speeds you up or slows you down, what interests you and what doesn't, what strategies you are comfortable with and which you aren't, and generally what works for you and what doesn't. I know some people want to know *the one way* to read faster, but the best I can offer those folks are the choices in this book. It's up to each one of you to decide how to put the strategies to work.

And the Results Are ...

Let's check in on your reading progress. Do either a One-Minute Timing or a 3-2-1 Drill found in Appendix B. Be aware of what slows you down and what speeds you up. Remember to record your progress on the appropriate charts in Appendix C.

The Least You Need to Know

- ◆ People believe that once they learn the speed reading strategies, they have to read everything fast all the time. Not true!

- ◆ You have control over your reading speed. Knowing what speeds you up and what slows you down is very helpful when monitoring your reading speed.

- ◆ Newsstands have great material for practicing speed reading.

- ◆ Approach Shakespeare, the Bible, poetry, study material, and dialogue with slower reading speeds.

- ◆ Knowing who you are as a reader and how you interact with your reading material can best dictate your speed.

12

Speed Reading On Screen

In This Chapter

- ◆ Reading on paper versus reading on screen
- ◆ On screen speed reading strategies
- ◆ Using pacers on screen
- ◆ Ergonomic suggestions for keeping your eyes happy
- ◆ Tips for reducing paper waste

The amount and range of information available online or as digital text can be overwhelming and at the same time gratifying. You can access a targeted selection of the Internet's millions of websites in the time it used to take to open one drawer of the library's card catalog. When you've found the information you're looking for online, the question then becomes: How are you going to read it? Will you print it out or read it online? And how can you read it fast if you read it on screen?

This chapter shows you how to adapt many of the speed strategies you have already learned for use when reading electronic text. Understanding why on screen reading is different and knowing how you can read it more efficiently can help you not only speed read on screen, but also read more comfortably, too.

What's Different About Reading On Screen

For many people, reading a document printed on paper is easier, faster, more familiar, and more comfortable than reading on a computer screen, but that's changing. Improvements in display technology, increases in the number of people who own or use computers, and the decrease in the age at which people start reading from a computer screen all affect the way people read digital text. If you're one of the stragglers, worried that you'll never be comfortable reading on screen or concerned that you won't be able to speed read on screen, rest assured you can efficiently, effectively, and comfortably handle the increased demands for reading on a computer screen while also reducing reliance on printed materials.

Keep in mind that online speed reading includes not only how fast you can read each word, but also how quickly you can …

- ◆ Access and sift through huge amounts of digital information.
- ◆ Process and evaluate the accuracy of that data.
- ◆ Communicate it in the right form to the right people.

Reading Is Reading Is Reading …

The process of reading follows the same fundamental steps whether on paper, on a computer screen, on a stone slab, or on a billboard. On a simple level, your eyes look at the letters that make up the words. Then your brain attempts to make meaning of the words. It sounds simple, but you may have noticed the profound difference you feel when you read online, and with good reason.

Critical differences exist when it comes to reading from a screen versus reading from paper. These differences alter the process and experience of reading.

Making Your On-Screen Text Look Good

How text on a screen is formatted effects how you read it. If the letters are placed too closely together, with very little white space between the letters, words, or lines, it's much harder to read. Increasing the white space between lines to double or 1.5 spaces makes for more readability than single spacing.

In the following paragraph, for example, the overall density of the text makes it more difficult to read. It's even more difficult to decipher when reading digital text.

An estimated 25,000 tattoos later, Hellenbrand recognizes how far she has drifted from her original art. "I'm not a good paper artist anymore. It isn't demanding enough for me. It's not nearly as thrilling. When I get it on the skin, that's when I become the artist. Skin is my medium."

The text margins can also affect how we read. Fully justified text, where both left and right margins are in a line tends to look better, but it's more difficult to read because it can distort the amount of white space in a line. (In addition to the full-justified text in the following paragraph, the spacing between lines is set at 1.5, which increases legibility.)

An estimated 25,000 tattoos later, Hellenbrand recognizes how far she has drifted from her original art. I'm not a good paper artist anymore. It isn't demanding enough for me. It's not nearly as thrilling. When I get it on the skin, that's when I become the artist. Skin is my medium."

Left justification, where the left text margin is in line and the right margin is "ragged" (like this book and most printed documents) is the easiest to read. To facilitate faster reading on screen, left justify your reading materials when you can and set your line spacing to 1.5.

The length of a line of text on a computer screen also impacts your reading speed. Oddly enough, the optimum line length for reading speed is not always the line length people prefer to read. You read faster when the line of text is approximately 10 inches wide, but most people often prefer lines between 4 and 6 inches. On the other hand, lines that are too short (narrower than 2.4 inches) can slow you down. Experiment with line lengths when you can to discover your preference.

When reading continuous text, you can read easier and faster if the text is a combination of upper and lowercase letters instead of ALL CAPITAL LETTERS because mixing cases creates a more distinctive word shape. When it comes to writing e-mails, USING ALL CAPITAL LETTERS IS JUST BAD MANNERS. READERS OFTEN FEEL AS THOUGH THE AUTHOR IS YELLING.

The Skinny on Fonts

The size and shape of a *font* can effect how quickly and efficiently you read on screen. One of the most frequently used fonts for printed matter is Times New Roman, a *serif* font, while the most readable fonts for on screen text are typically *sans serif* fonts. The straight, well-formed characters of sans serif fonts display more clearly on screen, improving the legibility of displayed text and, therefore, on screen reading speeds.

def•i•ni•tion

A **font** is a family of digital lettering and characters. Fonts are grouped into two categories: serif and sans serif. **Serif** fonts have little lines or tails as a part of the letters. Times Roman, `Courier`, and **Palatino** are serif fonts. **Sans serif** fonts such as **Arial**, Helvetica, and **Geneva** do not have the small lines or tails at the ends of characters.

Improvements in font design as well as monitor technology have helped textual displays more closely reflect reading paper documents. These advances help improve on screen reading comfort, experience, and ability.

The size at which the font is displayed also plays a role in reading speed and efficiency. The most readable font size depends on several factors:

◆ Your vision

◆ Your angle to the screen

◆ The font

In general, anything smaller than 10 point is too small to read at a comfortable distance from the screen. Anything larger than 18 point may be too large and may give the reader a sense that they're being shouted at. On average, 12-point font is the most widely used and preferred.

Font color can be used quite effectively to aid the reading process; however, what's pleasing to one reader might not be pleasing to another. Typically, dark text on a light background such as black or navy on white or gray is more readable. Any textured background makes the text placed on it less readable.

Play with all these presentation elements in your word processing program to help determine what works best for you because being aware of the physical appearance of on screen text, and changing it when possible, is a great way to increase your on screen reading speed.

Speed Tip

Some speed reading software programs offer the perfect opportunity for you to practice your speed reading skills. They're also a great place for adjusting the physical appearance of text to determine what display layouts work best for you. Free programs like Zap Reader (www.zapreader.com) and Spreeder (www.spreeder. com) enable you to set the physical appearance of text as well as the speed the text is displayed. If you want a program that offers more functionality, try AceReader's (www. acereader.com) 30-day free trial version or The Reader's Edge (www.readfaster.com) online demo version.

Adapting Paper Strategies to Screen

The best way to approach your on screen reading is armed with the same arsenal of reading techniques you use for your print reading. You will, however, need to slightly modify some of them.

You've probably realized that having a plan of attack for your reading is a critical element when trying to read quickly and efficiently. This is even more important when reading on screen. It's important to not only clearly define why you're reading something; you also need to define how long you'll spend on a given item. This is especially true online, where so much information competes for our attention.

To develop your on screen reading prowess, consider the following ideas.

> **Speed Secret**
>
> Having a strategy for reading your on-screen materials as well as the tools to speed up your reading are two of the best ways to block out online distractions.

Preview Your Digital Documents

Similar to cheat reading, the purpose of a preview is to gather as much information about the topic as possible without getting bogged down by the details. Most online documents are nonfiction in nature, making this strategy useable. You're primarily looking for the main ideas so you have a mental framework upon which to hang details if you choose to read the article in full.

Here are some preview tips:

◆ Look at any preliminary information, including the source, the author, the title, the date, and any introductory material.

◆ Scroll through the document and read the first paragraph, which is the introduction; the first sentences of each paragraph following; and the last paragraph,
which is typically the conclusion.

Speed Tip _____

If the article is spread out over
many screens, check to see if
there's a print-friendly version
or view of the entire document.
You don't need to print it, but it'll
be easier to preview and read
on screen and might be void of
any advertising, which is a defi-
nite plus.

◆ Be aware of advertising and unrelated links.

◆ Note anything that's highlighted, bold, itali-
cized, or in some way made to stand out from
the rest of the text—but only if it has to do with
the immediate topic. You can ignore banner
advertisements.

Previewing the material gives you the main points
of the article, without cluttering up your mind with
details. You can then decide if you need to read the
whole article.

Store Your Keepers

To effectively store articles, create folders using broad categories. Add and label subfolders with effective titles so you'll be able to easily find the information you need.
Your category folder headings will ideally have enough scope to include several articles
but shouldn't be so broad that you could put everything in them.

If you're exploring different home improvement projects, you might create one
electronic folder titled "Home Improvement." Within this main folder, you might
create subfolders with titles such as "Wall Coverings," "Plumbing," "Patio," "Room
Makeovers," etc. If you are simply saving links to websites that demonstrate particular
techniques, interesting colors or patterns, or complete project how-to's, create folders
as part of your favorites in your Internet browser.

If you already have a lot of articles in one folder and want to organize them better for
easier retrieval, try this:

1. Look at each article title and write down what broad category(ies) it might
   belong to.

Speed Tip _____

If you want, fast-forward to
Chapter 14 and take a look
at the LATCH concept. It can
help you keep your keepers—
and find them again!

2. Look at the category list and consolidate even
   more if possible.

3. Create folders with these category names and
   file articles in subfolders accordingly.

4. Make copies of the articles if they truly belong
   in one or more categories.

Taking Notes On Screen

Taking notes on material while reading on a computer screen can be tricky. The biggest questions, as with taking notes on hard-copy material, is "What do I write?" and "How do I write it?"

To remember and find relevant information, it's important, particularly for research reading, to store information in an organized manner and to document the sources of electronic information immediately.

Having an organized approach to your computer note-taking can save you a lot of time if you set up a folder designed to hold only information on the given research topic and restrict the contents to relevant information.

Knowing the documentation style for your given research also helps. Here are some common ones:

Speed Bump

Thanks to the copy and paste function, people tend to copy entire passages rather than gleaning the most important elements from a given document. Once copied and pasted into a new document, or downloaded and saved to your hard drive, information is often lost or forgotten entirely.

- ◆ Associated Press (AP)
- ◆ American Medical Association (AMA)
- ◆ American Psychological Association (APA)
- ◆ Chicago Manual of Style (CMS)
- ◆ Modern Language Association (MLA)

Be sure to gather all the relevant source information from any source you look at (even if you don't use it later) because it will help you avoid re-researching. Include this information with the information you save in your folder. If your research requires a "Works Cited" page, you might want to create a separate document in the folder and update it as you go.

You can also save the entire document. Then, when you read the document and take notes on it, save it as another document. In other words, keep the original intact and save a second copy on which you can highlight selected passages, write your comments, and generally respond to the material—electronically, of course. This way you can keep track of what information you want to use and how you want to use it (while avoiding inadvertent plagiarism).

Speed Tip _____

If an article you're reading on screen is a Microsoft Word document, you can make comments or notes in the margin with Word's Comment function. If you're reading a PDF file, you can also annotate it if you have Adobe Acrobat. Some programs have an AutoSummarize feature that automatically summarizes your document into an executive-type summary. If you have a nonchangeable document, you can use the full notes idea from Chapter 9, either on paper or by creating your own Word document, to hold ideas. File this notes document with the article on your computer. Look over your software to see what capabilities are available for you to work with.

Avoid Getting Sucked In

Following irrelevant links when reading online can become a big time waster. When you follow link upon link, you can easily lose sight of what you initially started looking for. It's essential to have a clear purpose in mind and to have a plan or strategy for

Speed Tip _____

Much of the reading you do on-screen, especially on the Internet, may not require detailed reading. Keep in mind that you can use skimming, scanning, or skipping effectively online, too!

your reading—especially online reading. It can get a little confusing if you follow several links to different articles, even if they're relevant. Try to stay on topic and finish one article before jumping off to another—even if you only preview the initial article.

When you're conducting online research, you'll likely have several online sessions. Remember to define your reason why before each session and do your best to stick to it.

Hands-Free On-Screen Pacing

In Chapter 2, I introduced to you the pacers, a series of hand and card methods for reading on paper. When you're reading on a computer screen, using a pacer can be more challenging. It would be impractical and uncomfortable to use your hand or a white card to follow the text on screen!

The following sections present some effective techniques that rely on computer technology to help you smooth out your eye movements for reading efficiently and effectively on screen.

The Highlighting Pacer

The following suggestion works best with Microsoft Word documents and others in "Read Only" mode. The pacing method works particularly well when you're tired. You won't necessarily read faster in the reverse text (white letters on a dark background), but it will help you keep your place.

To use this pacer …

1. Move your mouse pointer to the left of the target text. (The right side works, too, but highlighting from the left side ensures you get the start of the line, too.)

2. When you see a tilted arrow, click and hold your left mouse button and slowly drag your mouse down as you read. The text will continue to be highlighted until you click somewhere else to remove it.

3. Move your mouse down as you finish reading a line of text, keeping the mouse button pressed to keep the text highlighted.

Additionally, in many word-processing programs, when you double-click a word, the word is highlighted. If you're interrupted when you're reading a digital document, simply double-click the word where you stopped reading to highlight it. Then you can immediately return to where you left off when you're able to resume reading. Talk about a time-saver!

Speed Bump

Because you're highlighting all the text in your document, you run the risk of accidentally deleting all your text! Be sure your document is in "Read Only" mode, or use it carefully—and/or know how to use your Undo button!

The Scrolling Pacer

Many computer mice these days are equipped with a scroll wheel, or a button you can navigate with your finger to scroll up or down in the document. Take advantage of this technology to help you pace through your reading. Simply roll the ball to advance the text.

Speed Tip

If your mouse scrolls faster or slower than you want, you can change it. Whether you're on a Mac or PC, you can probably adjust the speed of the mouse in the System Preferences (Mac) or Control Panel (PC).

If you want to set the text to scroll automatically, simply click the ball and move your mouse down or up to control the speed and direction of the scrolling text. When the speed is set, you can take your hand off the mouse, sit back, relax, and read.

Using Your Cursor as a Pacer

Using your cursor as a pacer is similar to running your fingers under a line of text when you're reading printed text—much like Long-Smooth Underline and Short-Smooth Underline (see Chapter 2). It's likely to be the pacer that produces the most noticeable speed results.

When using your cursor as a pacer, it's important to hold your mouse gently and keep your arm supported in some way, such as on a table or desk. You might want to use a wrist support, too.

Here's how it works:

1. With your mouse, guide your cursor directly under the line of text you're reading.

2. "Underline" by moving your cursor under the center two-thirds of the line of text—especially when the line of text is long.

3. Read all the text, using your peripheral vision to read the third of the line of text you aren't specifically underlining with your cursor.

4. When you move your cursor to the next line, you can move your cursor faster because, at this stage, you're not reading.

5. When you've finished reading the screen of text, use your keyboard's page down button to advance to the next full screen of text.

Speed Tip

When using your cursor as a pacer, if you're using a mouse with a scroll wheel, you can roll the text forward as you continue to read rather than paging forward.

Using this pacing method serves the dual purpose of keeping your eyes moving in a directed pattern and helps you keep your place on a line of text, which is often even more difficult when you're reading on screen.

The Line-by-Line Pacers

The Line-by-Line Pacer methods are similar to the hardcopy pacing method of placing a blank white card above or under the line of text you're reading (see Chapter 2); using Line-by-Line on your computer screen provides a straight edge that serves as a guide for your eyes. You can use this method in two ways: Line-by-Line Top or Line-by-Line Bottom.

The Line-by-Line Top pacing method is like placing a white card *above* a line of text in a book you're reading. The card helps block out text that you've already read so your eyes can't wander back up to reread. For Line-by-Line Top:

1. Position the first line of the text you're reading at the top of your screen. This straight edge serves as a guide for your eyes.

2. Advance through the text by clicking one line at a time with your mouse in the scroll bar, using the down arrow on your keyboard, or scrolling with your mouse. The text you read goes "into the black," preventing you from rereading it.

The Line-by-Line Top method is most useful when …

♦ Eye-regression is a problem.

♦ Reading easier materials.

♦ Reading a narrow line of text.

♦ Skimming.

The Line-by-Line Bottom pacing method is like placing a white card *below* a line of text in a book you're reading. The card helps keep your place but allows for rereading if necessary. For Line-by-Line Bottom:

1. Position the first line of the text you're reading at the bottom of your screen. This straight edge serves as a guide for your eyes.

2. Advance through the text by clicking one line at a time with your mouse in the scroll bar, using the down arrow on your keyboard, or scrolling with your mouse. The text you read is like movie credits rolling from the bottom of the screen to the top.

The Line-by-Line Bottom method helps …

♦ Keep your place in your reading.

♦ Encourage active regression, allowing quick glances back when necessary, without having to scroll.

♦ When reading dense or difficult text.

♦ When reading wider lines of text.

Using pacers when reading on screen can feel a little awkward at first, but with some practice, it can significantly increase your reading speed as well as your concentration and comprehension.

Getting Your Eyes Comfortable

Your eye's comfort level when you're reading can be a key factor when deciding whether or not to read text electronically or print it and read it on paper. Following are some useful *ergonomic* suggestions for keeping your eyes comfortable for reading on screen:

def•i•ni•tion

Ergonomics is the science of workplace design factors that maximize productivity and minimize a worker's fatigue and discomfort.

Speed Secret

According to a study done at Cornell University, workers using computer reminders to take short rests and stretch breaks are more productive and 13 percent more accurate in their work than workers who were not reminded and who did not take breaks.

- Remember to go for regular eye exams. This is the first and most important element of keeping your eyes healthy.

- Take a break away from the computer screen every 30 to 60 minutes. This helps prevent visual fatigue, rather than repair it. If you wait until your eyes are really tired, they'll take longer to feel relief. Because computer users have limited eye movements while working on a computer, it's important to stretch your eye muscles on a regular basis.

- Place your monitor approximately 18 to 28 inches from your eyes.

- Position the top of the screen slightly below eye level. Bifocal wearers should have the screen top slightly lower.

- Use a paper document holder. Place it the same distance from your eyes and parallel to your monitor. Well-lit documents on the same parallel plane as your head minimize reflections and maximize legibility of print.

- Avoid glare and reflections. Place the screen at a right angle to windows and between overhead lights. When using a computer, the lighting should be about half the lighting used in a regular office setting. Try closing the drapes or blinds at high-glare times, and use fewer or lower-intensity lightbulbs. You can also try anti-glare screens or computer hoods to reduce glare and reflections or have an anti-reflective coating applied to your glasses.

- Adjust the brightness, contrast, and color on your monitor. The brightness of the environment and the computer screen should be similar. The contrast between the background and on screen characters should be high.

◆ Keep screen and eyeglasses clean. Use natural eye lubricants, when needed.

◆ Remember to use the eye relaxation strategies in Chapter 3.

As you continue to read more digital text, you'll realize that there's more to on screen reading than meets the eye.

Strategies for Going Paperless (or at Least Printing Less)

Everyone's "going green" these days, reducing their impact on the earth and the environment. You can, too, while still maintaining your goal for reading with speed and comprehension.

Some of the following rules were inspired by "Pulp Free," a digital column by Karl De Abrew at Planet PDF—my guru when it comes to doing it paperless! This guy didn't stop at reducing his paper usage; he claims to have eliminated it completely! While it might be hard to believe, De Abrew does not own a printer, fax, or photocopier.

De Abrew eliminated paper cold turkey a number of years ago, using most of the following eight rules. But for those of you who have one foot in print and the other in digital text, you have an escape hatch—you don't have to quit cold turkey like De Abrew did. The first three rules will do a lot to get you on your way to reducing your paper consumption. The next five are harder and more expensive:

Rule 1: If you can't go completely paperless, set a standard for when you will print—and stick to it. In general, people print anything over 2 pages long (or print simply because they always have). Not only does excessive printing kill trees and waste natural resources, it also wastes your time and resources.

Speed Tip _____

When you finish your e-mail or Internet research and have printed everything, you then have deal with the pile of paper sitting in your printer tray. Consider this a duplication of effort and a waste of precious time. The first step to reducing your dependence on printed materials is to be aware of your current printing habits. Cut it in half: if you normally print anything more than 2 pages long, set a new rule of only printing items more than 4 or 5 pages. After a couple weeks, set a new limit to printing only those items that are more than 8 or 10 pages long.

Rule 2: Do it yourself. Respond to your own e-mails—without printing them. In some business environments, people routinely print all their e-mails. In some cases, bosses might then hand-write the replies and have a secretary or assistant e-mail the responses. Of this practice, De Abrew says, "In this Brave New World, there should be no worker (executive or otherwise) too pompous to directly respond to their own messages. Modern businesses simply shouldn't pay for this kind of duplication. By handling your business interactions in bits and bytes, you'll save dollars and cents." I don't believe this practice of duplication is one of pomposity, but rather one of lack of ability in using the technology coupled with a high level of comfort using paper.

Rule 3: Fight the urge. Don't print just because you *can.* Using your printer just because it's there is a waste of precious resources—yours, your company's, and the earth's. Printing not only uses paper and ink, it wastes a lot of your time.

Speed Tip

> If you hit print every time you change a paragraph on a document you're writing, take the paper out of your printer. This will remind you of your goal to reduce your printing and help you fight the urge to print so frequently.
>
> If you don't want to clutter up your e-mail inbox with converted faxes, set up a rule to send all faxes to their own folder.

Rule 4: Don't skimp on a monitor. Buying a quality monitor may cost you a bit more, but it is well worth the price. A clear digital document on a readable screen reduces the urge to print because you can read from the screen more comfortably.

Rule 5: Get rid of your fax. If you have a line specifically designated to your fax, your fax tray may look about as cluttered as your e-mail inbox due to an increase in junk faxes. Unsolicited faxes cost you time and money and clutter up your important faxes. Explore the option of having your faxes delivered as e-mail.

Rule 6: Get a laptop or subnotebook. Subnotebooks are similar to laptops, but they are smaller and lighter, have fewer features and are less expensive. For people who travel frequently or those who have long commutes, purchasing a portable computer can mean extra productivity. With either portable device, you can store most (if not all) of the reading material you can handle for a trip or commute in 5 pounds (or less) without dragging all that heavy paper with you. It might also be possible, depending on the area you're traveling in, to have wireless Internet access so you can deal with e-mail and other online content.

Rule 7: Centralize your information. Store all your digital information in one place. There are many companies that offer online storage capabilities—some of it for free. If this is of interest to you, check out if your employer offers digital storage or do an Internet search to find the service right for you.

Rule 8: Don't stop at just one monitor. This is probably one of the more extreme and expensive suggestions, but if you truly go paperless, the expense will be made up eventually. As you may have already figured out, going truly paperless would be difficult when the need arises to refer to two documents on your computer screen at the same time. It is possible to view multiple documents at the same time on one monitor, but it can be difficult and frustrating, depending on your screen size and the complexity of the documents. De Abrew suggests buying a second monitor for this purpose. If you have the money and the space, it may be the best way to go paperless.

It's up to you to decide how much of a paper reductionist you want to be. The more you feel comfortable speed reading on screen, the less you can rely on paper.

Speed Read Just the Good Stuff

Despite the amazing benefits of speed reading online, be sure to evaluate the validity of the websites you use. Unlike printed documents such as textbooks and most magazines, which are professionally written and checked for accuracy, anyone can post documents on the Internet. No organization or agency polices the Internet to be sure all the information there is correct. You may not know whether a seventh-grader or a national expert has written the site you visit. Assessing online sources helps you quickly reduce your reading load by eliminating invalid sources.

Whether you're reading short articles or conducting detailed research online, it's important to know whether the information is credible.

Consider using the *D-SOURCE* acronym to help you remember to evaluate the source before accepting information gathered digitally:

D = Dependable

S = Says Who?

O = Objective

U = Understandable

R = Recent

C = Complete

E = Evidence

Start your professional or research reading project by questioning the validity of online information by following these suggestions:

D = Dependable   Ask these important questions to test the dependability of an electronic source:

◆ Is the information located on a site created by a known entity? For example, is an article from a printed national, international, or local newspaper or magazine?

◆ Is there a non-Internet equivalent of the material you can find to verify its legitimacy?

◆ Does the material contain a lot of spelling, typographical or grammatical errors? If so, the information probably hasn't been properly edited, which brings the quality of the information into question. These types of errors can also result in incorrect information.

◆ Are the charts, graphs, maps, and photos clear and clearly labeled?

S = Says Who?   On whose authority is the information being presented? Look for the following information about the author:

◆ Who wrote it?

◆ What are his or her credentials?

◆ What else has he or she written on the topic?

◆ What are the author's affiliations (university department, organization, corporate title, etc.)?

◆ Is contact information available?

If you can't find sufficient credibility in the author's background, consider disqualifying him or her as a source.

O = Objective   Ask yourself, *How objective is this author?* Practically everything you read has some sort of bias or particular personal slant. Think critically about the information the author provides as well as the information *not* provided to help determine level of bias.

U = Understandable   Ask yourself, *Is this information easy to understand?* If you find that the material uses very difficult vocabulary or a lot of jargon, you might want to find material targeted to a different audience.

R = Recent   Ask yourself, *How old is this information?* Most articles provide a date, but that date could have different meanings. It may indicate …

◆ When the article was first published.

◆ When it was first placed on the web.

◆ When the most recent revision was done.

Decide how relevant the information is for your purpose.

C = Complete   Ask yourself, *Is that all there is?* Some online information is a work in progress, or has a sense of incompleteness about it. Look for …

◆ How thoroughly the author deals with the topic.

◆ A sense of completeness.

◆ The depth of the material.

◆ New information. (Or is it a summary of other research?)

◆ An "under construction" icon.

◆ A printed equivalent.

◆ Differences between digital and print versions.

E = Evidence   Ask yourself, *Where's the beef?* Some online materials can appear quite flashy but contain very little valuable substance. Look for whether or not …

◆ The author referred to other sources to substantiate his or her claims.

◆ The sources used are noteworthy.

◆ The material contains a bibliography.

◆ The material contains footnotes.

◆ The references within the text are reliable.

◆ The hyperlinks are to credible sources.

And the Results Are …

In this chapter, you've learned how to adapt your paper reading strategies to your on screen reading. By doing so, you can increase your reading speed while reducing your reliance on printed materials. You've also learned about keeping your eyes refreshed and how to evaluate the validity of materials online.

It's now time to check in on your reading progress. This is your chance to find out your online reading rate and practice some of the pacing strategies for on screen text. Choose one of these two articles from Fast Company (www.fastcompany.com):

"What Should I Do with My Life?" by Po Bronson
4,669 words/average 16 words per line
www.fastcompany.com/magazine/66/mylife.html

"Masters of the (Information) Universe" by Mark Fischetti
1,831 words/average 13 words per line
www.fastcompany.com/magazine/10/masters.html

Speed Tip

You can choose any other online articles you like; however, you'll need to determine the average number of words per line to calculate your words per minute (see Appendix D).

When you reach the article page, click on "Printable page" to get the text in a single column width without illustrations or ads. Consider warming up your eyes using the Discipline Your Eyes Exercise in Chapter 3. Conduct a One-Minute Timing exercise using your on screen pacer of choice and any other reading strategy you like. Track your words per minute (multiply the numbers of lines you read on screen × the average number of words per line listed with the article information above) and comprehension on the appropriate charts in Appendix C.

The Least You Need to Know

◆ You can use most of the same strategies when reading on screen as you use when reading paper documents; you just have to modify them to suit the digital text.

◆ It's worth your time to get comfortable with a few on screen pacers to increase your on screen reading speed.

◆ Following ergonomic guidelines can improve your eye and body comfort when reading on screen.

◆ There are ways to go completely paperless, and there are ways to simply reduce your usage of paper.

◆ When evaluating the validity of online content, try using the D—SOURCE acronym before accepting information gathered digitally.

Kick Your Bad Habits, and Watch Your Speed Soar

In This Chapter

- ◆ Identifying your bad reading habits (everyone has them!)
- ◆ Knock out the daydreaming
- ◆ Going backward doesn't work
- ◆ Word-for-word reading slows you down
- ◆ Reading faster reduces bad habits

Anyone who learns a new skill benefits from fine-tuning their abilities. Imagine how effective the tennis player is who learns a new backhand and then fine-tunes it to know when best to use it. Imagine the beautiful sound of the musician who learns to play the violin and then fine-tunes it so he doesn't squeak the strings when bowing. Imagine the gracefulness of the gymnast who learns how to work the parallel bars and then fine-tunes it to perfect her dismount.

As a new speed reader, you can benefit from learning how to fine-tune your abilities by understanding the three habits all readers share—daydreaming, back-skipping, and subvocalization—and how they affect your reading abilities. All three habits are very normal and very human.

As much as you'd like to get rid of these habits, you can really only reduce them, not get rid of them completely. Using speed reading strategies helps.

Daydreaming 101

Have you ever tried to tell someone about a dream you had and found that you couldn't really describe all you saw, thought, and felt in detail as you experienced it? One of the reasons for this is because we think faster than we talk.

If you recall from Chapter 1, the rate at which a person talks is 150 words per minute (an average between 100 and 200) and the rate at which a person thinks is upward of 300 words per minute. There's a minimal difference of about 150 words per minute, which is why, when you read or listen to someone talk, you have the possibility of *daydreaming:* you can think faster than you can talk, listen, or read!

def•i•ni•tion

Daydreaming is a spontaneous mental fantasy—while awake—about whimsical thoughts connected to some emotion, typically lasting only a short period of time. Daydreaming is frequently caused by not paying attention and may or may not be related to what's going on around you.

If the person you're listening to isn't engaging you with his or her words or actions, or if you're choosing not to pay attention—maybe because your mind is preoccupied or you're tired—daydreaming is inevitable. This might be one explanation why students are expert daydreamers; the instructors are either not engaging or not interesting, or the students' minds are thinking at speeds faster than their spoken thoughts. Students need to literally pay more attention to their inattention to stay on task!

Benefits of Daydreaming

Daydreaming is a natural human event and has long been ridiculed as a lazy or nonproductive activity. It is, however, beneficial in many ways:

◆ *It helps you relax.* Daydreaming enables your mind to take a minivacation, which releases tension and anxiety.

◆ *It helps you solve problems.* You might review the problem in your daydream and then envision what you can do to resolve the problem.

◆ *It strengthens relationships.* This occurs when you think about what you'll be doing with a friend or lover, what you'll say, and what he or she might say in return.

♦ *It enhances productivity.* By allowing yourself to daydream, you help your preoccupied mind solve a problem, plan ahead, or revisit a pleasant experience.

♦ *It helps you achieve a goal.* When you envision yourself reaching a goal—getting a college degree, climbing that mountain, or making a gourmet meal—it's almost as if you've reached it and you just need to take the steps to make it.

♦ *It relieves boredom.* You're human; you'll get bored with whatever activity you're engaged in, perhaps because the activity doesn't engage you or interest you. When reading, you might daydream because you're reading too slowly!

Causes of Daydreaming

To get even more specific about daydreaming, let's apply it to the task of reading. When reading, daydreaming is inevitable at times because …

♦ The speed you're reading is slower than your speed of thinking.

♦ The material doesn't engage your mind.

♦ You're preoccupied.

♦ You're tired.

♦ You aren't interested.

♦ Your mental to-do list is taking over.

♦ The material triggers a memory, causing you to go off task.

♦ You aren't paying attention.

♦ You're bored.

There are more reasons, but you get the picture: daydreaming happens. So if daydreaming happens, let's look at how to identify it, when to stop it, when to encourage it, and what to do to capitalize on it.

> **Speed Secret**
>
> Psychologists estimate that we daydream for $\frac{1}{3}$ to $\frac{1}{2}$ of our waking hours, although a single daydream lasts only a few seconds to a few minutes.

The Bad and the Good

Daydreaming really isn't as difficult to deal with as you might think. You first need to become aware of when you're daydreaming, as soon as possible, followed by deciding whether it's good or bad daydreaming. If you're thinking about things unrelated to your reading materials—you need to fold laundry, make phone calls, or go grocery shopping—this is obviously bad daydreaming, or not a good use of your reading time. It's probably unrelated to the reason why you're reading any given material.

If, however, you're thinking about how what you're reading relates to what you already know, that kind of daydreaming has everything to do with comprehension and building more background knowledge when reading. It's a great use of your time to allow your mind to relate what you're reading to what you already know. For example, let's say you're reading an article about proven strategies for finding a job in a down market. You're reading it because you were recently downsized and are now looking for a job. While reading, you might recall the resumé writing process and getting references from your previous employers. Maybe you recall the wonderful interview you had with a company that you hope hires you. Or maybe you remember the late nights of Internet searching to locate appropriate positions. This extraneous thinking, not relevant to the task of just reading, is helpful to your learning because you have a previous memory to relate the information to.

> **Speed Tip**
>
> If your mind is racing with your to-do list and preventing you from paying attention to your reading, try dumping it out onto a piece of paper. The mind keeps interrupting to remind you about your to-do's, so by writing them down, your mind will rest easy.

Reducing Daydreaming

You can prevent daydreaming while reading. Being well rested, putting yourself in a place conducive for concentrating, reading material you're interested in, and so on all help (see Chapter 6). Nevertheless, here are two basic strategies you can put into place right away, regardless of your other influences:

Catch yourself doing it. Decide quickly if your daydream is helping or hurting your reading process, and decide whether you should continue to daydream or get back to paying attention to the material.

> **Speed Secret**
>
> You'll daydream more during tasks you're familiar with, like making a bed or driving a car, and will tend to concentrate better when given something new.

Use speed reading strategies. When you use a hand or card pacer or any of the eye strategies, you naturally have to focus on what you're doing, which greatly reduces your tendency to daydream. By cheat reading, you build interest in (or get rid of) material, enabling you to focus more on the reading content than on what you're doing later that day.

Back-Skipping 101

If you ever get the chance to watch someone's eyes as they read silently, you'll see the eyes move forward but also twitch backward from time to time as well. This "twitching" is called *back-skipping* and is a natural human event, but in excess, it can prevent the ability to read fast and can especially reduce comprehension.

def•i•ni•tion

Back-skipping, also known as *regression*, is when your eyes go back over words they've already read. Done in excess, it can hinder reading speed and comprehension.

The Bad and the Good

Think about walking—you want to walk one step at a time, one foot after the other in a forward direction. The idea of walking a few steps forward, going back a step or two, and proceeding forward again isn't something most of us do. But many of us do it with our eyes when we read.

Back-skipping, when done unconsciously, means going back over material you've already read, either out of habit or because you don't trust that your brain got it the first time. Slower readers do this more than faster readers because going backward while speeding forward is harder than when just slowly moving forward.

When done consciously, back-skipping indicates that you recognize you missed something when you were reading, forcing you to return to look for what you missed. You might have done this when you got to the bottom of a page and realized you didn't understand anything because your eyes were looking at the words but your brain wasn't engaged. So you go back, looking for what you missed. This makes an unconscious event more conscious. More commonly, speed readers go back consciously because they want to be sure they understood a concept they sped read through or because they missed an important word—like *not*—and want to go back to find it.

Reducing Back-Skipping

Although back-skipping can be helpful when you consciously miss information, it's more commonly hurtful if you do it unintentionally. Similar to daydreaming, you can't get rid of the habit, but you can reduce back-skipping:

Catch yourself doing it. When you're aware of your back-skipping, you can do something about it.

Speed Tip _____

Ask someone to watch you read silently to see how many times your eyes back-skip in a minute. The more you do it, the more you need speed strategies to keep your eyes moving forward!

Use speed reading strategies. The faster you move forward, the harder it is to stop and go back, so using speed reading strategies makes sense. Most hand and card strategies are helpful, particularly the Blank White Card because it covers up the words you already read, leaving open the words yet to read, reducing the tendency to go back.

Treat your reading like watching a movie. Even if you miss something, don't go back. Continue on and expect to understand what you missed or find out it really wasn't important.

Subvocalization 101

If you read fewer than 200 words per minute, you have intimate knowledge about what pure subvocalization is. (Remember from Chapter 1 that subvocalization is when you either move your lips while you read in an attempt to say the words you're reading or you mentally whisper every word you read inside your head.)

When you first learned how to read, you needed all four steps of the subvocalization process:

1. You see a word on the page.

2. You then say it, either by moving your lips or whispering it mentally.

3. Then you hear the word with your ears.

4. Finally, you understand it with your brain.

However, now that you're a mature reader, you don't need to say or hear the words mentally. Your eyes and brain are quite capable of recognizing most words without saying or hearing them because of your vast experience with reading.

The Bad and the Good

Subvocalizing every word slows you down and limits you to the same speed that you talk out loud, which is around 150 words per minute. It also works your brain much harder than necessary, forcing it to process or decode one word at a time. When you learn to read in thought chunks (see Chapter 4), your brain works less and understands more as it processes more words at a time.

Subvocalizing tends to bore you because the voice you hear is your own and it's usually speaking in a monotone, expressionless manner. Some people say they get bored and then daydream as a result—not a good thing!

At times, however, slowing down your reading and intentionally subvocalizing is smart and a good use of your time:

Speed Tip

If you move your lips when you read, try this: gently press your index fingers over your lips so you won't be tempted to move them while reading. Although it might feel uncomfortable at first, within a short time, you'll begin to feel the path of reading going from your eyes, to the page, and directly to your brain.

- When material is really important, such as any legal or insurance agreement, especially if you're not a lawyer or insurance agent

- When material is unusually challenging

- When you want to memorize

- When you're studying

- When you read things like the Bible, Shakespeare, plays, and other dialogue

- When you're reading in a distracting or loud environment and you can't concentrate any other way

Reducing Subvocalizing

Just like daydreaming and back-skipping, you can't completely get rid of subvocalization, but you can certainly reduce it:

Catch yourself doing it. When you're aware of your word-for-word mental talking, you can do something about it.

Use speed reading strategies. The faster you move forward, the harder it is to stop and go back, so using speed reading strategies greatly reduces your tendency to read word for word. Reading key words is a great method to start with for word-for-word readers because it naturally reduces the number of words you mentally talk while

Speed Tip

In addition to using speed reading strategies, try pressing your tongue to the roof of your mouth while you read to resist the temptation to sound out the words. You can also try humming or chewing gum to occupy your vocal cords or your mouth instead of pronouncing the words in the text.

keeping comprehension. It also helps you feel comfortable in that you still subvocalize some but you aren't talking every word in your head. Any of the hand and card strategies are very helpful as well (see Chapter 2). The point is simply to see the text faster than you can read out loud so you can unlearn the habit of sounding the words to comprehend.

And the Results Are ...

Check in on your speed reading progress now. Choose to do either a One-Minute Timing or a 3-2-1 Drill found in Appendix B. Consider first warming up your eyes using the Discipline Your Eyes Exercise in Chapter 3. While you read, use your preferred pacer method. Be sure to record your progress in Appendix C.

The Least You Need to Know

♦ Be aware of three reading habits all humans share: daydreaming, back-skipping, and subvocalization.

♦ You're more likely to daydream when you're not paying attention. Good daydreaming happens when you relate something you're reading to what you already know.

♦ By learning to trust your brain, you can reduce back-skipping.

♦ Subvocalization, or talking the words you're reading in your head, slows you down when done purely by habit.

♦ By catching yourself doing these bad habits, you can reduce them and read faster!

Part 4

Overload Management

In this information age, having a "to-read" pile—or several—is very common. If you look at your reading workload, either on paper or on screen, and immediately feel overwhelmed, stressed, guilty, frustrated, or inadequate, Part 4 helps you feel much better.

In the following chapters, I introduce to you many simple yet effective organizing and prioritizing strategies you can immediately put to good use for your paper and on-screen workload. Mix them with the speed reading strategies you learned in earlier parts, and you have an amazing formula for reading success.

Embrace Your Paper Reading Piles

In This Chapter

- You have permission *not* to read it all!
- Get a realistic grip on all you have to read
- Gain control of your paper reading piles
- Prioritize your reading based on your time
- Get organized with LATCH

Are you a "later" kind of person? Do you put reading in a pile you tell yourself you'll "get to later"? Anyone who has a reading pile of any size knows who they are. There's nothing wrong with having piles; it's the thoughts and feelings you get when you look at the piles that's the trouble.

Now please understand, there's nothing wrong with being a "later" piler or even just having a paper reading pile. Every knowledge-hungry professional, student, or individual *should* have one. However, for most people, the pile is problematic:

- It consists of too much quantity and not enough quality.
- It makes you feel guilty for not reading it all.

- ◆ It makes you feel inadequate for not making the time to get to it.

- ◆ It almost always makes you feel overwhelmed and hopeless about ever getting caught up.

- ◆ You know there's valuable information in there, but you feel helpless to get to it.

We stack up magazines thinking that just because we receive it, we should read it. We buy books that look interesting, or that we heard about on *Oprah*, or a friend told us about, thinking we really have time to read them. We subscribe to e-zines (online magazines or newsletters) because we have a genuine interest, but don't think about the time it will take to read them. *Then*, we spend time reading articles that bore us just because they're there.

Out of all this, all we really want is to find just a few golden information nuggets that will make our personal or professional lives easier, less expensive, or more enjoyable. It often feels like a lot of work for such a small but useful reward. Let's see what choices we have in making this a better experience.

Weed Your Magazines

That pile of magazines growing on your desk, nightstand, bathroom floor, and/or kitchen counter (did I find them all?!) is like an overgrowth of weeds in a garden. The weeds dull the beauty of the flowers, and we stay away from the garden because we know it will take work, and time, to make it beautiful and inviting again. But what can we do? Weeds are inevitable, right? Not so fast.

More than 10 years ago, I looked at a pile of magazines growing on my nightstand and became confused as to why someone like me, an efficient and skilled reader, still had a huge pile of reading. So I took the idea to task and came up with a simple solution that has now worked for me, and those I teach it to, for years. The process can easily be modified for other types of materials in your pile.

Gather All Your Weeds

Right now, your magazine pile is probably overgrown. You can see just how over-grown it is by putting *all* the reading material you have to read in *one* place. That means taking all your piles and consolidating them, say, on the kitchen table or your desk. (Now might be a good time to have a good laugh as you look at all you have while scratching your head and saying to yourself, *What was I thinking?! I can't read all of this!*)

It helps to know exactly all you have by taking some sort of inventory of what you have in front of you. Either write down your own inventory list or just stack like titles together. Note how often you receive them: daily, monthly, quarterly, etc.

What's Their Value?

It's a given that some pieces of material in your pile are more valuable to you than others. By picking up each one at a time and evaluating the magazine either by your previous experience with it or the cover stories, decide its value to you on a scale of 1 to 10.

Set 1 as the lowest, least useful rating you can give. A 1 means every time you read that magazine, you feel like you're wasting time, you rarely find any good information nuggets inside, and you don't feel any satisfaction when you read it.

Make 10 the highest, most useful rating. A 10 means you absolutely *love* this magazine and it doesn't matter what the articles are about, you want to read it. When a 10 arrives, you're tempted to stop what you're doing to read it *right now* or, at the very least, place it on top of your reading pile to get to it first when time allows.

You can place a Post-it on the cover of each with your rating, write the number in marker on the cover, or just stack them in two piles: anything with a number *under 6* in one pile and anything *6 and over* in another.

Get Rid of the Undesirables

One of the piles is ready to go. Can you guess which one? You got it—the under-6 pile. You've deemed it unimportant and not of comparative value to you. So why keep the magazines in it?

Get rid of the under-6 pile! How is up to you:

- ◆ Throw it away!
- ◆ Recycle the pile (if you can).
- ◆ Donate it to a homeless shelter.
- ◆ Share the magazines with your local school or senior center for art projects.
- ◆ Give them to a new business in town with a waiting room.

- Tie them together to make a footrest under your desk.

- Any other creative idea you can come up with!

If you consistently have the same title in your under-6 pile, seriously consider unsubscribing to the magazine. The less valuable material you initially add to your pile, the better!

Weigh Your Pile to Match Your Time

You're not done, yet! You've definitely made your pile more appealing and inviting, but you have to remember one important detail: when do you have time to read it all?

If you give 3 hours a month to reading magazines and you have 10 magazines in your pile, chances are you'll still have large piles. Most people can't and don't read 10 magazines in 3 hours. They might read three to five, depending on their reading speed, how much content they like to read, and how fast they turn the pages.

Match your reading time on a monthly basis with the amount you have chosen to read. If you have more reading material than time, weed out more to match your time. If you're one of the lucky ones who has more time than reading material, add more good stuff to your pile! Ask your friends and colleagues what they read. They might just turn you on to your next number 10! (For more about this reading time issue, see Chapter 6.)

My Reading Pile

I'd like to share my current magazine reading pile with you to provide a point of comparison. Consider that I am a self-employed corporate trainer working out of my home office. I travel overnights at least 6 to 12 times each year for business. I am a wife and mother of two children whom I feed and take care of while also managing the school carpool, after-school sports activities, and social schedule. Like many of you, I do the food shopping, food preparation, laundry, and general household cleaning. My current monthly magazine reading pile (which doesn't include the one to three books per month I read for personal or professional development, or my online newsletters) consists of the following:

- Two newspapers (one daily, one Sunday)

- Eight professional journals (all monthly)

- Three personal magazines (most monthly)

I admit I don't always get to the daily or Sunday papers, and sometimes I immediately recycle a magazine that doesn't hold my interest or becomes too old. I do sometimes pick up a magazine I don't subscribe to in the airport or supermarket when I have time and interest.

You might think this pile is a lot, or a little, depending on your own pile. But considering that more than 18,000 titles of magazines are printed in this country every year, I've chosen only 11 per month, which some might say is a very small amount. But it is perfect for me.

My small pile is all I need to feed my personal and professional soul. I'm not afraid of it, and I'm eager to get to it. I also don't read everything in each magazine and use other reading strategies (see Chapters 7 and 10) to quickly get through it.

I place my magazines in a stand-up cardboard catalog holder. If the cardboard starts to bend because it's getting too full, I know I either need to make more time to read or get rid of some magazines. I limit myself to one catalog holder's worth—no more.

Lastly, I only keep a maximum of 4 months' worth of my chosen magazines. If I have five back issues of the same monthly magazine, either because I didn't make enough time to read or that title hasn't interested me as much lately, I get rid of one. Ideally, I love to read this month's magazine in this month! But life doesn't always work out that way ….

Prioritize Your Books

A pile of books is sometimes more threatening than a pile of magazines. One professional woman I worked with had bought so many business and how-to books from an online bookstore that when people came into her office, there was no place to sit down! She had stacked books on her guest chair as well as all around it. She had read only a few of them and wanted to know what to do. I told her the first thing that came to my mind: stop buying books!

Get a Bookcase ... or Two

The second thing I suggested was to get a three-tiered bookcase to put the books on and organize them according to her own value system. Just like the strategy I shared earlier in this chapter about placing a value on each magazine, I asked her to hold each book, quickly thumb through it, and decide, on a scale of 1 to 10 (1 being low, 10 being high) what value she wanted to place on it. Then I suggested she place all those books with a value of 9 or 10 on the top shelf, placing them in the order she wanted to read them. Books with 6 through 8 went on the middle shelf, and books under a 6 went on the bottom shelf.

She'd bought some of the books recently so the personal value was high; others were bought years ago when she was into different things so their value had gone down over time.

Carve Out Time

The third part of the process was to figure out when she would make the time to read any of the books based on her schedule. If she was unable or unwilling to give time for reading, then why keep any of them at all?

She confided that she really liked the insights books offered, but she felt inadequate and slow as a reader. She procrastinated heavily and found a million other things to do instead of read. No wonder she had an uncontrollable stack!

Decide What *Not* to Read

It might seem that she still has the same number of books to read as she did in the beginning, but she can now intelligently choose which ones *not* to read based on her value system rating. (She ended up giving away most of the unread books from the bottom shelf and some from the middle to her corporate library.)

She doesn't read a book anymore just because it's there; instead, she picks a book she feels has some real personal or professional value for her. And she makes sure now if she buys a book, she has the time to read it. This saves her, and her company, a lot of money.

She's now motivated to read more frequently and not procrastinate nearly as much. She feels much more satisfied when she reads and finds it a good use of her time.

Newspaper Reading Made Easy(er)

As a college student, I didn't understand why anyone would want to read a newspaper every day. At the time, I was the type of reader who only read when I had to and avoided it like the plague if unnecessary. The newspaper used to be in the "unnecessary" category. When I learned the secrets of faster reading, I found reading a daily newspaper a welcome change of pace and a great way to get a broader view of this crazy world. I was better able to make conversation and understand what others were talking about. It was also easier material to practice my faster reading strategies on.

I'd like to share with you an efficient process I have created to help me get through a Sunday paper. Some of this process can be used for your daily reading as well.

1. Get rid of the clutter. Start your process by getting rid of the unwanted circulars and sections you don't need or want to spend your time on. They get in your way and distract you. I immediately remove the real estate section (unless I'm looking to buy some), help wanted, and sports (I hear enough from my husband and sons!).

2. Set up the paper for faster reading. Lay it flat out on a cleared-off table with all the sections neatly underneath.

3. Organize the sections based on your interests. Looking at the cover page of each section, decide which ones intrigue you the most, and prioritize them accordingly. This way, if you run out of time, you've read the sections of most value to you.

4. Quickly skim the headlines. Look for articles of interest, and disregard those you have no interest in.

5. Read the first few paragraphs or just the first sentences of paragraphs. Most newspaper articles are written in an A-frame style, with the most important, new information upfront, followed by the other, unimportant or older news details. Start reading the first few paragraphs in their entirety and then continue reading just the first sentence of every paragraph thereafter, if you want to see if there is anything new.

6. Use a faster reading strategy. Some of the best strategies for reading newspapers based on their narrow column width include the following:

   ◆ Reading key words (Chapter 4)

   ◆ Using a white card (Chapter 2)

   ◆ Center Pointer Pull (Chapter 2)

   ◆ The Left or Right Pointer Pull (Chapter 2)

   ◆ The S or Z pattern (Chapter 2)

   ◆ Open Hand Wiggle (Chapter 2)

If you're partial to another method not mentioned, try it. If it works, use it. And enjoy the rest of your day!

Clippings and More Clippings

What if, while reading your magazines and newspapers, you come across an article you want to keep? What do you do with it? The best solution is to clip it out and save it. But what if you save a lot of articles? What do you do with them?

Weed to Make the Information Useable

I recently worked with a gentleman who admitted that he had 10 years of back issues of the monthly *Gourmet* magazine sitting in boxes in his garage. (His wife was understandably upset when he suggested that they move to a bigger home to accommodate his boxes!) When I asked him why, he said, "Someday, maybe when I retire, I will use the recipes and ideas. I love making chocolate and might want to start a chocolate business."

I probed a little further and asked how he might go about finding those chocolate recipes after he retired. He looked at me a little perplexed and said as if trying to convince himself, "I guess I'll have to read them all?" I then suggested he not wait until retirement and consider the following:

1. Get rid of 80 percent of the magazines, or 8 years' worth. According to Barbara Hemphill, author of *Taming the Paper Tiger*, most people use only 20 percent of what they keep so it makes sense to get rid of the other 80 percent. He could have just kept the most recent 2 years, but instead chose to look at the cover graphic and magazine focus to quickly decide whether he wanted to keep it or not. He forced himself to keep just 24 issues, which is 2 years' worth.

2. Of the remaining 2 years' worth, take one magazine at a time, when time allows, and locate the chocolate recipes and other interesting information, using the table of contents as a quick guide.

3. Tear out the relevant recipes and information. Throw away the remaining part of the magazine and, as always, recycle when possible.

4. Repeat steps 2 and 3 with any new issues that comes in.

I reminded him that any recipe he might want and doesn't have can most likely be found on the magazine's website or located online after a quick search.

So now he has a collection of recipes and other information clipped out. He put the clippings in a pile, all in one place. I said he had a great start. Then I asked how he might find that great chocolate torte recipe he might want to make. He said he'd have to look through them all. I said there is a much better way: archive them in a simple-to-find file scheme so he can make this information useable.

Find the Clip When You Want Using LATCH

I share this great idea with you from *Information Anxiety 2* by Richard Saul Wurman, one of the best books I have read on understanding information overload. In it, Wurman says there are *only* five ways information can be organized—LATCH:

Location   This is by place, either physical or relational. For example, if you want to keep your recipes by region, you can create files for French recipes, Italian recipes, etc. If you're a human resources director, you can create global files for the company's various physical locations. If you're a medical student, you might create resource files for the locations in the human body, from the head to the toes.

Alphabet   This provides you with 26 familiar and ordered subcategories to file in. You probably already use this for the names in your address book, but you can also use it for your CD collection or office supplies log. My friend from earlier can file his chocolate recipes in alphabetical order or subfile them this way under broader categories.

Time   Anything that has a timeline fits in this organizational scheme. In the example of the chocolate recipes, they could be organized by how long each recipe takes to make. So if you only have 30 minutes, look for the 30-minute recipes. If you have 2 hours, look for the 2-hour recipes. Long-term projects, conference planning, and quarterly reports also fit in here.

Category   This is probably the first area to look at when you need to organize a lot of information. Think about under what categories the information falls. For the chocolate lover, you could use cakes, soufflés, candies, puddings, and so on. You could use various types of products or clients, different medical plans, and assorted types of insurances.

Hierarchy   Think about size in this area. Anything you can list from small to large or least to most (and visa versa) fits this area. Although many things don't need this possibility, the chocolate recipe saver could list the recipes from smallest products to largest, say from chocolate jellybeans, to candies, to brownies, to cakes.

Source: Wurman, Richard S. Information Anxiety 2, © 2000, pages 40 to 42. Reprinted with permission of Pearson Education, Inc., Upper Saddle River, NJ.

Let's look at how my friend could organize his chocolate recipes using LATCH:

American Recipes

> Brownies
>
>> Small pan
>>
>> Large pan
>
> Cakes
>
>> With frosting
>>
>> Without frosting
>
> Candy

French Recipes

> Cakes
>
>> Jelly filled
>>
>> Mousse filled
>
> Candy
>
> Mousse
>
> Petit fours

Swiss Recipes

> Cakes
>
> Chocolate bars
>
> Pudding

I have applied Wurman's philosophy to my business and topic files with much success. But it's important to mention here that there's no one best way to file anything, as long as the system works for you and makes your information easily accessible and useable, then it's "right."

Even the Bills Can Be Appealing

So far, you've read about different ways to make and manage your reading piles to make them more inviting and faster to get through. In addition, you might find a few other strategies useful:

Make the bills easier to pay. When you receive a bill, don't just put it on a pile. Open it up, throw away the advertising inserts (okay, quickly look at them if you must), and place the bill with the envelope together with the amount you need to pay facing out. Then file or pile them by the date they're due. (You can buy a 30-day file jacket at a local office supply store to keep them in.) When it comes time to pay the bills, you can "speed" through them, or at least faster than if you just piled them without opening them.

Handle each piece of paper only once. This is a popular time management credo that many use and an equal amount cannot understand. It doesn't mean you literally only touch the material one time. It means that every time you touch a piece of reading material, don't do nothing. Rather, take some action that advances it one step closer to its final destination.

For example, when a magazine comes in, decide on your scale of 1 to 10 if it even makes your pile. Assuming it does, the next time you touch it, quickly look over the table of contents and highlight the articles you're most interested in. Or place a sticky note on the article you want to read so you know where to turn when you have time. The next time you touch it, turn to an article of interest and read it. If you can read all that is of interest and finish it, then recycle it or throw it away. If you want to file it, do so.

Manage catalogs better. For you catalog shoppers, it can be very easy to amass a threatening stack of catalogs, many of which you may never buy from. They just keep coming and coming. And that's the beauty of it! You don't need to keep them all, just the most recent one, so consider throwing away the older one when the newer one comes in. And if you receive one you don't ever envision yourself buying from, immediately throw it away (or even better, recycle it!).

Use organizing software. If you need to track large amounts of reference material on your computer, try Barbara Hemphill's *Taming the Paper Tiger* software available at www.thepapertiger.com. Researchers, engineers, educators, and others who read widely or need to have an easy reference database will find this software a powerful tracking tool.

So now you have choices that perhaps you didn't know about before. By making your paper piles more inviting, you just might find more time to read, find more nuggets, and enjoy your reading more!

And the Results Are ...

Once again, it's time to check in on your speed reading progress now. Choose to do either a One-Minute Timing or a 3-2-1 Drill found in Appendix B. Consider first warming up your eyes using the Discipline Your Eyes Exercise in Chapter 3. While you read, use your preferred pacer method. Be sure to record your progress in Appendix C.

The Least You Need to Know

♦ Understanding that you can't read it all is the first step to deciding what you want to read and what's most valuable to you.

♦ Placing a personal value on all your reading material makes your reading pile more interesting and makes your reading time much more enjoyable.

♦ Organizing your books to read based on your current interest levels encourages you to read and greatly reduces your feelings of overload.

♦ Reading newspapers can be overwhelming because of the amount of information they hold. Approaching them in an organized way helps you get through them quicker.

♦ Using the LATCH system, you can create a filing scheme that makes finding your nuggets easier.

Chapter 15

Making Your Electronic Piles Inviting

In This Chapter

♦ Master your on screen reading workload

♦ Manage your online subscriptions

♦ E-books 101

♦ Let technology be your news clipping service

♦ Blogging made easy(er)

Just when you think you have your paper reading workload under control, you open your e-mail inbox or surf the Internet and find more to read and manage! If you think about it, reading a paper workload isn't that different from an on screen one; it's just on screen! (Chapter 12 has some great suggestions for reading better and faster on screen.)

Getting your on screen reading workload under control can be quite empowering. Most people are slaves to their screens where they really need to be masters. This chapter helps anyone tied to his or her on screen workload loosen their chains in the quest of becoming an on screen reading workload master!

What's in an Electronic Pile?

Countless types of reading materials are available today, both on paper and on screen. Although many started out in a paper version, they have quickly progressed to electronic versions. Take books, for instance. Just when you thought a paperback was portable, handheld devices like PDAs, pocket PCs, and other designated reading devices came along to enable you to download a book's text (or an *e-book*) onto the machine.

def•i•ni•tion

E-books are books produced in digital format. They can be ordered online and delivered electronically to your computer. Many e-books are now available on audio CD or as MP3 files you can download to an iPod or MP3 player. **E-zines** are electronically published magazines or newsletters available online.

Thinking a page newsletter was cumbersome and expensive to mail by traditional means, the computer came along and added the concept of *e-zines*, or online newsletters, that for the most part are available free of charge. Even those who formerly thought preparing and mailing a traditional newsletter was too much find the electronic version easier to manage. The end result for you? More to read!

And whoever thought a paper brochure would become, for the most part, unnecessary? Since the advent of websites, they are! Websites are interactive brochures.

The same is true for the office memo—what was wrong with that? It wasn't fast enough! So now we have e-mail to zip documents all over the world.

And if reading your morning paper or a magazine doesn't fit in your hands anymore, you can most likely read it—archived for years—on your computer screen.

 ## Speed Tip

If you're still struggling to manage your paper reading workload and need some additional help, consider learning more about two important areas: time management and organization. Sometimes what may appear to be too much may mean just too many choices and not enough targeted decisions. In Appendix B, I've reprinted an article from Julie Morgenstern, a time management and organizing expert. She has written books on both topics, which I highly recommend. (And for those who would like a break from reading, consider the audio book versions!)

Embrace Your Electronic Reading Pile

With all that's available for you to read on screen, what and how much do you subscribe to? If you frequently subscribe to daily, weekly, or monthly mailing lists from every interesting website you visit, you definitely have more to read on screen than a person probably needs. And if you purchase anything on the Internet, you'll also be bombarded with the retailer's promotions. It ends up just like the paper piles; you have more to read than time available.

Managing Your Subscriptions

Let's do a quick revisit to the weeding concept talked about in Chapter 14, this time applying it to your electronic reading pile:

1. Gather all your weeds. Identify all that you have coming in electronically. Make a list.

2. What's their value? Rank the importance of each on a scale of 1 to 10, with 1 being low and 10 being high.

3. Get rid of the undesirables. Anything you rank under a 6, get rid of or unsubscribe to; keep anything 6 and over.

> **Speed Bump**
>
> When buying anything online, pay attention to whether you check or uncheck the "Yes, send me e-mails!" box. Some manufacturers phrase their offer positively ("Yes, I want to receive your stuff") and automatically have it prechecked. Others phrase it negatively ("No, I don't want to receive your stuff") and don't have it automatically checked.

4. Weigh your pile to match your time. Based on the amount of time you want to be reading on screen on either a daily, weekly, or monthly basis, match it to how much information you're signed up to receive.

I continually revisit this process when I find I've been overzealous and have subscribed to too many things that look interesting. I used to receive information like a word of the day, feeling of the moment, inspiration for the week, and so on and found them great ... for a little while. Then it seemed that I just didn't find value in them anymore and was often deleting them without reading them. That's when I was sure it was time to unsubscribe!

Getting Started Reading E-Books

When e-books became a reading option in the late 1990s, technology's early adopters were eager to try this new medium. Internet bookstores offered them for sale, and other specialized websites popped up selling e-books as well. Unfortunately, e-books were not embraced by many others and online sellers stopped offering them for sale. As a result, fortunately for you, is that e-books are now widely available for personal download at no charge!

An *e-book reader*, such as a pocket PC or PDA (personal digital assistant), is mobile; it fits into a small bag, and can be used almost anywhere (although its batteries sometimes run out!). It is light, thin, and has some paper-like qualities. It isn't made of paper, however, which for some readers is just too different to work with.

def•i•ni•tion

An **e-book reader** is a device used to read e-books. It may be a device specifically designed for that purpose, or one intended for other purposes as well, like the PDA (personal digital assistant). Some devices, like the Sony Reader Digital Book, can hold upward of 160 books!

E-books have many features traditional paper books do not: the author or e-publisher has the freedom to control the look and feel of the e-book through fonts, colors, images, and in some cases, bookmarks, notes, and annotations from the author.

I suggest you try reading an e-book on an e-reader before deciding whether or not e-books are for you.

E-Book Reader Options

Today, you can find many different *e-book readers*, some more expensive than others. What has changed considerably in the past few years are both the software and the reading device options available that support e-books and documents.

What makes e-books come to life are the applications, or software, used to read the e-books. As of this writing, here are a few of the more popular and widely available e-book applications:

- ◆ Microsoft Reader with ClearType technology can be used on your PC, laptop, or pocket PC. Features include highlighting, bookmarks, notes, and drawings. Microsoft e-book readers are available for free download on pocket PC devices manufactured by Hewlett Packard, Casio, and Compaq. Go to www.microsoft.com/reader.

- ◆ Palm Reader is an award-winning application used to read Palm Digital Media e-books on your Palm OS handheld. The Palm Reader is free, but an upgrade called Palm Reader Pro isn't. It does come with a free 15-day trial. Go to www.ereader.com and click on the software link.

- ◆ The Mobipocket eBook Reader can be used on Palm OS, Psion, Franklin eBookman, and Windows CE PDAs. It comes with a free 14-day trial. Go to www.mobipocket.com and click on the software link.

◆ Adobe Acrobat eBook Reader has a
new software application built from
the ground up for acquiring, managing, and reading e-books, digital
newspapers, and other digital publications called Adobe Digital Editions.
It's available as a free download for
Microsoft Windows and Mac systems.
Go to www.adobe.com and click on the
download link.

Speed Tip

Check out www.eReader.com
for a worthwhile, one-stop
e-book shop and information
center about e-readers.

Other E-Book Resources

If you go to your favorite search engine and type in *e-books*, you'll get more results
than you have time in this lifetime to look through!

To help you get started, try these select few:

◆ www.ebooks.com is a digital bookstore that carries 102,000 popular, professional,
and academic e-books from the world's leading publishers. Most can be downloaded for an average of $10 to $20 each and work with the Microsoft Reader
and Adobe Reader applications.

◆ The World Public Library, found at
www.netlibrary.net, carries the world's
largest digital archive of more than
500,000 *portable digital format* (PDF) e-
books and documents. They have audio
MP3 download options as well. You
can join for under $10 a year to receive
unlimited downloads from the site.

◆ Microsoft (www.microsoft.com) and
Adobe (www.adobe.com) also offer
free e-book downloads for their reader
formats. On the main page, enter "free
e-books" in the search bar.

def•i•ni•tion

**Portable document format
(PDF)** is an electronic document
format that's different from other
documents because it allows a
certain amount of versatility while
retaining the original document
formatting. You can download
a PDF reader for free at www.
adobe.com.

Streamline Your On-Screen Inflow

Are you a news, *blog*, or *podcast* junkie? If so, you need to know about *RSS* feeds and *XML*. These are free subscriptions to a wide variety of websites and blogs in specific areas such as business, technology, science, education, humor, and more. Instead of you going out to search websites, you receive the news, blog posts, and podcasts you want through your RSS subscriptions.

def•i•ni•tion

A **blog,** shortened from *web log*, is a journal-type series of entries posted online. A **podcast** is a web-based audio broadcast via an RSS feed, accessed by subscription over the Internet. **RSS** stands for "real simple syndication" and is a quick way for you to get updates, headlines, or even full articles culled from the web and delivered to your computer. (You might also see an **XML** button, which stands for extensible markup language. That's just another way to read RSS feeds.)

An RSS document, also called a feed, is delivered as a summary of a website headline or update and is sometimes delivered in full text. RSS makes it possible for you to stay current with your favorite websites and blogs in an automated manner that's easier than checking them manually.

You can also streamline your on screen inflow by subscribing, at no charge, to Google Alert. At www.googlealert.com, you can sign up to receive information about any key word(s) you select. I have several feeds that keep me abreast of websites, blogs, and news postings about topics I'm interested in. I do suggest, however, that you get the daily (or weekly) compilation instead of the individual e-mails! If there are 20 notices in 1 day on your key words, that's 20 e-mails for you to sort through!

Speed Tip

If you want more functionality than the freeware RSS feed, consider paying for software such as Feed Demon owned by www.newsgator.com. It makes it fast to scan headlines of the RSS feeds or blogs you follow or any website with RSS feeds, and it only drills down and reads the entries for the posts you're interested in.

Also, many large newspapers such as *The New York Times* have news-clipping services focused specifically on their publication. Some are available at no charge and others are on a subscription fee basis. Check the website of your favorite newspaper to see what's available.

I'd rather have information that I've selected come to me rather than be inundated with all the possibilities out there. Taking advantage of RSS feeds and other alert services ensures that I read the best and don't even see the rest!

E-Mail Reading Made Easy(er)

I teach a workshop called "Slaying the E-Mail Dragon" in which I spend about third of the time teaching participants how to move their eyes more efficiently across a computer screen, another third about managing e-mail time, and the last third about how to use e-mail software better. Smart reading and processing takes using smart strategies!

Lucky for you, you know the first third already: how to use key words, thought chunks (see Chapter 4), and on screen pacers (see Chapter 12). But you must *use* them! Reading on screen can make for slower reading speeds, so using your speed strategies can prevent this problem.

An e-mail is anywhere from 18 to 25 words per line across your screen, while a newspaper column is around six words per line. This means keeping your place while you read e-mail can be somewhat challenging. On screen pacers can help. You should be able to read most of your e-mails on screen. The only time they need to be printed is for portability (i.e., to bring to a meeting) or to keep in a permanent paper file.

To make e-mails more readable and easier to respond to, consider setting a good example to those you e-mail to in the hopes they will do the same:

♦ Keep it short, sweet, and to the point. If you think of an e-mail like a postcard, you'll need to think and communicate efficiently.

♦ Create great subject lines. Be as specific as possible in the subject so the receiver has a strong clue about what's in the communication and, more importantly, what they need to do with it. For example, "Meeting Time Change" can be more specific if the subject line read: "9/15 planning meeting now 10 A.M."

♦ Write short subject lines. Subject lines need to be limited to 6 to 8 words or 30 to 40 characters for the readability. Excessively long subject lines either get cut off when received or are frequently ignored by the receiver.

> **Speed Bump**
>
> E-mails are as public as a postcard, so avoid sending *anything* you'd be bothered that anyone might read. Avoid sending gossip, bad news, inappropriate jokes, etc., via e-mail. Also be careful about replying to all recipients on an e-mail distribution list if you only need to respond to the sender.

◆ Leave space. No one likes to read a thick chunk of text on screen (or on paper, for that matter!), so when possible, include only two or three lines in each paragraph and then separate your paragraphs with a space.

◆ Number questions for easier response. If you have two questions on the same topic to ask the same person, number them and separate them by a space. He or she can then respond directly by replying with the answers typed after the original text or by saying something like: "In response to question 1 ...." If you have two questions on two separate topics, consider two separate e-mails. It will keep your communications easier.

◆ Put the main point upfront. Many e-mail writers bury their main point somewhere in the e-mail or save it to the end. If you put it in the first sentence or two, the receiver knows why you're writing.

◆ Use the preview pane. The preview pane helps you decide which e-mails you want to read now. If the writer did put the main point up front, then you would know what the email is about before you open it.

◆ Remember that e-mail begets e-mail. The more e-mails you write, the more you get, so if you want less e-mail, write less!

Better Blogging

If you're a *blogger*—and you know who you are—you may have found that you have quickly become inundated with *blog posts*, not only from your own blog, but from others you subscribe to. Depending on your blog involvement, consider some of these ideas:

◆ Investigate different blog readers. For example, check out www.bloglines.com.

◆ Try resizing your browser or news reader to narrower columns (approximately 8 words per line).

◆ Limit your blog reading time. This can be an addiction for some, which, like Internet surfing, sucks away time!

def·i·ni·tion

One entry in a blog is called a **blog post**. A **blogger** is someone who adds or edits a post.

◆ Limit the number of feeds you subscribe to on a particular topic. If you add a new feed, consider unsubscribing to an old one.

◆ Don't read a feed for a week and then do a quick catch-up to see it if was really worth your time. If so, keep it; if not, unsubscribe.

◆ Organize your categories by importance or frequency, not by topic. Some breakdowns include "must read," "daily," "Mondays only," "Fridays only," "weekly," and "monthly."

◆ Quarantine new blogs for a week to decide if you really want to add them to your *aggregator*.

◆ Add an "ignore" category for blogs you no longer read so you remember those that aren't worth your time. Or even better, just delete them.

def•i•ni•tion

An **aggregator** is a program that watches for new content at user-specified RSS feeds. An example is www.bottomfeeder.com.

Get to Know Your Software

You can read and process information faster when you know how to use the software you're working with. You could read the thick software manual (and maybe fall asleep in the process!), or you could try one or more of these ideas:

◆ Subscribe to Microsoft's e-Newsletter at www.office.microsoft.com. The monthly e-newsletter is chock-full of tips and ideas for working better with your software.

◆ Become friendly with your local software training company and consider signing up for a course or two.

◆ Talk to others who use your software. They might know things you don't, and you can share things you know with them.

And the Results Are ...

This is your last formal opportunity to check in on your reading progress. Do either a One-Minute Timing or a 3-2-1 Drill found in Appendix B. Remember to warm up your eyes using the Discipline Your Eyes Exercise in Chapter 3. While you read, use your preferred pacer method. Be sure to record your progress on the appropriate charts in Appendix C.

Now that you've completed your last timing exercise, take a look at your results. Look at the first timing you did and compare it to where you are now. What do you see?

What seemed to work best? What didn't? What more do you want to work on? What topics or strategies do you need to revisit?

Hopefully, you're pleased with your results and ready to continue experimenting with these strategies to make them even more effective and efficient. Here's to speeding through your reading!

The Least You Need to Know

◆ You can remedy an overwhelming electronic reading pile by using the same paper-handling strategies of matching your reading quantity to your available reading time.

◆ Reading e-books is as easy as knowing about e-book reading devices and the available software formats.

◆ Keeping up to date with topics of interest is as easy as subscribing to news-clipping services available on the web, many at no charge.

◆ Make your e-mails look good and easier to read. Hopefully, those who send you e-mail back will do the same!

◆ Blogs are web logs you can subscribe to through RSS feeds.

◆ Know how to use your software better and smarter and see how fast you can speed through your reading.

Appendix A

Glossary

accelerated learning   A teaching approach designed to make learning happen faster.

acquisition   The ability to come into possession of a skill or knowledge.

aggregator   A program that watches for new content at user-specified RSS feeds.

auto-summarize   A feature available on some word processing programs that allows you to create an executive-type summary of a longer document.

background knowledge   The accumulation of knowledge gained through personal experiences, either informal or formal. The trips you take, the people you talk to, the teachers you learn from all contribute to your background knowledge. In your day-to-day life, and especially when you read, you are constantly learning new things, creating more background knowledge.

back-skipping   When your eyes go back over words they already read. Done in excess, it can hinder reading speed and comprehension.

Blank Card Method   A reading pacer method where the reader uses a blank white card placed above the line to force the reader to concentrate and focus while reducing back-skipping.

blog   Shortened from *web log*, a blog is a journal-type series of entries posted online.

blog post   One entry of a blog.

blogger   Someone who adds or edits a blog post.

building bridges of knowledge   Applying some new piece of information to what you already know.

Center Pointer Pull   A reading pacer method where you place the index finger of either hand in the center of the reading material. You read moving the finger down the center of the column and moving your eyes from left to right.

cheat reading   A reading strategy where you look for and read primarily the writer's outline.

comprehension   The process of understanding what you read; the brain's role in the reading process.

Cursor as pacer   An on-screen pacer method of using your cursor to underline the center $2/3$ of the lines.

daydreaming   A spontaneous mental fantasy—while awake—about whimsical thoughts connected to some emotion, typically for a short period of time. It is frequently caused by not paying attention and may or may not be related to what is going on around you.

discomfort zone   The uneasy feeling you get when you try something new. Most new speed readers feel it the first time they try to read fast and discover an issue with comprehension.

Double Pointer Pull   A reading pacer method where you place the left pointer finger on the left margin of text and your right pointer finger on the right margin of text. Then move your fingers straight down the text moving your eyes across each line reading from fingertip to fingertip.

e-book   A book that is produced in digital format. E-books can be ordered online with no shipping, no taxes—many times for free—and delivered electronically to your computer. Many e-books are now available on audio CD or as MP3 files you can download to an iPod or MP3 player.

e-book reader   A device used to store and read e-books. It may be a device specifically designed for that purpose, or one intended for other purposes as well, like the PDA (personal digital assistant). Some devices, like the Sony Reader Digital Book, can hold upward of 160 books!

ergonomics   The science of workplace design factors that maximize productivity and minimize a worker's fatigue and discomfort.

eye jump *See* saccade.

eye stop *See* fixation.

e-zine An electronically published magazine (or newsletter), especially on the Internet.

fiction Literary works whose content is produced by the imagination and are not necessarily based on fact, such as novels and short stories. Books can be either fiction or nonfiction.

fixation A coordinated positioning and focusing of both eyes on a word. Also called an *eye stop*.

font A family of digital lettering and characters.

Forgetting Curve Discovered by Ebbinghaus, it shows that humans tend to halve their memory of newly learned knowledge in a matter of days or weeks unless they consciously review the learned material.

hemisphericity A brain theory discovered by Roger Sperry that in the two sides of the brain (right and left), one is more dominant.

highlighting pacer An on-screen pacer where you "highlight" each line of text as your eyes read.

keeper A new idea, typically some piece of information, you want to "keep" and remember. Keepers should always be written down, looked at again, and/or used for future reference.

key words Words that are typically three letters long or longer and carry the most meaning of a sentence.

LATCH system A five-part system for organizing files, both paper and electronic.

Left Pointer Pull A reading pacer method where you place the index finger of either hand along the left margin of the reading material. You read moving the finger down the left margin and moving your eyes from left to right.

Line-by-Line Pacers Two on-screen pacer methods where you use the upper or lower straight-edge of the screen to help you keep your place and read faster.

Long-Smooth Underline A reading pacer method where you move your three middle fingers under the lines of text moving across from one margin to the other.

memory The ability of the mind to retain learned information and knowledge of past events and experiences coupled with the ability to retrieve that information and knowledge. *Short-term memory* ranges from 5 to 8 seconds to a day or two. *Long-term memory* comprises our background knowledge.

mental whispering   *See* subvocalization.

mind map   A hand-drawn diagram used to represent the ideas in a reading and arranged around a central topic. It is used to visually see a writing's structure and serves as a study aid.

narrow eye span   Reading word for word, seeing and processing just one word at a time. *See also* wide eye span.

nonfiction   Writing that gives facts and provides information, such as a newspaper or magazine. Most business reading is considered nonfiction. Books can be either fiction or nonfiction.

Open Hand Wiggle   A reading pacer method where you lay your hand on top of the reading material and slowly pull it down using a wiggle movement down the page.

organizational pattern   The author's plan of action for getting his or her thoughts across. If you can identify it in your reading, you will be able to anticipate the order in which the material will be presented.

pacer   A card or even your hands used to mark the line you're reading. A visual guide provided by your fingers, whole hand, or a card to move your eyes down and across the lines of text with the results of increased concentration and faster reading speeds.

portable document format (PDF)   An electronic document format that's different from other documents because it allows a certain amount of versatility while retaining the original document formatting.

peripheral vision   What your eyes see outside the central area of focus. You can widen your central area of focus because of your peripheral vision.

phonics   A method of reading that breaks language down into its simplest phonetic components. Children learn the sounds of individual letters first, then the sounds of letters in combination and in simple words. Some know this method as the "look and say" method of reading.

podcast   A web-based audio broadcast via an RSS feed, accessed by subscription over the Internet.

Point-to-Point   A reading pacer method where you use your pointer and pinky to alternately point to text on the line, one finger about $1/3$ in and the other about $1/3$ from the end of the line.

reading speed   The rate at which your eyes and brain decode and understand words. Word-for-word readers have a slower reading speed than those who read more than one word at a time.

regression   When your eyes go back over words they've already read. *See also* back-skipping.

retention   Your ability to recall or recognize what has been learned or experienced.

retrieval   Your ability to bring stored information into consciousness. It's like a (search and) recovery mission for your brain.

Right Pointer Pull   A reading pacer method where you place the index finger of either hand along the right margin of the reading material. You read moving the finger down the right margin and moving your eyes from left to right.

RSS (real simple syndication) feed   A quick way to get updates, headlines, or even full articles culled from the web and delivered to your computer.

S Pattern   A reading pacer method where you pull your pointer finger down the page in an S curve through the text.

saccade   The series of small, jerky movements the eyes make when changing focus from one point to another. Also called an *eye jump*.

sans serif   A font that does not have little lines or tails as part of the letters. Sans serif fonts include Arial, Helvetica, and Geneva. *See also* serif.

scanning   When you are looking for specific information.

scrolling pacer   An on-screen pacer method where you use the scroll wheel on a computer mouse to advance the text while reading.

serif   A font that has little lines or tails as part of the letters. Serif fonts include Times Roman, Courier, and Palatino. *See also* sans serif.

Short-Smooth Underline   A reading pacer method where you move your three middle fingers under the lines of text starting about $\frac{1}{4}$ the way into the line and stopping your fingers before the last $\frac{1}{4}$ of the line.

sight vocabulary   The ability to see a word and immediately understand what it is and what it means.

signal word   A reading road sign; it indicates where you are or where you are headed. Signal words are conjunctions or words that join phrases, sentences, or paragraphs.

skimming   When you are looking for general or main ideas.

skipping   Deciding not to read something or skipping it.

speed looking   The name for what you are doing when you read quickly to the bottom of a page and have no idea what you just read. It does not complete the act of reading because your brain wasn't engaged.

speed reading   A series of active, mindful, and conscious reading strategies that enable readers to read efficiently and effectively.

study reading   Anything you read and learn from that you need or want to use later on. (For students it's usually for tests and papers. For business people, it's typically for sharing at meetings, writing reports and giving presentations. Some people just like to learn new things so they spend time study reading what they are interested in.)

subvocalization   The learned habit of reading word for word, either mentally or physically. This is also sometimes referred to as *mental whispering*. It can also mean you are either moving your lips while you read in an attempt to say the words you are reading, or mentally whispering every word you read inside your head.

technical material   Writing that includes vocabulary specific to a particular field, profession, or trade.

tellback   A verbal or written summary of something you read.

thought chunking   A reading strategy in which you learn to look for the groups of words that form thoughts in a sentence.

topic sentence   The first sentence of a paragraph that contains the main idea.

Vulcan   A reading pacer method where you use your index finger and pinky finger to frame the line of text and pull your eyes down the page.

wide eye span   Reading more than one word at a time. Faster readers pick up more words in an eye stop than slower readers do. *See also* narrow eye span.

words per minute (WPM)   The average number of words you read in one minute's time.

XML (extensible markup language)   Another way to read an RSS feed.

Z Pattern   A reading pacer method where you pull your pointer finger down the page in a Z pattern across and down through the text.

Timed Reading Exercises

The way to perfect a skill is to practice, practice, practice, and that's what this appendix is all about! In the following pages, you'll find instructions for conducting both a One-Minute Timing exercise and a 3-2-1 Drill. And then, to give you some practice timing your reading, I've included seven articles. These articles have been carefully chosen for their content, relevance, length, and general interest, and I've listed them in order from shortest length to longest. Here's what you'll find:

1. "Homeopathy 101" by Amy Rothenberg, N.D., DHANP: 1,486 words, 13 words per line

2. "Paradigm Shifting American Health" by Mark Pettus, M.D., FCAP: 1,766 words, 14 words per line

3. "Give Us This Day Our Global Bread" by Ron Lieber: 1,921 words, 6 words per line

4. "The Power of Time Management" by Julie Morgenstern: 2,648 words, 6 words per line

5. "Creating a Paperless Office" by Bill Gates: 3,469 words, 13 words per line

6. "Tattoo Pioneer: Shanghai Kate Hellenbrand" by Christine Braunberger, Ph.D.: 3,588 words, 13 words per line

7. "Sleep Deficit: The Performance Killer" by Dr. Charles A. Czeisler: 3,679 words, 6 words per line

Speed Tip

If your reading speed is already more than 400 words per minute, consider using a longer article for your 3-2-1 Drill. It will give you more material to read in your 3 minutes.

Note that some are printed in single columns (wider column width) while others are in double columns (narrow column width). Experiment with all the speed strategies on both types of material to see which methods and layouts work better for you.

When you decide on an article to read, review the directions for the exercise you want to do. Remember to add speed strategies!

How to Do a One-Minute Timing

One-Minute Timings are a quick and easy way to see how you interact with your speed strategies. Consider doing many of them as you advance through the material to quickly learn what works best for you. Here's what to do:

1. Choose an article to read.

2. With your timing device (a clock with a second hand, a stopwatch, or another digital timer), time yourself reading silently for *exactly* 1 minute. (Read normally for your first reading; for subsequent readings, use a speed strategy or two and aim to read faster than you are comfortable.) At the end of 1 minute, mark the line you're on.

3. On a separate piece of paper, write down as many key points as you can remember *without* looking back at the reading (that's cheating!).

4. Calculate your words per minute (WPM) by counting the number of lines you've read and multiplying that by the number of words per line listed under the title of the article. (When counting lines, include a subhead as a line.)

$$WPM = \text{\# of lines read} \times \text{number of words per line}$$

5. Now gauge your percent of comprehension on a scale from 0 to 100 percent of how much you think you understood based on the key points you wrote down.

6. Turn to the "One-Minute Timing Progress Chart" in Appendix C and record your results.

How to Do a 3-2-1 Drill

The 3-2-1 Drills are a great way to learn how to break out of your slow reading habits. It also allows you to become more of a visual reader than a verbal reader. Here's what to do for a 3-2-1 Drill:

1. Choose an article to read.

2. With your timing device (a clock with a second hand, a stopwatch, or another digital timer), time yourself reading as quickly as you can with your chosen speed method(s) *with comprehension* for 3 minutes. (If you finish the article and the 3 minutes aren't up yet, return to the beginning of the article and read until the 3 minutes are up.) When your time is up, mark the line you are on.

3. On a separate piece of paper, and *without* looking back at the reading (that's cheating!), write down as many key comprehension points as you remember.

Speed Tip

If you like, you can tally your words per minute (WPM) using this simple formula: WPM = # of lines read × # of words per line.

4. Now go back to where you started and reread the same text using your chosen speed method(s), this time only giving yourself 2 minutes to reach the same point. You will of course have to speed up your reading! At the end of 2 minutes, add more key points to your comprehension sheet, if you can.

5. Now, to really challenge yourself, go back to where you first started and read using your chosen speed method(s) for just 1 minute, stopping at your original 3-minute ending point. Add more key points to your comprehension sheet, if you can.

6. Turn to the "3-2-1 Drill Progress Chart" in Appendix C and record your results.

Article 1, "Homeopathy 101"

by Amy Rothenberg, N.D., DHANP

1,486 words, 13 words per line

Reprinted with permission by Amy Rothenberg, www.nesh.com.

You may hear about people using homeopathy to help with medical problems or maybe you have seen advertisements about homeopathy. How can you tell if the remedies are safe, effective or cause side-effects? Is there a time when your medical doctor might choose to refer a patient to a qualified practitioner of homeopathy? It is the purpose of this article to offer general information about homeopathy and to answer the above questions.

Homeopathy is a unique system of medicine which addresses the whole patient—physically, mentally and emotionally. Symptoms are understood according to the classic physiologic model taught to all health care providers. As the patient strains against both internal and external stressors, the patient develops symptoms; the symptoms are seen as the person's way of handling these stressors. It is the gleaning and understanding of the details and connections among these symptoms that lead the homeopath to prescribe a particular remedy.[1]

Homeopathy was first conceived by Samuel Hahnemann (1755–1843) a German physician and chemist. Troubled by the harshness of medical protocols of his time as well as by personal family tragedies, he turned away from medical practice and devoted himself to the work of scientific translation. It was during his work on a translation of a popular book on botanical medicine, *Cullen's Materia Medica* from the English into German where he became intrigued with the portion written on Cinchona bark. Cinchona bark is where quinine is derived—and the close relationship between its effectiveness and its capability to poison. His curiosity was ignited.

He undertook what was essentially the first drug trial, known as a *proving*[2] giving healthy subjects samples of the substance in question and seeing what, if any, effect it had upon them. To his surprise, in the case of the Cinchona bark, a number of participants developed the very same symptoms that the herbal preparation was known to help.

From this observation was born "*similia similibus curantur*" from the Latin, "likes are cured by likes." This essential underpinning of homeopathic practice can be further defined as follows: Any drug which is capable of producing symptoms in the healthy will remove similar symptoms occurring as an expression of disease.[3]

In his lifetime, Hahnemann conducted provings on some 106 substances. He worked diligently and wrote prolifically on topics of homeopathic philosophy, the treatment of chronic disease as well as the *Materia Medica Pura*, one of the earliest compilations of homeopathic drug lists available.

Hahnemann also set out to determine what the optimal dosage of medication would be to achieve both for best clinical outcomes and for the least side effects. His ideas about using the minimal dose whenever possible have stood the test of time. His experimentations led to the potentization process which is the process of diluting and vigorously shaking a homeopathic remedy, designed to intentionally lessen its strength. At this time, homeopathic remedies are made in accordance to the United States Homeopathic Pharmacopoeia and are produced from plant, mineral and animal sources. Homeopathic remedies are available through homeopathic pharmacies as well as over-the-counter in some pharmacies and health food stores.

Homeopathy is used to treat first aid problems as well as acute and chronic disease. First aid problems are addressed in rather "cookbook" fashion. For example, many may have heard of using the homeopathic remedy *Arnica Montana* for the treatment of trauma. Because traumatic events impact most people in a similar fashion, *Arnica* is one of only a handful of remedies to be considered. In other words, when the stress from the outside is very severe, most individuals respond in a similar fashion. That response will point to one of only a few remedies.

For acute, self-limited problems such as ear infections, laryngitis or hives, people's symptoms present in a more individualized manner. For instance, one person with hives might have small raised red bumps where cold applications and itching makes it feel better, while another might have white large welts where itching makes it worse but warm applications make them better. Though both have hives, they would require and respond to two different homeopathic remedies. The homeopath is addressing the whole person at any one time. With most acute conditions there are a limited number of remedies to choose from because there are only so many ways an acute problem can manifest.

For illnesses which are more chronic in nature, homeopathic practitioners prescribe *constitutional* remedies which are based on the whole person. There are many homeo-pathic remedies to be considered.

Remedies are given for particular people as opposed to particular diagnoses. One could have five patients with arthritis and they might receive five different homeo-pathic remedies depending on *how* they experience the problem; i.e. how it actually feels, the type of pain or discomfort, what makes it better, what makes it worse, was there a clear initial cause, do they have any other symptoms simultaneously, etc. The homeopath is interested in *how* the arthritis fits into the rest of the person's physical health. In addition, it is central to perceive how those physical characteristics sit in regards to the patients' mental and emotional health.

To the homeopath, all symptoms are context dependent; one cannot see a symptom standing by itself, rather the homeopath seeks to understand each symptom a patient reports as it relates to the whole person. The typical first appointment for a homeopathic physician is one and half to two hours, allowing enough time to fully understand the patient and all aspects of their lifestyle and health. Thus, the doctor-patient relationship is an important component of the homeopathic process.

This individualized approach would be utilized whether the presenting complaint was cardiovascular in nature or a condition relating to the gastrointestinal tract, urinary system or the skin. For some patients, there are very few outward symptoms related to their condition making it seemingly difficult for the homeopath to prescribe upon such a complaint. However, the homeopath can prescribe based on *presenting symptoms from all systems of the body* and from general physical characteristics of the patient as well as from their mental and emotional make-up. Homeopathic physicians give a remedy for the patient and expect their overall health to improve.

As with many modalities in complementary medicine it could be asked, who goes to a homeopath? Most practitioners of homeopathy see a wide range of patients similar to that which a family doctor would encounter. Perhaps nothing else is working for a particular patient. For some known and some unknown reasons, there are patients who do not respond well to medications, some have contradictory reactions to drugs, some are allergic to pharmaceuticals or do not tolerate them well. Some patients merely want their medicine to be in accord with an overall health-oriented, "natural" lifestyle.

Some patients visit homeopaths because they have incurable conditions and are strictly seeking symptomatic relief. Some seek to enhance immune function thereby reducing susceptibility to acute illness from which they suffer along with chronic complaints. Others come to help address underlying mental or emotional concerns which accompany chronic physical complaints. Some patients present with concerns about medication they are on. Perhaps it is not working well or well enough or is causing intolerable side-effects.

The last group the homeopath may see are patients who do not feel well, yet there is nothing diagnostically wrong: the lab work, physical exam and health history are typical, yet their energy is diminished, there are low grade symptoms on various body systems and the mood is depressed. Some of these patients have clear and intense subjective symptoms, but they continue to pass all exams. Homeopathy can offer that person increased energy and a feeling of well-being. Many or most of their symptoms will go away. This is one of the unique benefits of homeopathic care. Since we treat the patient, we do not have to wait until they present with a large compliment of symptoms. The fact that there aren't specific remedies for specific diagnoses may make some uncomfortable; it is contrary to the modern medical model where drug prescriptions are frequently diagnosis-driven. But, if there is no clear disease or diagnosis, it can become difficult to choose correct medications or sometimes to provide any treatment at all. This is an added advantage of homeopathic medicine: as a method of primary prevention, it can offer treatment to patients *before* they become severely ill.

There are currently over 3000 homeopathic remedies for a homeopath to choose from. It is the individualizing nature of the physical symptoms as well as the mental and emotional characteristics of the patient which lead to finding the best homeopathic remedy for each person.

References:

[1]Herscu, Paul. *Stramonium, with an Introduction to Analysis Using Cycles and Segments.* Amherst, Massachusetts: New England School of Homeopathy Press, 1996.

[2]———. *Provings, with a Proving of Alcoholus.* Amherst, Massachusetts: New England School of Homeopathy Press, 1996.

[3]Hahnemann, Samuel, and Wenda Brewster O'Reilley, Ph.D., ed. *The Organon of the Medical Art.* Redmond, Washington: Birdcage Books, 1996.

Article 2, "Paradigm Shifting American Health"

by Mark Pettus, M.D., FCAP

1,766 words, 14 words per line

Most of us want to live as long and as well as possible. We want strong, healthy bodies and agile minds that maintain their ability to remember, reason, and communicate. We want to share life's joys and sorrows with loved ones, participate in our communities in a meaningful way, and come to the end of our lives satisfied and fulfilled.

Unfortunately, for many of us, this won't be how it happens. In my experience as a practicing physician for more than 20 years, it is increasingly common for people to live too short and die too long. In fact, despite a doubling of the life expectancy over the last 150 years, the sobering reality is that it is now estimated that this trend will begin to reverse itself, and life expectancy for future generations will be lower than for their parents.

What's going wrong?

There are many factors contributing to the decline in American health, including the growing epidemic of obesity, poor nutritional choices, inactivity, unprecedented toxic exposure, and unrelenting stress. According to the National Institutes of Health, 60 percent of Americans are overweight and 30 percent are considered obese. Lifestyle Syndrome, characterized by abdominal fat, elevation of blood pressure, pre-diabetes, high insulin levels, and abnormal blood fat, affects 30 to 40 percent of adults. Alarmingly, Lifestyle Syndrome signals a trajectory that leads to many of the age-related diseases, diminished quality of life, and shorter life expectancy.

Five years ago, I was on this trajectory. I had little to no structured physical activity, I ate plenty of sugars and processed foods, and I lived a fast-paced life in which I always felt that there wasn't enough time. This was coupled with a family history that included diabetes, high blood pressure, kidney disease, and premature death. The "tipping point" for me came at an annual visit to my primary-care provider. My blood pressure was up, my weight was up, and my cholesterol panel was as high as it had ever been. When we began discussing medications to control some of my risk factors, I realized I needed to take stock before things got worse.

A critical issue we are facing is that our systems of health care are more designed to address diseases once they manifest rather than they are to promote optimal health and prevent diseases from occurring in the first place. Doctors and patients alike are now trained to turn to medications and interventions after symptoms become severe or the disease has presented itself, often not taking seriously enough the warning signs and borderline readings that signal future distress. In truth, many devastating health outcomes, like heart attack, stroke, and Alzheimer's disease, have multiple contributing risk factors that are treatable and reversible—but silent—by their very nature. Feeling well does not equal good health.

Ironically, medical progress itself is also resulting in higher percentages of people with diseases: as people live longer, they develop many of the chronic age-related diseases along the way. And tragically, nearly all age-related diseases—high blood pressure, diabetes, cholesterol imbalance, cancer, Alzheimer's, and cardiovascular diseases such as heart attack, stroke, and chronic kidney disease—have major lifestyle, behavioral, and stress components to them.

Unfortunately, in our current medical model there is insufficient time and resources to appropriately educate, inspire, and motivate the necessary lifestyle and behavioral changes people need. Integrative and preventative approaches to health, including healthy nutrition, fitness programs, yoga and mindfulness activities, and the healing arts, are often overlooked and usually not covered by health-care insurance. The potential for these dimensions of living to profoundly transform all dimensions of health and healing and the magnitude to which they do is often underappreciated.

In my case, as I considered the options before me, I realized that my underlying assumption was that I believed that a decline in some aspects of my health and quality of life as I aged was inevitable. I thought that high blood pressure, high cholesterol, a drop-off in my conditioning, a few inches more around my abdomen, fatigue, and an inability to stop and smell the roses were irreconcilable manifestations of my genetic legacy and the aging program I was locked into. My passive approach to self-care was certainly contributing to making that happen. I decided to get active.

I took inventory of my life and targeted the "low-hanging fruit"—those things that would be easiest to change. I cut out sugar-sweetened drinks. I started walking in my neighborhood. I chose daily push-ups and abdominal exercises for light resistance work. And I learned some simple—and portable—breathing and relaxation techniques. My research and reading interests shifted to the science of mind-body interaction and practice. I began to broaden my knowledge about integrated health, the science and philosophy of Eastern approaches to health, and how people create effective and sustainable change. My connection to my own spirituality deepened and it became my mission to better understand how I could be a more effective steward of the precious gifts of which I had ownership.

What's the solution?

It is increasingly clear that most of the health and quality-of-life issues we are likely to confront during our lives can be prevented or reversed with greater attention to self-care. Therefore the single most effective medicine that health care has to offer today is education—about how the body works and how the beliefs we hold in our mind play out in our lives; about nutrition, how foods affects the body, and how to cook for maximum nourishment and pleasure; about physical fitness, exercise strategies, and enjoyable ways to combine getting active and getting outdoors. We need to learn to take care of ourselves.

This can be easier said than done. Even when health-care professionals provide the health-promoting messages of exercise and good nutrition, the advice is heeded less than five percent of the time! Most people don't lack knowledge about what they need to do; what they lack is the bridge to effective execution. What people need is practice in living in healthy, life-promoting ways that lead to optimal vitality and fulfillment—which is exactly what Kripalu, a center for yoga and health in the Berkshires of Massachusetts, has been specializing in for more than 30 years.

The medical center of the future

Education at Kripalu is experiential, which means that people learn by doing, by experiencing what they are learning. The experiential immersion offered in the Institute for Integrated Healing programs enables people to fully live and realize the benefits of healthy living. This is the only way we are going to help people transform their underlying beliefs and overcome the challenge of creating critical lifestyle changes.

The driving principles of Kripalu's Institute for Integrated Healing are that most of the symptoms and chronic diseases we attribute to the natural and inevitable processes of aging are not inevitable or natural at all and that their root causes can usually be understood, prevented, treated, and reversed by addressing lifestyle, behavior, and stress. We also seek to cultivate emotional and spiritual health—to address the sense of disconnection and loss of meaning that is so prevalent in modern society and that can often contribute to poor health. We believe circumstances can be created to unleash the full human potential for health and healing.

Research is revealing the biology of why patterns of thinking, feeling, and doing are so hard to change. Research is also telling us that profound and enduring change is possible at any time in one's life. In fact, we are designed for just that!

We live on the cusp of a new frontier of understanding the natural processes that promote and maintain health, longevity, and quality of life. The science of the mind has opened a window into the biological underpinnings of thought, feeling, and behavior and their connection to health and the experience of life. These recent discoveries are revealing a new understanding of who we are as human beings. And the implications are extremely compelling.

The doctor of the future

Consider the following: National Public Radio recently ran a report on research conducted in a diabetes prevention program at Washington Hospital Center in Washington DC, which found that diet and exercise programs can be just as effective as medicine in reducing the risk of developing Type 2 Diabetes. The results were surprising to physician Meeta Sharma and her colleagues, who thought it likely that drugs would work better. "Our own intrinsic appreciation of it was that just medical therapy is going to be the way to go in terms of prevention," she said.

The Institute for Integrated Healing is being designed to bring experiential education and training not only to patients but also to medical professionals, many of whom, like I was myself, are in need of shifting the paradigm that guides their work. As Thomas Edison predicted, the doctor of the future "will interest his patients in the care of the human frame, in diet, and in the cause and prevention of disease."

When I began to reclaim my health—and my life—I was astonished by three things: The first was how quickly I began to feel better. The second was how effective small changes actually were. And the third was how addictive these changes became. After about three weeks, the more I changed, the more I desired to change, and my motivation, courage, resolve, and follow-through grew. Five years later, my cholesterol and blood pressure levels are better than ever. I run 20 miles a week, I crave green, leafy vegetables, and I have cultivated a lifestyle that has less stress and includes more of the things that I value—family time, friendships, and community. Helping others to become better stewards of their precious gifts is my unrelenting calling, and I have also become a better doctor, one who is walking his talk.

Dr. Mark Pettus is a board-certified internist and nephrologist who did his postdoctoral training at Harvard Medical School. The ultimate "patient's doctor" (he has been voted top physician more than once), he is passionately dedicated to health care that works. In addition to turning his own health around, he has helped thousands of people change their lives. Former chief of staff at Berkshire Medical Center, Dr. Pettus is the author of The Savvy Patient *and* It's All in Your Head: Change Your Mind, Change Your Health *and has appeared on numerous radio and television programs. You can find out more about Dr. Pettus at his website, www.savvypatient.com.*

Article 3, "Give Us This Day Our Global Bread"

by Ron Lieber

1,921 words, 6 words per line

Used with permission of Fast Company, Copyright © 2007. All rights reserved.

Think of a product that is so local, it could never go global. So basic, it could never be branded. So fundamental, it could never be reinvented. Now think about bread—Lionel Poilâne's bread, that is.

Lionel Poilâne sells the most famous bread in Paris. In fact, he sells 15,000 loaves of bread each day—2.5% of all bread sold in Paris, by weight. But he doesn't think of himself as a mere baker. Most bakers simply mix dough, shape loaves, and shove them into the oven. And while for many years he did all of those things every day, that still doesn't make him a baker.

Ever since Poilâne, 55, took over the family bakery from his father roughly 30 years ago, his life's work has been to elevate the level of his own craft. In doing so, he has adopted an approach to his art and his business that is equal parts ancient and modern, historically grounded and technologically sophisticated, locally based and globally aware, product-oriented and philosophically informed. Poilâne somehow manages to bring all of those elements together in a simple, delicious loaf of bread.

The bread itself is decidedly old school: Thick, chewy, and rich with a dark, fire-tinged flavor, Poilâne's bread traces its heritage back to the original French bread. But his business is remarkably modern. Today, Poilâne has a new shop in London and two older ones in Paris. And on the outskirts of the City of Light, he has his own global baking facility, where 40 bakers work at 16th-century ovens in teams of 2. Each day, Poilâne-branded bread travels by company-owned trucks to more than 2,500 shops and restaurants throughout Paris, and by FedEx delivery to Poilâne aficionados in roughly 20 countries around the world.

Poilâne's secret isn't hidden in a recipe. After all, there are only four ingredients in his basic loaf: flour, water, salt, and the starter (which provides the yeast). Poilâne's secret is in his philosophy and creativity. Armed with a deep knowledge of how bread has changed over time, Poilâne has developed an approach that he calls "retro-innovation," and it has made him successful in a city where people take bread very, very seriously. "Retro-innovation takes the best of the old and the best of the new," Poilâne explains. "You can only do it if you free your mind, if you don't belong to anything."

Old Bread, New Bread

When Poilâne first became an apprentice to his father at 14, the family business was still quite small. There was just one Poilâne bakery in Paris, and it was only in the previous few years that Lionel's father had started experimenting with the large, dark, old-fashioned loaves that are a Poilâne trademark today. Intrigued, Lionel threw himself into the project—even though nearby bakeries had long abandoned the older styles of bread. "There are many ways to solve a problem," he says. "In baking, people are always looking for the new bread. But it exists already. Using old ways is a glorious way to make new things. The man with the best future is the one with the longest memory."

In the early 1980s, Poilâne decided to tap into the memories of the oldest bakers in the country to see if they could give him advice on how to reproduce the older styles of bread. With the help of two students, he contacted more than 10,000 bakers over a two-year period. "I conducted an ethnography of my own business," he says.

Most of the bakers had only fading memories to offer, but some were thrilled that he was trying to revive older bread-making traditions and offered to bake him sample loaves.

By the time he was finished with his study, Poilâne had tried more than 75 different types of bread that he'd never tasted before. He eventually wrote up his findings in a book—a study that is still used today in baking schools throughout France. He also amassed a library full of books on bread, which today contains more than 2,000 volumes.

Armed with all of this information, Poilâne perfected his father's technique. Then he waited, hoping eventually to persuade others to try it out. "Regional, dark French bread had almost disappeared because it was once the bread of the poor people," Poilâne explains. "After World War II, the chic bread was white. It became the rich bread. It was new, and it represented freedom, even though it wasn't really French." According to Poilâne, the white bread that became most popular—the baguette—actually originated in Austria.

Today, the baguette remains popular; it is impossible to walk more than a block or two in Paris without crossing paths with someone who is toting one. But with a texture somewhere between cotton and marshmallows, and with a taste that barely registers wheat, the vast majority of Parisian baguettes work best as a staging ground for sandwiches or as a tool to sop up soup. Poilâne refuses to make them.

This deep understanding of history gives Poilâne and his bakers the background—and the inspiration—that they need to make old-fashioned bread each day. The bakers' work doesn't look particularly complicated or difficult, but small subtleties can make a huge difference. "You can make thousands of products with only three ingredients," Poilâne says. "The water and flour can, of course, be very different. Then there are the conditions: the geography and the climate. There's yeast, fermentation, time, oven, and shape. Manipulation is important too."

Poilâne is a stickler for many of those details, but he's surprisingly lax about others. The flour is a combination of wheat mixes from four different mills, and the sea salt absolutely must come from Brittany. The water, however, comes from the tap at the three storefront shops and from a well at the larger bakery. The bakers shape the loaves loosely by hand, paying no mind to the odd bumps and imperfections that emerge. The wood-fired clay-and-brick ovens, however, must be perfect—and Poilâne has spent years designing the specifications. "They take one month to build, one month to dry, and one month to heat to 240 degrees Celsius," he explains. "If you try to warm them up more quickly, the clay cracks: Pop!"

As the business has grown, Poilâne has begrudgingly added croissants, tarts, a brioche, and a few other breads to his repertoire. While all are high-quality products, the old-fashioned, oversized, wood-fired country loaf still far outsells all of the other products combined. "If you start to make too many things, that's extension," he says. "My motto is do things with intention, not with extension."

Loaves and FedExes

When it comes to bread, Poilâne is set in his ways. When it comes to distribution, however, he has a more innovative operation than any other baker on Earth—which is to say, he is one of the few bakers on Earth to take his bread global.

Poilâne's desire to ship his bread stemmed initially from his lack of interest in owning more stores. Last June, Poilâne finally opened a bakery in London—but there probably won't be too many more such openings soon. "I can get on the train and be in London in three hours," he says, explaining why he decided to open there. "But I'm not eager to have a business card that says 'Paris, London, New York' on it. We thought about opening in Japan, but we couldn't have a wood fire there. It's important in business to be able to say no when you feel like saying yes would mean losing your soul."

Instead of building little bakeries all over the globe, Poilâne built one big one on the outskirts of Paris. When it first opened 18 years ago, it was designed to fill orders from other shops and restaurants in Paris. "We wanted to take an ancient product and reproduce it on an industrial, multiplied level," explains Ibu Poilâne, 52, Lionel's wife, an artist and designer who helped him design the building.

To the Poilânes, the round structure is anything but a factory—and one visit makes the difference clear. Instead of building a production line, the Poilânes simply put 24 identical ovens—duplicates of the 100-ton ones in the basement of the storefront bakeries—in a circle. In the middle is an atrium with enormous piles of wood to heat the ovens. Workers use a ceiling-mounted remote-controlled crane to pick it up and deposit it in chutes that lead to the ovens.

Poilâne's global bread business developed as a natural response to customer demand: Stores and individuals started calling from abroad to ask Poilâne to ship them bread, so he started to take advantage of the large FedEx hub at nearby Roissy-Charles-de-Gaulle airport. FedEx allows Poilâne's bread to leave the bakery in the early morning and be on dinner tables in the United States the next night. All it takes is a quick warm-up

in the oven to make the bread taste as good as it does in Paris. And the size of the basic Poilâne loaf—about 4 pounds—helps the bread travel well and last longer. Global bread sales are growing: Last year, exports were up 30%. Poilâne has also long sold his loaves over the Internet.

Poilâne's bread has won him famous fans over the years: Frank Sinatra and Lauren Bacall used to enjoy a loaf from time to time, and Robert De Niro is a customer. The most devoted patron, however, is a gentleman in New York who wants to remain anonymous. In 1997, he agreed to pay Poilâne $100,000, asking that his children and grandchildren receive a loaf a week for the rest of their lives. "Can you imagine?" Poilâne says, with obvious pride. "In 50 years, he'll be dead, but his grandchildren will be feeding our bread to their children and explaining how they are eating the bread of their great-grandfather!"

As the business has gone global, Poilâne has become an ambassador of sorts. This suits him fine, since 10 or 12 years stoking the subterranean ovens was plenty for him. "When I first started as an apprentice, I was a very bitter boy stuck down in the basement with the bread," he says. "I thought I was outside of the world." Now people from all over the world seek him out. He keeps his office in a lofty space on the top floor of the building that houses the original bakery and store, so he can come down and meet customers when they visit. "The pleasure of life is in meeting people, and the shop is open to the street, so it's a great social space," he says.

Baker or builder? Ambassador or philosopher? Even Poilâne's friend Salvador Dali couldn't figure it out. "He thought I was an artist who happened to work on bread," Poilâne says. "In fact, I was just a baker who was interested in artistic projects. But that confusion led to a good relationship. In some ways, every businessman needs to learn how to be an artist. It's crucial when you're leading a project."

One of Poilâne's favorite projects is the cage that he and Dali made together out of bread dough. "The bird could eat its way out of the cage," Poilâne explains. "That was very real to me. As an apprentice, I too felt like a bird in a cage made out of bread. I just fed on my limits."

Article 4, "The Power of Time Management"

by Julie Morgenstern

2,648 words, 6 words per line

Reprinted with permission from Julie Morgenstern Enterprises. Adapted from "Time Management from the Inside Out," Henry Holt/Owl Books, 2000. All Rights Reserved.

I was not always an organized person. In my first book, *Organizing from the Inside Out*, I shared the story of how I struggled with clutter and time management my whole life, and reached my turning point when my daughter was born. When she was three weeks old, she awoke from a nap on a beautiful summer day and I knew it was a golden opportunity to take her for her first walk.

Unfortunately, it took me two and a half hours to gather supplies for our outing: blankets, bottles, pacifiers, diapers, toys, a sweater, booties ... where were they all? By the time I was ready to go, she had fallen fast asleep. I had missed the moment. Disappointed and deflated, I looked down at my innocent babe asleep in her crib and thought, *If I don't get my act together, this child will never see the light of day.*

And so I conquered the chaos, starting first with the diaper bag and eventually tackling every other area of my home, office, and life. In the process, I discovered that organizing is not a mysterious talent but rather a completely learnable skill. I had just been going about it backward: I'd been diving into the piles instead of starting with a plan. I learned that by investing a little bit of time analyzing and strategizing beforehand, I could design a system that would last.

About three years later, I founded my company, Task Masters, a service that helps people get organized so that they may lead more gratifying lives. My staff and I provide one-on-one organizing services and seminars to thousands each year. My work with clients who come from all age ranges, genders, and personality types has enabled me to deepen my understanding of the organizing process and develop my emphasis on customizing the solution to each individual. In 1998 an editor at Henry Holt and Company asked me to write a book on my techniques. The result was my first book, *Organizing from the Inside Out*, which has become a *New York Times* best-seller.

Fourteen years after that diaper-bag fiasco, I was given the opportunity to see just how far I'd come with my organizing skills. Less than two weeks before my daughter's Bat Mitzvah (a huge affair that, as a single parent, I had coordinated by myself), I got the call every author dreams of—it was from the Oprah Winfrey show. They wanted to fly me out to organize their offices as well as several viewers' homes for their big "Spring Clean-up" show ... all within the next ten days!

Was I ready to jump on this fantastic opportunity without hesitation? Was I organized enough to manage all of the details involved in pulling off both the Bat Mitzvah and the Oprah show simultaneously? The answer was a resounding yes! Because I was more organized, most of the details regarding the Bat Mitzvah were done. What wasn't done was written on a list, and I could do a quick scan to see exactly where I stood. My planning and delegation skills came in very handy—I was able to prioritize the tasks and decide what my staff and friends could do in my place. My files and database were very organized, so any information I needed for either event was at my fingertips. And during the whirlwind of the next two weeks, my planner kept me very focused on everything I had to do and every place I had to be. I didn't miss a beat.

My suitcase was packed in a flash and I was on the next plane to Chicago. Instead of missing the moment, I was able to embrace this unexpected convergence of priorities. The result was one of the most glorious weeks in my life—celebrating a momentous,

spiritual occasion with my daughter, and appearing on the most coveted TV show in the world. Here's to the power of time management!

Being organized, whether with your space or time, is all about being ready. It's about feeling in command so that you are prepared to handle all of the opportunities, distractions, and surprises life throws your way. We live in a complex, fast-paced world filled with infinite possibilities and opportunities. When you develop good time-management skills, instead of being overwhelmed by it all, you can celebrate it. You know what to choose. You feel clear and focused, ready to take on life.

So what makes time management so difficult? It is my observation that the single most common obstacle people face in managing their days lies in the way they view time. Therefore, the very first step in taking control of time is to challenge your very perception of it.

Most people think of time as intangible. In the journey from chaos to order, it is often easier to organize space than time, because space is something you can actually see. Time, on the other hand, is completely invisible. You can't see it or hold it in your hands. It's not something that piles up or that you can physically move around.

Time is something you feel, and it feels ... utterly amorphous. Some days go whizzing by while others crawl painfully along. Even your tasks seem hard to measure—infinite and endless in both quantity and duration.

As long as time remains slippery, elusive, and hard to conceptualize, you will have difficulty managing your days. You need to change your perception of time and develop a more tangible view of it. You need to learn to see time in more visual, measurable terms.

In my own journey to getting organized, my biggest breakthrough came when I realized that organizing time really is no different than organizing space. Once you understand that time has boundaries, you begin to look at your to-dos much differently. Tasks are the objects that you must fit into your space. Each one has a size, and arranging them in your day becomes a mathematical equation. As you evaluate what you need to do, you begin to calculate the size of each task and whether you can fit it into the space.

When you start seeing time as having borders, just as a space does, you will become much more realistic about what you can accomplish, and much more motivated to master various time-management tools and techniques to help you make the most of your time.

What's Holding You Back?

When people struggle to manage their time, they very often jump to the conclusion that they are internally flawed somehow, that they are born incompetent in this area of life. Or they throw their hands up in resignation, convinced that "out of control" is just how life is supposed to be in the modern world. Both of these perceptions are totally inaccurate and self-defeating.

Once you learn the skill of diagnosing time-management problems, you will stop wasting time and energy beating yourself up or working yourself to exhaustion.

There are a variety of reasons you may be held back from managing your time. In my work with hundred of clients, I have found there are generally three main causes: external realities, technical errors, and psychological obstacles.

External Realities are environmental factors that are actually beyond your control. You didn't create them, and they put a limit on how organized you can be. By recognizing these you can stop blaming yourself and find a more direct way to manage or eliminate them.

Technical Errors are easily resolved mechanical mistakes. You just need a skill or a technique you don't have. Once you understand these errors, you simply make the appropriate adjustments to your approach and you're all set. Problem solved. Here are a few common technical errors people face:

Tasks Have No "Home"

One of the most common reasons you may not be getting to things that are important to you is that you haven't set aside a specific time in which to do them. Too often, people make lists of what they want to do, without asking the next essential question: When am I going to do this? Unless a task has a "home," that is, a time slot clearly blocked out in your schedule, you won't get to it.

If you think you will get to anything in your "spare time," keep in mind that there is no such thing as spare time! As it is, our days are packed with more things to do than there will ever be time for. The only chance we end up with a free moment is when something we planned falls through at the last minute. Then, we usually can't think of what to do with those unexpected moments because we were caught off guard. So if something is really important to you, set aside a specific time in your schedule to make it happen.

You've Set Aside the Wrong Time

If you've set aside time to do something but find yourself still not getting to it, it's possible that you've set aside the wrong time. We all have energy and concentration cycles: Some of us are morning people, some of us are most energetic at night. Some of us feel motivated to begin big, new projects at certain times of the year, such as January, September (when we're in a back-to-school mind-set), or when the warm weather begins. Some women find that there are times of the month when they are better able to handle projects requiring focus or patience.

If you are working against your own energy or concentration cycles, it will be hard to effectively tackle a task when you've planned to. If you can't bring yourself to balance your checkbook each month as you promised yourself, maybe the problem is that you're always trying to do it at night after work, when your mental energy is low. If you schedule the task in the morning instead you'll probably find yourself more motivated to tackle those figures.

You've Miscalculated How Long Tasks Take

Most people are very unrealistic about what they can accomplish in a day. If the time required to complete your to-dos exceeds the time you have available, you simply won't get to it all and you'll end up feeling frustrated and demoralized. This is completely avoidable. If you get better at calculating how long tasks take, you can plan a realistic workload. Learning how to estimate how long tasks take is a skill anyone can learn …. Furthermore, when you know what your big-picture goals are, it will be much easier to eliminate, shorten, or delegate tasks that don't serve your goals.

Psychological Obstacles are hidden, internal forces that prevent you from achieving the life you desire. If you have conquered all of your technical errors and external realities and are still feeling out of control, it's likely that you have a psychological force working against you. When you realize what's causing certain self-sabotaging habits, you can begin to break free of their control.

Sometimes we don't allow ourselves to improve our time-management skills to make time for what's really important to us because of psychological obstacles. We know what we need to do, but resist taking action because our time-management problems are serving us somehow—they are fulfilling some deep-seated need we may not even be aware of. Without awareness, these forces will sabotage your efforts to take control of your time. These psychological obstacles often don't reveal themselves until after you've conquered the technical errors and external realities. In fact,

it's often best to deal with time-management problems on a very practical level first. Frequently, once you begin experiencing the benefits of managing your time from the inside out, many of the psychological resistances melt away. Here are some examples of common psychological obstacles:

You Are a Conquistador of Chaos

If you constantly keep your schedule packed beyond the scope of reality, if you always leave everything to the very last minute, and if your life feels like one urgent calamity after another, chances are you are a "conquistador of chaos." You set your life up to be in constant disaster mode because, quite frankly, you are a wonderful crisis manager. You feel so good conquering the impossible that you keep creating it, just so that you can rescue yourself. You pull it off every time—though not necessarily without some "fallout" along the way.

If you are a conquistador of chaos, chances are you got your training for this role when you were a child. Perhaps you were raised in a difficult environment where you were the organizer, peacemaker, or the problem solver. You learned to feel a certain comfort in crisis, and you felt good about your ability to handle chaos. Now your job is to learn how to feel good about that ability without having to test on a daily basis.

You Have a Need for Perfection

If you're a perfectionist, you feel compelled to do everything at the same level of excellence. Good time-managers keep things in perspective. They set priorities rather than give every task equal weight. If you demand extremely high standards for every single task you undertake, you simply won't get everything done.

The need for perfection often comes out of a need for approval. It could also come from a fear of criticism, humiliation, or harsh judgment. It could be that you grew up conditioned by a well-meaning teacher or a parent who drummed into your head, "If you're going to do things, do things right!" You didn't learn how to evaluate which tasks were worth a huge amount of exertion and which weren't. Or it could be that you feel more secure when everything seems to be under your control. For your own sake, you need to adjust your standards based on the specific task at hand. Some tasks are worth your finest effort, and others just need to get done.

You Have a Fear of Losing Creativity

Many creative or "right-brained" people fear that imposing structure in their lives will squelch their creativity or their free-spirited personality.

As a result, their personal and business lives are chaotic and cause them tremendous stress. If this is your situation, be assured that imposing structure can actually be liberating. Many of the most successful creative writers, artists, and musicians find great freedom in structure and discipline. They write or paint or draw at the same time every day. Some days the creativity flows, others it trickles out, but the consistency of their schedule assures that they make time for what is important to them.

Structure doesn't destroy your creative impulses, it allows them to flourish. After all, when your schedule is free-form, you often don't get to the things that are most important to you. Your creative work takes a backseat to the more urgent demands of other people, and you neglect your own needs, such as paying your bills and making doctors' appointments.

You need to learn to trust that you can put structure into your schedule and still have enough freedom to hear the call of your muse, or respond to opportunities that crop up, or spend time with your friends, customers, and associates. You don't have to plan every hour, but you can map out a general rhythm to your day.

Regardless of which challenges you face, true time management from the inside out is about designing a schedule that is a custom fit for you. It's about identifying what's important to you and giving those activities a place in your schedule based on your unique personality needs and goals. And it's about feeling deeply satisfied at the end of each day. Tune in to who you are and what you want, and then integrate practical time management tools to build your life around your unique personality.

Julie Morgenstern is a productivity expert and author of Time Management from the Inside Out, Organizing from the Inside Out, *and* Never Check E-Mail in the Morning. *For more, visit www. juliemorgenstern.com.*

Article 5, "Creating a Paperless Office"

by Bill Gates

3,469 words, 13 words per line

From Business @ the Speed of Thought *by Bill Gates with Collins Hemingway. Copyright © 1999 by William H. Gates III. Reprinted by permission of Grand Central Publishing.*

Digital technology can transform your production processes and your business processes. It can also free workers from slow and inflexible paper processes. Replacing paper processes with digital processes liberates knowledge workers to do productive work. The all-digital workplace is usually called "the paperless office," a phrase that goes back to at least 1973. It's a great vision. No more stacks of paper in which you can't find what you need. No more pawing through piles of books and reports to find marketing information or a sales number. No more misrouted forms, lost invoices, redundant entries, missing checks, or delays caused by incomplete paperwork.

But the paperless office, like artificial intelligence, is one of those "any day now" phenomena that somehow never seem to actually arrive. The first use of the phrase *paperless office* appeared in a headline a quarter of a century ago in a trade publication for phone companies. The Xerox Corporation (although it never called it a "paperless office") did more to promote the concept than anyone else. In 1974–75 the company was talking about "the office of the future" that would have computers and e-mail with information online. Between 1975 and 1987 several business publications promised that the paperless office wasn't far off and would radically change the workplace, but in 1988 I told a reporter, "This vision of a paperless office is still very, very far away …. Computers today are not yet fulfilling this vision."[1]

Today we have all the pieces in place to make the vision a reality. Graphical computing and better analytical tools make it easy to integrate data of various types. Highly capable, networked PCs are ubiquitous in the office environment. The Internet is connecting PCs around the world. Yet paper consumption has continued to double every four years, and 95 percent of all information in the United States remains on paper, compared with just 1 percent stored electronically. Paperwork is increasing faster than digital technology can eliminate it!

In 1996 I decided to look into the ways that Microsoft, a big advocate of replacing paper with electronic forms, was still using paper. To my surprise, we had printed 350,000 paper copies of sales reports that year. I asked for a copy of every paper form we used. The thick binder that landed on my desk contained hundreds and hundreds of forms. At corporate headquarters we had 114 forms in Procurement alone. Our 401(k) retirement plan had 8 different paper forms—for entering and exiting the plan, for changing employee information, and for changing employee investments or contributions. Every time the government changed the rules, we'd have to update and reprint the forms and recycle thousands of old ones. Paper consumption was only a symptom of a bigger problem, though: administrative processes that were too complicated and time-intensive.

I looked at this binder of forms and wondered, "Why do we have all of these forms? Everybody here has a PC. We're connected up. Why aren't we using electronic forms and e-mail to streamline our processes and replace all this paper?"

Well, I exercised the privilege of my job and banned all unnecessary forms. In place of all that paper, systems grew up that were far more accurate and far easier to work with and all that empowered our people to do more interesting work.

STARTING A JOURNEY WITH A SINGLE CLICK

Now, even before a new employee is hired, he or she embarks on an electronic journey. We receive 600 to 900 resumes from job applicants every day by postal mail, by e-mail, or via our Resume Builder on the Microsoft Web site.[2] Seventy percent of the resumes arrive electronically via e-mail or the Web, up from 6 percent two years ago and rising. Our software automatically acknowledges every electronic submission. Our recruiting database, from Restrac of Lexington, Massachusetts, directly accepts information from resumes created at our Resume Builder Web site; e-mail submissions are parsed to deliver candidate information to Restrac. A paper resume is scanned and converted into text that can go into the database. All resumes are electronically matched with open job positions within twenty-four to forty-eight hours of receipt.

Human Resources specialists search the Restrac database for promising candidates, consulting with hiring managers in person or over e-mail. They use scheduling software to set up job interviews. Every interviewer gets a copy of a resume and any other background information in e-mail. After meeting with a prospect, each interviewer e-mails comments about the candidate to Human Resources, the hiring manager, and other interviewers, suggesting follow-up questions to later interviewers. This real-time sharing of interview information ensures that interviewers build on one another's work rather than duplicate it. One interviewer might suggest to the next that she probe for a better sense of how the person would work on a team, for example. For obvious hires, the e-mail alerts help us focus our time on explaining to the recruits why Microsoft is a good choice for them.

Let's say that an applicant named Sharon Holloway accepts our job offer. Sharon is a hypothetical new hire, but the description of her experience at Microsoft is typical of the experience of the 85 people we hire each week. While our intranet is a global solution for all 28,000-plus Microsoft employees worldwide, in this example we'll assume that Sharon is based at our main campus in Redmond, Washington.

Before Sharon arrives at Microsoft, an administrative assistant in her new group fills out the electronic New Hire Setup form on Microsoft's intranet to request a voice-mail account, an e-mail account, office furniture, and a computer with preinstalled software to be ready on Sharon's arrival. The same form ensures that Sharon gets added to the company phone list, receives a nameplate for her office door, and gets a mailbox in her building's mailroom. The single electronic form goes directly to the groups responsible for taking care of these items. Electronic logs ensure that everything is tracked.

After an orientation session with a Human Resources manager on the company's general approach to business and employee issues, Sharon and the other new employees are directed to the company's internal Web site for most of their administrative needs. Sharon goes online to review the employee handbook (it no longer exists in paper form), download any software she needs beyond the standard setup, and fill out her electronic W-4 form.

Next Sharon uses a procurement tool on our intranet called MS Market to order office supplies, books, a whiteboard, and business cards. MS Market automatically fills in her name, her e-mail alias, the name of her approving manager, and other standard information for the order. Sharon has to enter only the information unique to the purchase into a few designated fields. The vendors receive her order electronically and deliver the order to her office. An order above a certain amount of money requires additional levels of management approval before processing. Our electronic system routes the form to the right people for an electronic okay.

Sharon visits the Microsoft Archives, Library, and company newsletter sites to read up on Microsoft. By signing up for one or more of our library's news services, she sees the latest news about the company and the industry in electronic versions of publications such as *The Wall Street Journal, The New York Times, CNet,* and so on. The availability of these services online has increased the number of our subscribing employees from 250 to 8,000 for the *Journal* alone. The online library lists books, software, and videos that employees can check out online for delivery to their offices. Librarians also maintain Web pages containing news and research for each Microsoft product group.

New employees don't follow a standard route on our intranet site. We hire people who are intellectually curious, and they explore freely. After they get their basics set up, they'll dive into business or technical areas that relate to their jobs and interests. Our new employees use the site the way it's meant to be used: to learn and to get things done.

When Sharon's first paycheck "arrives," the payroll amount is deposited automatically into her checking account, and she can view her deposit confirmation and the details of her pay stub on a secure intranet page. As her banking needs change, Sharon can change her financial institutions online.

For travel, Sharon handles plane and hotel reservations online with a booking tool designed by Microsoft in partnership with American Express. AXI, available online twenty-four hours a day, seven days a week, gives Sharon direct access to corporate-negotiated airline fares and flight availability information, a low-fare search tool, airline seat maps, corporate-preferred hotels, and the ability to check a flight's status or request an upgrade. Microsoft's travel policies are embedded in the AXI software as business rules. Any nonstandard travel request triggers e-mail from AXI to a manager for review. Travel expenses are submitted digitally to her manager for electronic approval. We deposit the reimbursement into Sharon's checking account electronically within three business days of approval.

SUPPORTING CHANGING LIFESTYLES

Contrary to popular perception, Microsofties do have a life outside the company. Sharon gets married and after her honeymoon enters her vacation time online. When she and her husband move into a new house, Sharon submits her new address via an online form that automatically distributes the information to all of the organizations that need her address, such as Payroll, Benefits, and the vendors managing our retirement and employee stock option programs. She visits our intranet to get information about bus routes and ridesharing in her new neighborhood.

When Sharon and her husband have a baby, she goes online to learn about benefits such as parenting seminars, paid parental leave, and day care referrals. Sharon electronically submits the medical claims associated with the birth and goes online to change her benefits to accommodate the new baby. Microsoft has a "cafeteria"-style benefits program that pays a certain dollar amount of benefits to each employee. An employee can model different what-if scenarios to decide how the dollars should be allocated—with choices for medical, dental, and optical coverage, life and disability insurance, health club membership, and legal services—and see how an increase or a decrease in one benefit affects the entire package. She can set up a payroll deduction for any benefit combination that costs more than the company contribution.

An online tool is also the means for Sharon to manage her 401(k) retirement plan, her employee stock purchases, and her stock option grants. She can direct the total percentage of her salary to be withheld for retirement or stock purchases and can alter the percentage to be allocated to each retirement investment option. Fidelity Investments' Web site for the plan enables Sharon to view current account information and market indexes, to model loans, and to review her transaction history. The stock purchase tool enables Sharon to view the number and price of shares she's purchased, change her withholding amount during enrollment periods, or cancel participation. The stock option tool enables her to accept a grant with a secure electronic signature and view her options summary and exercise history. Salomon Smith Barney, the brokerage firm that handles Microsoft stock options, is creating a Web site that will enable Sharon to run scenarios to see how many shares she needs to exercise for such things as remodeling her house for her growing family. All employees can exercise their stock options online unless they live in countries that require paper forms.

As an employee and a shareholder, Sharon receives the company's annual report online—our income statement is shown according to the conventions and in the currencies of seven different countries, and my letter to shareholders is available in ten languages—and she can vote her proxy online. Microsoft was the first company to offer paperless proxy voting to employee shareholders, a step that has increased our employee participation from 15 percent to more than 60 percent.

USING ONE TOOL FOR MULTIPLE PLANNING NEEDS

One of Sharon's jobs as a marketer is product planning. Most of the management and financial information she needs is accessible from MS Reports, a single interface to many databases such as expense, customer, contract, and budget. MS Reports can also be used to access MS Sales, our sales reporting system; HeadTrax, our head count system; and a financial management system that includes general ledger, fixed asset, project accounting, and statutory information and management reports. MS Reports uses Excel pivot tables to show data from multiple views, enabling Sharon to focus on analysis instead of data structures. She can review revenue projections for her product from sales locations worldwide as the projections are updated. She can view historical information about previous marketing campaigns such as personnel, capital expenses, and marketing expenses.

With the relevant data from MS Reports to help her plan, Sharon uses an online budgeting application to enter her projected head count and expenses for her new product, then is able to track her marketing budget throughout the project, answering questions such as "What is my spend rate?" "Where am I spending money?" and "How can I reallocate resources for new projects?"

Sharon may use an additional planning tool, OnTarget, to track expenses in more detail. OnTarget provides project accounting. A manager can get complete project expenses across multiple cost centers or across fiscal years.

REWARDING STAFF WHILE FOLLOWING POLICY

When Sharon is promoted to manager, one new duty is conducting performance reviews for each of her "reports" every six months. Each employee writes a self-evaluation, and Sharon adds her own performance evaluation to the original document. Sharon's evaluation of an employee incorporates peer review, and e-mail makes it easy to get feedback from people in other divisions or even around the world. Sharon and her manager review her appraisals of the work of her employees and her proposed ratings for them. Then Sharon meets each employee face-to-face to discuss performance and new objectives.

Microsoft managers used to spend more time on the paperwork for reviews than on the reviews themselves. Our review application simplifies the work of managers while ensuring that they follow company policies. The application calculates a default merit increase and bonus for each person based on Sharon's rating and on the employee's job level and current salary. Overriding the defaults is possible (for example, to "load up" the salary and bonus for a star performer), but managers have to adhere to the company's overall percentage guidelines. As Sharon enters the numbers for each employee, the tool automatically calculates the new group average. If she comes in too low or too high, she can go back and redo the numbers. After senior managers review the numbers electronically, compensation changes feed directly into the master employee data and stock option systems.

By translating a rating into compensation and by enabling the manager to visually compare such figures as ranking by performance and by salary, the review application helps managers to grade employees consistently according to both performance and policy. We estimate that the application also reduces managers' time spent on review administration by at least 50 percent.

SAVING AGGRAVATION AND $40 MILLION

Using our intranet to replace paper forms has produced striking results for us. As this book goes to press, we have reduced the number of paper forms from more than 1,000 to a company-wide total of 60 forms. Among those groups that started out with the most forms, Procurement has dropped from 114 to 1; and Human Resources is down to 39. Of the 60 remaining paper forms, 10 are required by law and 40 are required by outside parties because their systems are still based on paper. The last 10 paper forms are used so seldom that we haven't bothered to make them electronic, yet. Businesses have an incentive to persuade partners and governments to accept information electronically so that everybody can get to a fully digital approach with no paper.

Overall, the savings from our using the electronic forms I've described in this chapter amounted to at least $40 million in our first twelve months of use in 1997–98. The biggest savings came from the reduction in processing costs. Accounting firms put the cost of paper orders—mostly the time of all the people handling the paper—at about $145 per transaction. Electronic processing at Microsoft, by comparison, runs less than $5 per transaction. In its first year MS Market alone handled 250,000 transactions involving more than $1.6 billion, saving our company at least $35 million in processing. Transaction volumes are increasing significantly. The $35 million figure includes $3 million saved through the reassignment of twenty-two procurement personnel worldwide. MS Market also directs employees to vendors with whom we've negotiated volume discounts, which saves us money on many purchases.

Using electronic forms for just the 401(k) plan, the employee stock purchase plan, and the stock options plan saved us another $1 million annually in labor. Attrition took care of some of the reduction in head count, but most of the staff moved on to more important tasks they weren't doing before because they'd had to spend so much time on rote administrative chores. One person who had been spending each day answering routine questions now manages the content for the Web page that provides the answers. Within a year, the number of employees using the online system to obtain account information and ask questions regarding Microsoft's 401(k) plan doubled from 24 percent to 51 percent. As a result, during the same period, assistance by service representatives decreased by half, from 35 percent to 17 percent.

Our new online travel system is expected to reduce overhead in our corporate travel group and to triple travel agent productivity from an average of eight to twenty-five completed itineraries (usually hotel, rental car, and airfare) per agent per day. Consistent employee use of preferred vendors will save us millions of dollars per year.

The average time it takes an employee to make a domestic travel reservation is projected to go from seventeen minutes and six phone calls or e-mails to approximately five minutes.

All of the administrative applications and content I've talked about in this chapter run on a total of twelve servers, either dual-processor or quad-processor systems. Total cost for the hardware was about $765,000 annually. Though far lower than comparable costs on other systems, our expenses were still higher than companies will see today because we pioneered a lot of solutions. There were no standards, for instance, for integrating third-party systems inexpensively; software products such as our commerce server provide this integration today. Companies will see lower costs going forward as the result of standards and of increased functionality in commercial software packages.

Even as we pioneered solutions, our central IT budget, which covers these and other major business applications, decreased 3 percent between 1996 and 1999, mostly from standardizing data and consolidating the number of information systems we have.

PUTTING RESPONSIBILITY INTO THE HANDS OF THOSE AFFECTED

Electronic tools give us benefits beyond reducing transaction costs. For example, by requiring proper sign-off before a request is processed, MS Market prevents inappropriate purchases that can easily slip through a paper-based system. Shipping information is typed instead of handwritten, so routing errors are almost nonexistent. Communication with our suppliers is documented, and we know the costs in advance so that there are no surprises. Our suppliers get paid faster, too, which motivates them to make swift deliveries. Business rules are implemented up front so that, for example, the system won't accept an order that has an incorrect budget code. This requirement eliminates hours and hours our finance group used to spend "scrubbing" records. Employee buying patterns can be tracked and used in vendor negotiations, too. The list of benefits goes on. We're always discovering new ones.

In our Human Resources, Procurement, and Employee Services groups and in the functions they touch throughout Microsoft, going digital has given us a mechanism for changing how we work. By enabling our employees to directly control such processes as entering address changes and making and changing retirement investments, we've put responsibility directly into the hands of the people most motivated to act. Self-service administration of benefits enables Human Resources staff to spend more of their energy on strategic personnel issues such as recruitment and training.

This fundamental process issue—how to get bureaucracy out of the way—is one that our Human Resources staff itself is driving. Human Resources had conducted a number of classic reengineering studies to understand what routine processes can be automated and what processes require their professional skills. Human Resources wants to do "thinking work, not manual work."

[1]James E. LaLonde, "Gates Computers Still Too Hard to Use," *Seattle Times*, 1 June 1988.

[2]People mail their resumes to resume@microsoft.com. The link to Resume Builder is at www.microsoft.com/jobs.

Article 6, "Tattoo Pioneer: Shanghai Kate Hellenbrand"

by Christine Braunberger, Ph.D.

3,588 words, 13 words per line

Reprinted with permission by Christine Braunberger, Ph.D.

In the summer of 1971, *The Wall Street Journal* and jewelers Tiffany and Co. had a public disagreement over tattooed women. Kate Hellenbrand, a young graphic artist on Fifth Avenue's advertising scene, likely set too fast a pace past the newsstands to notice the interplay. But it was a quarrel she soon would be immersed in for the rest of her life.

The Wall Street Journal's front page story heralded tattoos as "the perfect gift ... [for] the lady of your life." Catering to its affluent readership, the story is couched in terms of market scarcity—tattooists are a "vanishing breed,"—while at the same time, trend setting—"she'll be the first in her crowd." Three days after the story ran, Tiffany & Co. took out a small ad, which appeared on page four, admonishing the *Journal* on grounds of bad taste. In a plain san serif typeface, it reads: "We take exception to *The Wall Street Journal's* front-page article on July 6th which says that tattooing on female posteriors or any other part of the anatomy is 'tasteful.' We think it is the absolute height of bad taste." The ad is signed by the Tiffany & Co. logo. Their fear was plain: the man who gives his wife a tattoo as a gift is not giving her a tennis bracelet, and Tiffany & Co. could begin to lose business to the then-illegal NYC tattoo artists. Little did they know how many women would begin to adorn their bodies—or who would provide the adornment.

Manhattan, and its tussles concerning who is the ascendant arbiter of taste, was a world away from the rugged rural farm outside Salt Lake City, Utah, where Hellenbrand (born Kathryn Ann Barton) grew up. There, as her step-father's helper, Hellenbrand grew to love the tools used on the farm and learned how to handle everything from the plow to the jigsaw. This love of tools led her to the field of graphic arts when she moved to Los Angeles in 1964 to take classes at the revered Art Center School of Design and Chouinard's School of Fine Arts.

In Los Angeles, Hellenbrand became part of that magical group of original hippies, culminating at the first Monterey Pop Festival. She also developed an addiction to surfing, which she supported through typesetting and technical illustration work for the US Department of Defense via Volt Technical Corporation. It also appealed to her sense of irony to occasionally run marijuana over the Mexican border. But it was the tools of her day job that took her back to the intrigue of the tools on the farm. She excelled at the use of the X-Acto Knife, Rapidiograph pen, border tapes and French curves. In another bit of situational irony, many of these tools that have been discarded by graphic artists in favor of computer wizardry continue to serve tattoo artists.

Hellenbrand's work with Volt brought her to NYC in the late 1960s, where she befriended the artists and activists whose work dovetailed with her own surfer ideology. As she describes it, Hellenbrand became "politicized" that first year when she met Christopher Robert Gay McClaren John Pollock (more judiciously known as "Kit"), a poet and the private assistant to David Dillinger—one of the Yippee's Chicago Eight—who, along with Abbie Hoffman, Jerry Rubin, and Bobby Seale went to the 1968 Democratic Convention, to nominate a Pig for President. An unsung peace activist during the war, Dillinger made many self-funded trips to Hanoi, Vietnam, to negotiate the release of US MIA and POWs. "Kit and I fell madly in love, and it was through him that I began to read such incredibly courageous and powerful journalists like I.F. Stone."

The work she was doing for the government became increasingly distasteful to Hellenbrand as she determined she could no longer support the Vietnam War and actions of the US Government. Rejecting her Top Secret classified clearance, Hellenbrand embarked on a series of typesetting jobs, which landed her at Muller, Jordan, & Herrick, an advertising agency on the corner of 53rd and Fifth Avenue, whose clients included Avon, McKesson Liquors, and Head Skiis. To Hellenbrand, she had achieved the ultimate in her field by working at an ad agency on Fifth Avenue.

As a salaried employee, Hellenbrand could come and go as the work demanded. During lulls she began wandering across the street to the Museum of Modern Art and the nearby Museum of American Folk Art. When not prowling the Museum's hallways and exhibits, she was lunching with such models as Lauren Hutton, Pat Cleveland, and Ingrid Polk. Meanwhile, at home in her West 15th St. apartment, Hellenbrand was getting to know the photographer next door, Michael Malone. Hellenbrand remembers him as "stunningly gorgeous," a California native with movie star looks:

> Because we shared the same floor, Malone with the front apartment and with me holding down the rear apartment, we became good friends. Malone was struggling to find his way. He was a carpenter/light show technician/fledgling photographer. He was energetic, funny, sexy, smart and connected. I adored him from the second I set eyes on him. He wore cowboy clothes, had lots of hair everywhere and possessed boyish charm. Because he was so poor, I hired him

to help me in my apartment. He painted the rooms, built bookcases, shelves, whatever I needed. I paid him a day rate. He would often have his electricity turned off because of nonpayment of his bill. Those times would find him running long extension cords into my apartment to tap off of my power. He would borrow my little TV, he had a key to my apartment and would forage through my fridge. I didn't mind. We became close. He had a lot of friends who were musicians: Jerry Jeff Walker, Linda Ronstadt, Gary B. White, Nicholas Holmes, "Baby" Keith Sykes, Rosalie Sorrels, Dave Von Ronk, Loudon Wainwright III, Kate McGarriigale, Townes Van Zant and Guy Clark. I'd go with Michael to the old Kettle of Fish tavern in the West Village almost every night. After Bob Dylan's gigantic impact on the "Roots" music scene in NYC, small clubs like Gertie's Folk City and the CaféWha and the Gaslight popped up all over Bleeker and MacDougal Street. Our singer/songwriter friends were all 'rockin' their way to stardom' doing night sets at one club or another. Between their sets, they'd meet for a drink at the Kettle. Now I was in Folk Music Alley drinking with Kris Kristofferson and going to Bob Dylan's birthday party. How is it that it all seems so normal?

That the intensity of these terribly talented men and women could seem normal drew Hellenbrand in, fueling her creativity and need for art as a way of living.

One day, while out photographing plants that struggle though the cracks in New York's city street concrete, Malone's viewfinder focused on a brilliant dragon tattoo on the calf of a lower east side underground tattoo artist, Thom Devita. Devita was sitting on the stoop at St. Mark's Place, flashing work by Paul Rogers—arguably the best color man of the time. Malone was inspired to shift the focus of his photo essay from struggling plants to struggling artists. Hellenbrand and Malone began to go to tattoo parties to document this illegal (banned in NYC in 1961 after an alleged hepatitis outbreak) "lowbrow" art wherever they could. Soon, Hellenbrand found it more expedient to forego fancy lunches with models to do freelance graphic work for the museums around the agency. In the course of designing grant material for the Museum of American Folk Art, Hellenbrand learned of the museum's plan to mount a show they would call "Tattoo!"

Hellenbrand's initial involvement was to suggest that the exhibit feature current artists, rather than focus exclusively on C.F. Fellows, whose 1931 *Tattoo Book* was their inspiration. The curators were apprehensive; they said that they couldn't work with living outlaws. Did Walter Hoving, the chair of Tiffany & Co. and writer of the advertisement, know he was brandishing a diamond-encrusted shield of taste against a then-illegal industry? Certainly exhibition directors, Herbert Hemphill, Jr. and Frederick Fried, didn't know that they were in the founding moments of a truly fresh, young talented tattoo artist. While the museum's leadership was reluctant to get involved with the underground artists that Hellenbrand and Malone were discovering, they thought it would be a great idea for these two to co-produce a contemporary section of the show, and they were given a room to fill. Due to their relentless pursuit of the best tattoo artists in the world for inclusion, their piece of the museum's show crept out of that one side room and into the main hall. Ultimately, their contribution included a slide-show, large color prints of tattoos, interviews, anecdotal statements and drawings from some 20 artists worldwide: Sailor Jerry Collins from Hawaii; Don Ed Hardy from California; Horiyoshi II from Japan; Don Nolan from California; Cliff Raven from Chicago; Huck Spaulding from upstate New York; Paul Rogers from Florida; Zeke Owen from California; Smokey Nightingale from Washington, D.C.; and Johnny Walker from Washington, D.C. Some artists were reluctant to get very involved. There had been little previous interest in the art of tattooing by any legitimate museum or gallery before, and the artists were distrustful that their work would be treated with respect. They didn't have to worry.

There were worries, though.

Hellenbrand remembers preparing for opening night, when the curators were stunned to see three NYC detectives marching up the steps with arrest warrants in hand. The directors had recreated an old-style tattoo studio in their front windows, based on photos from Huck Spaulding, and the police thought that a real tattoo shop had opened. Such a public mistake provided the museum with the kind of publicity it couldn't afford to buy. The show became a huge success, and the museum extended it for three additional months.

As the show was developing, Malone began to spend time with DeVita in what Hellenbrand recalls as a squatter's tenement, where he lived and worked. In order to find DeVita's clandestine quarters, one had to sidestep a fairly significant waterfall from a broken water pipe. In the winter, it would freeze into a solid cone of ice. The room opened into a baroque chaos of found objects; in the middle, Thom worked on his clients—from immigrant day laborers to municipal employees—by a single overhead light. Hellenbrand would accompany Malone on his shoots to DeVita's East 8th St., home/studio, where the speakeasy environment was charged with excitement, emotion, and drama. Hellenbrand learned another side of the city from DeVita, who knew how to scrounge all the necessities of life—from food and books to the ingredients of his art—for free from the streets. The DeVita that Hellenbrand knew never seemed to hold a "real" job, but lived well by virtue of his scrounging skills.

During this time, they were also getting to know the Reverend Richard O. Tyler at the Gnostic Lyceum, a loosely constructed Buddhist enclave housed in an old Jewish synagogue. The Reverend's Lyceum added another dimension to Hellenbrand's education in eccentricities: one paid dues to the Lyceum or fees to stay in its hostel only in gold, drank homemade apple moonshine, and could participate in free-form jazz jams and various pagan rituals. Here too, the environment was "a madhouse of decoration" with the yard a testimonial to outsider art. Joining the inner circle, or cong, included a tattoo ritual, and Hellenbrand still bears the faint white Om symbol on her hand.

Eventually, DeVita bought the Lyceum's East 4th St. building and began tattooing there. Though the world was clearly masculine, Hellenbrand was drawn in and soon used her stable job for the credit needed to purchase a nine-seat VW bus for tattoo travels. At first, she was driving DeVita and Malone upstate, near Albany, so that DeVita could get tattoo work from Huck Spaulding on the weekends. Spaulding, a master tattoo artist from the carnival era and sometimes partner of Paul Rogers, was to become the tattoo world's largest equipment supplier.

Malone was the first to succumb to his new friend's emerging business, and he bought a starter kit from Spaulding. When the kit arrived, Malone convinced Hellenbrand to spare some skin. Thus he began his tattoo career by carving a small red heart on Kate's ankle. Soon, Malone undertook some illegal renovations; he took the walls around a bedroom halfway down to create a bay for tattooing. After lugging away many a bag of plaster after dark, Hellenbrand and Malone created the Catfish Tattoo Studio, named after the first tattoo DeVita did for Malone. From Huck Spaulding they learned how a tattoo studio should look. From Tony "the Pirate" Cambria they learned to paint flash on white vinyl roll-up shades, which could be rolled up quickly if the police visited.

At the advertising agency during the day Hellenbrand continued to work as a typesetter and graphic designer; meanwhile, Malone would roam the streets handing out their new business cards. In the evenings Hellenbrand would hand-color the catfish on those business cards and continue to write to other tattoo artists, inviting them to be part of the Museum of American Folk Art Show.

Primary among these correspondences was Don Ed Hardy, a young surfer-style tattoo artist from San Francisco with a fine arts background. He was a prolific and promising talent even in his early twenties. His association with Sailor Jerry and Zeke Owen created a sort of Pacific Rim triumvirate blending Japanese/Chinese/Hawaiian/Californian; together they were rediscovering and reinventing the technology as well as the art. Hardy made a trip to NYC where he met with Malone and Hellenbrand,

and they began photographing root material for this new kind of tattooing—this West Coast style. Horimono was the term Sailor Jerry and Hardy applied to it.

Malone, Hardy, and Hellenbrand visited the Springfield, MA, Museum of Fine Art, which housed a stockpile of wood block prints by Kuniyoshi. Perhaps the most recognized artist of the Ukiyo-e period of Japanese art (17th–20th Centuries), Ukiyo-e in general and Kuniyoshi's archive in particular were a tremendous influence on Horimono. Malone shot print after print all day—by the end the three had formed a bond that would secure their friendship. Thereafter, Hardy made several trips to NYC to see Malone and Hellenbrand, often bringing his wife, Christine, with him.

Hellenbrand describes herself as thrust into the museum show's secretarial and production roles, but the number of hats she was wearing was multiplying fast. When Hellenbrand would come home from a day at the agency, she never knew whom she'd find at the Catfish Studio. Now it seems audacious to have opened their home to tattoo strangers, but "our desire outweighed our common sense," and they were never the worse for it. At first she acted as a kind of hostess. Angelo, a Bronx artist, was a frequent visitor, accompanied by Tom King, a Vietnam vet and avid tattoo collector. King asked Hellenbrand if she'd ever thought about tattooing. "No, that's Michael's thing," she replied, "I don't want to be anyone's Yoko Ono."

Still, King pushed because he knew Hellenbrand had a strong art background, and he said he thought she'd "do a good job." Hellenbrand's love of tools had made her curious about the small machine, and she wondered how it would feel to tattoo someone. A small flower image was chosen—nothing too difficult—and the preparations were made in "a somewhat religious manner."

"I remember only bits of that first piece," says Hellenbrand. "I had watched so many tattoos go on for so long, I sort of knew how to move my hands, etc. But it is all a blur to me—sort of white noise. And I had a kind of out-of-body experience, I was so nervous. And immediately taken with the entire process."

Life went on as usual for two weeks—until King returned with a healed and vibrant tattoo on his calf. "I was so excited at the finished product; I knew this was it. This was something I could do and wanted to do. It was magical; those strong, bright colors beaming back at me. Once I picked up the machine I realized what power I had and that I had to have it in my life." King loved the piece and immediately wanted Hellenbrand to create another. The second was a large peacock (6×8") in the middle of King's chest. This time Hellenbrand dug in her heels and did the outline and shading in one sitting, then the color followed in a second sitting a month later. Her third tattoo was a large dragon snaking around King's existing tattoos on his right arm—a sort of sleeve. "On that tattoo I started at 8:30 in the morning and the next time I looked up it was 1:30. And I thought anything that can make time and space fall away like this is for me. I quit my job and began to tattoo full time."

It was 1972 when Hellenbrand left the advertising agency so that she could devote herself to tattooing. She knew of only two other women in the world who tattooed: Cindy Ray (Bev Robinson) who still works in Australia and Rusty Skuse, who worked in England. Although these women were not close enough to guide her, many of the challenges she might have faced were eased by the strong alliances she had formed with artists included in the museum show. Malone and Hellenbrand had earned trust, and a measure of gratitude, in their efforts to legitimize their art form.

> I know how extremely lucky I am to have had this trust in the beginning. To be a young female (two of the most hated elements for a newcomer to the field) and to be granted total acceptance and access by the giants like Sailor Jerry and Huck Spaulding and Paul Rogers is beyond anything anyone else has done before or since. No one has had such a gilded resume and I don't take it for granted. Whenever I hit a snag or needed supplies, I simply had to ask. And they were also open to having me come into their shops.

To get their first real "official" tattoos, Malone and Hellenbrand traveled to Chicago to meet Cliff Raven, one of the first tattoo artists (along with Hardy) to enter the field with a Bachelor of Fine Arts Degree.

The experience for Hellenbrand wasn't totally satisfying:

> When I went to Cliff Raven in Chicago, Malone had already found his image—a small Japanese demon shooting lightning from the palm of his hand. I was unsure of what I wanted so while Malone was getting his piece, I was searching the designs for something I could live with forever. I found a small clipper ship that I wanted on the top of my thigh.

Hellenbrand always had been curious, mesmerized by foreign travel and unknown places.

> My favorite book as a child was my *Collier's Atlas*. To me it's all about exploring. So that's what I wanted, a little clipper ship on my thigh to symbolize my love of adventure and they said, "No, you're a girl and girls can only get a rabbit, a squirrel, or a skunk named Stinky." I was heartbroken. As an ex-farmer's daughter, I surely wasn't going to get any kind of yard varmint, especially a skunk

named Stinky. So I went back to hotel, and Malone finally suggested that I get cherry blossoms on my chest. The next night I went back and got the blossoms. They were lovely but not connected to me.

It wasn't until 2005 that Hellenbrand finally got her clipper ship. Ironically, it was from Zeke Owen, one of the few men who did resist Hellenbrand's entry into the world of tattoo.

> He would tell me, "Put down your machines, you are bad luck in this business." Of course, that's because it was a military business at that time and sailors and soldiers would stand in line for hours to get tattooed by a woman—any age, any degree of attractiveness—because of the novelty, or because they hadn't been near a woman for weeks or months. She could be a reminder of their mother, grandmother, sister or wife. It was an economic issue I think. Or if it was something else, I was never told. So, to have Zeke, who is one of the grand masters of the art, do my heart's desire tattoo on me was a tremendous validation.

Even though friends attempted to curtail Hellenbrand's choice of gender-appropriate imagery, and a potential mentor turned her away, she was far too enamored to walk away. Not only was she developing a reputation as part of this "hot new couple," she was learning the trade and the history, while living the art's next chapter.

As Zeke Owen and Sailor Jerry were developing the hygiene protocols that would set the standard for the industry, Sailor Jerry joined Paul Rogers and Huck Spaudling in their color experiments. Hellenbrand created letterhead for a non-existent sign company so they could order raw pigments. Free samples came in five-pound bags, which the men would grind up and tattoo into their legs, searching for non-reactive colors.

An estimated 25,000 tattoos later, Hellenbrand recognizes how far she has drifted from her original art. "I'm not a good paper artist anymore. It isn't demanding enough for me. It's not nearly as thrilling. When I get it on the skin that's when I become the artist. Skin is my medium."

Article 7, "Sleep Deficit: The Performance Killer"

A conversation with Dr. Charles A. Czeisler

3,679 words, 6 words per line

Reprinted by permission of Harvard Business Review. *Copyright © October 2006 by the Harvard Business School Publishing Corporation. All rights reserved.*

At 12:30 am on June 10, 2002, Israel Lane Joubert and his family of seven set out for a long drive home following a family reunion in Beaumont, Texas. Joubert, who had hoped to reach home in faraway Fort Worth in time to get to work by 8 am, fell asleep at the wheel, plowing the family's Chevy Suburban into the rear of a parked 18-wheeler. He survived, but his wife and five of his six children were killed.

The Joubert tragedy underscores a problem of epidemic proportions among workers who get too little sleep. In the past five years, driver fatigue has accounted for more than 1.35 million automobile accidents in the United States alone, according to the National Highway Traffic Safety Administration. The general effect of sleep deprivation on cognitive performance is well-known: Stay awake longer than 18 consecutive hours, and your reaction speed, short-term and long-term memory, ability to focus, decision-making capacity, math processing, cognitive speed, and spatial orientation all start to suffer. Cut sleep back to five or six hours a night for several days in a row, and the accumulated sleep deficit magnifies these negative effects. (Sleep deprivation is implicated in all kinds of physical maladies, too, from high blood pressure to obesity.)

Nevertheless, frenzied corporate cultures still confuse sleeplessness with vitality and high performance. An ambitious manager logs 80-hour work weeks, surviving on five or six hours of sleep a night and eight cups of coffee (the world's second-most widely sold commodity, after oil) a day. A Wall Street trader goes to bed at 11 or midnight and wakes to his BlackBerry buzz at 2:30 am to track opening activity on the DAX. A road warrior lives out of a suitcase while traveling to Tokyo, St. Louis, Miami, and Zurich, conducting business in a cloud of caffeinated jet lag. A negotiator takes a red-eye flight, hops into a rental car, and zooms through an unfamiliar city to make a delicate M&A meeting at 8 in the morning.

People like this put themselves, their teams, their companies, and the general public in serious jeopardy, says Dr. Charles A. Czeisler, the Baldino Professor of Sleep Medicine at Harvard Medical School.[1] To him, encouraging a culture of sleepless machismo is worse than nonsensical; it is downright dangerous, and the antithesis of intelligent management. He notes that while corporations have all kinds of policies designed to prevent employee endangerment—rules against workplace smoking, drinking, drugs, sexual harassment, and so on—they sometimes push employees to the brink of self-destruction. Being "on" pretty much around the clock induces a level of impairment every bit as risky as intoxication.

As one of the world's leading authorities on human sleep cycles and the biology of sleep and wakefulness, Dr. Czeisler understands the physiological bases of the sleep imperative better than almost anyone. His message to corporate leaders is simple: If you want to raise performance—both your own and your organization's—you need to pay attention to this fundamental biological issue. In this edited interview with senior editor Bronwyn Fryer, Czeisler observes that top executives now have a critical responsibility to take sleeplessness seriously.

What does the most recent research tell us about the physiology of sleep and cognitive performance?

Four major sleep-related factors affect our cognitive performance. The kinds of work and travel schedules required of business executives today pose a severe challenge to their ability to function well, given each of these factors.

The first has to do with the homeostatic drive for sleep at night, determined largely by the number of consecutive hours that we've been awake. Throughout the waking day, human beings build up a stronger and stronger drive for sleep. Most of us think we're in control of sleep—that we choose when to go to sleep and when to wake up. The fact is that when we are drowsy, the brain can seize control involuntarily. When the homeostatic pressure to sleep becomes high enough, a couple thousand neurons in the brain's "sleep switch" ignite, as discovered by Dr. Clif Saper at Harvard Medical School. Once that happens, sleep seizes the brain like a pilot grabbing the controls. If you're behind the wheel of a car at the time, it takes just three or four seconds to be off the road.

The second major factor that determines our ability to sustain attention and maintain peak cognitive performance has to do with the total amount of sleep you manage to get over several days. If you get at least eight hours of sleep a night, your level of alertness should remain stable throughout the day, but if you have a sleep disorder or get less than that for several days, you start building a sleep deficit that makes it more difficult for the brain to function. Executives I've observed tend to burn the candle at both ends, with 7 am breakfast meetings and dinners that run late, for days and days. Most people can't get to sleep without some wind-down time, even if they are very tired, so these executives may not doze off until 2 in the morning. If they average four hours of sleep a night for four or five days, they develop the same level of cognitive impairment as if they'd been awake for 24 hours—equivalent to legal drunkenness. Within ten days, the level of impairment is the same as you'd have going 48 hours without sleep. This greatly lengthens reaction time, impedes judgment, and interferes with problem solving. In such a state of sleep deprivation, a single beer can have the same impact on our ability to sustain performance as a whole six-pack can have on someone who's well rested.

The third factor has to do with circadian phase—the time of day in the human body that says "it's midnight" or "it's dawn." A neurological timing device called the "circadian pacemaker" works alongside but, paradoxically, in opposition to the homeostatic drive for sleep. This circadian pacemaker sends out its strongest drive for sleep just before we habitually wake up, and its strongest drive for waking one to three hours before we usually

go to bed, just when the homeostatic drive for sleep is peaking. We don't know why it's set up this way, but we can speculate that it has to do with the fact that, unlike other animals, we don't take frequent catnaps throughout the day. The circadian pacemaker may help us to focus on that big project by enabling us to stay awake throughout the day in one long interval and by allowing us to consolidate sleep into one long interval at night.

In the mid-afternoon, when we've already built up substantial homeostatic sleep drive, the circadian system has not yet come to the rescue. That's typically the time when people are tempted to take a nap or head for the closest Starbucks or soda machine. The caffeine in the coffee temporarily blocks receptors in the brain that regulate sleep drive. Thereafter, the circadian pacemaker sends out a stronger and stronger drive for waking as the day progresses. Provided you're keeping a regular schedule, the rise in the sleep-facilitating hormone melatonin will then quiet the circadian pacemaker one to two hours before your habitual bedtime, enabling the homeostatic sleep drive to take over and allow you to get to sleep. As the homeostatic drive dissipates midway through the sleep episode, the circadian drive for sleep increases toward morning, maintaining our ability to obtain a full night of sleep. After our usual wake time, the levels of melatonin begin to decline. Normally, the two mutually opposing processes work well together, sustaining alertness throughout the day and promoting a solid night of sleep.

The fourth factor affecting performance has to do with what's called "sleep inertia," the grogginess most people experience when they first wake up. Just like a car engine, the brain needs time to "warm up" when you awaken. The part of your brain responsible for memory consolidation doesn't function well for five to 20 minutes after you wake up and doesn't reach its peak efficiency for a couple of hours. But if you sleep on the airplane and the flight attendant wakes you up suddenly upon landing, you may find yourself at the customs station before you realize you've left your laptop and your passport behind. There is a transitional period between the time you wake up and the time your brain becomes fully functional. This is why you never want to make an important decision as soon as you are suddenly awakened—ask any nurse who's had to awaken a physician at night about a patient.

Most top executives are over 40. Isn't it true that sleeping also becomes more difficult with age?

Yes, that's true. When we're past the age of 40, sleep is much more fragmented than when we're younger. We are more easily awakened by disturbances such as noise from the external environment and from our own increasing aches and pains. Another thing that increases with age is the risk of sleep disorders such as restless legs syndrome, insomnia, and sleep apnea—the cessation of breathing during sleep, which can occur when the airway collapses many times per hour and shuts off the flow of oxygen to the heart and brain, leading to many brief awakenings.

Many people gain weight as they age, too. Interestingly, chronic sleep restriction increases levels of appetite and stress hormones; it also reduces one's ability to metabolize glucose and increases the production of the hormone ghrelin, which makes people crave carbohydrates and sugars, so they get heavier, which in turn raises the risk of sleep apnea, creating a vicious cycle. Some researchers speculate that the epidemic of obesity in the U.S. and elsewhere may be related to chronic sleep loss. Moreover, sleep-disordered breathing increases the risk of high blood pressure and heart disease due to the strain of starving the heart of oxygen many times per hour throughout the night.

As we age, the circadian window during which we maintain consolidated sleep also narrows. That's why airline travel across time zones can be so brutal as we get older. Attempting to sleep at an adverse circadian phase—that is, during our biological daytime—becomes much more difficult. Thus, if you take a 7 pm flight from New York to London, you typically land about midnight in your home time zone, when the homeostatic drive for sleep is very strong, but the local time is 5 am. Exposure to daylight—the principal circadian synchronizer—at this time shifts you toward Hawaiian time rather than toward London time. In this circumstance, the worst possible thing you can do is rent a car and drive to a meeting where you have to impress people with your mental acuity at the equivalent of 3 or 4 in the morning. You might not even make the meeting, because you very easily could wrap your car around a tree. Fourteen or 15 hours later, if you're trying to go to bed at 11 pm in the local time zone, you'll have a more difficult time maintaining a consolidated night's sleep.

So sleep deprivation, in your opinion, is a far more serious issue than most executives think it is.

Yes, indeed. Putting yourself or others at risk while driving or working at an impaired level is bad enough; expecting your employees to do the same is just irresponsible. It amazes me that contemporary work and social culture glorifies sleeplessness in the way we once glorified people who could hold their liquor. We now know that 24 hours without sleep or a week of sleeping four or five hours a night induces an impairment equivalent to a blood alcohol level of .1%. We would never say, "This person is a great worker! He's drunk all the time!" yet we continue to celebrate people who sacrifice sleep. The analogy to drunkenness is real because, like a drunk, a person who is sleep deprived has no idea how functionally impaired he or she truly is. Moreover, their efficiency at work will suffer substantially, contributing to the phenomenon of "presenteeism," which, exacts a large economic toll on business.

Sleep deprivation is not just an individual health hazard; it's a public one. Consider the risk of occupational injury and driver fatigue. In a study our research team conducted of hospital interns who had been scheduled to work for at least 24 consecutive hours, we found that their odds of stabbing themselves with a needle or scalpel increased 61%, their risk of crashing a motor vehicle increased 168%, and their risk of a near miss increased 460%. In the U.S., drowsy drivers are responsible for a fifth of all motor vehicle accidents and some 8,000 deaths annually. It is estimated that 80,000 drivers fall asleep at the wheel every day, 10% of them run off the road, and every two minutes, one of them crashes. Countless innocent people are hurt. There's now a vehicular homicide law in New Jersey (and some pending in other states) that includes driving without sleep for more than 24 hours in its definition of recklessness. There's a man in Florida who's serving a 15-year prison term for vehicular homicide—he'd been awake for 30-some hours when he crashed his company's truck into a group of cars waiting for a light to change, killing three people. I would not want to be the CEO of the company bearing responsibility for those preventable deaths.

Sleep deprivation among employees poses other kinds of risks to companies as well. With too little sleep, people do things that no CEO in his or her right mind would allow. All over the world, people are running heavy and dangerous machinery or guarding secure sites and buildings while they're exhausted. Otherwise intelligent, well-mannered managers do all kinds of things they'd never do if they were rested—they may get angry at employees, make unsound decisions that affect the future of their companies, and give muddled presentations before their colleagues, customers, the press, or shareholders.

What should companies be doing to address the sleep problem?

People in executive positions should set behavioral expectations and develop corporate sleep policies, just as they already have concerning behaviors like smoking or sexual harassment. It's important to have a policy limiting scheduled work—ideally to no more than 12 hours a day, and exceptionally to no more than 16 consecutive hours. At least 11 consecutive hours of rest should be provided every 24 hours. Furthermore, employees should not be scheduled to work more than 60 hours a week and not be permitted to work more than 80 hours a week. When working at night or on extended shifts, employees should not be scheduled to work more than four or five consecutive days, and certainly no more than six consecutive days. People need at least one day off a week, and ideally two in a row, in order to avoid building up a sleep deficit.

Now, managers will often rationalize overscheduling employees. I hear them say that if their employees aren't working, they will be out partying and not sleeping anyway. That may be true for some irresponsible individuals, but it doesn't justify scheduling employees to work a hundred hours a week so that they can't possibly get an adequate amount of sleep. Of course, some circumstances may arise in which you need someone to remain at work for more than 16 consecutive hours. The night security guard, for example, can't just walk off the job if his replacement isn't there, so you will need to have a provision for exceptional circumstances, such as offering transportation home for a sleep-deprived worker.

Companies also need executive policies. For example, I would advise executives to avoid taking red-eye flights, which severely disrupt sleep. If someone must travel overnight internationally, the policy should allow the executive to take at least a day to adapt to the sleep deprivation associated with the flight and the new time zone before driving or conducting business. Such a policy requires some good schedule planning, but the time spent making the adjustments will be worth it, for the traveler will be more functional before going into that important meeting. And the sleep policy should not permit anyone, under any circumstances, to take an overnight flight and then drive to a business meeting somewhere—period. He or she should at least be provided a taxi, car service, or shuttle.

Companies can do other things to promote healthy sleep practices among employees. Educational programs about sleep, health, and safety

should be mandatory. Employees should learn to set aside an adequate amount of time for sleep each night and to keep their bedrooms dark and quiet and free of all electronic devices—televisions, BlackBerries, and so on. They should learn about the ways alcohol and caffeine interfere with sleep. When someone is sleep deprived, drinking alcohol only makes things worse, further eroding performance and increasing the propensity to fall asleep while also interfering with the ability to stay asleep. Additionally, companies should provide annual screening for sleep disorders in order to identify those who might be at risk. For example, this past year our team launched a Web-based screening survey that any law enforcement officer in the U.S. can take to help identify whether he or she is suffering from sleep apnea, restless legs syndrome, narcolepsy, or other sleep disorders. Those whose answers place them at high risk are referred for evaluation and treatment by a specialist accredited by the American Academy of Sleep Medicine. [Accredited sleep centers may be found at www.sleepcenters. org.]

Finally, I would recommend that supervisors undergo training in sleep and fatigue management and that they promote good sleep behavior. People should learn to treat sleep as a serious matter. Both the company and the employees bear a shared responsibility to ensure that everyone comes to work well rested.

This corporate sleep policy of yours sounds a little draconian, if not impossible, given people's crazy schedules.

I don't think it's draconian at all. Business travelers expect that their pilots won't drink before flying an airplane, and all of us expect that no driver on the highway will have a blood alcohol level above the legal limit. Many executives already realize that the immediate effect of sleep loss on individuals and on overall corporate performance is just as important. A good sleep policy is smart business strategy. People think they're saving time and being more productive by not sleeping, but in fact they are cutting their productivity drastically. Someone who has adequate sleep doesn't nod off in an important meeting with a customer. She can pay attention to her task for longer periods of time and bring her whole intelligence and creativity to bear on the project at hand.

What do you think about the use of drugs that help people fall asleep or that shut off the urge to sleep?

These agents should be used only after a thorough evaluation of the causes of insomnia or excessive daytime sleepiness. Patients too often think there's a silver bullet for a problem like insomnia, and doctors too easily prescribe pills as part of a knee-jerk reaction to patient requests during the final minutes of an office visit. The causes of insomnia are subtle and need to be carefully investigated. These can be from too much caffeine, an irregular schedule, anxiety or depression, physical problems such as arthritis, use of other medications, and so on—and only a careful evaluation by a doctor experienced in sleep medicine can uncover the causes. I once saw a professor who complained of difficulty sleeping at night, and only after taking a careful history did we find that he was drinking 20 cups of coffee a day. He didn't even realize he was drinking that much and didn't think about the fact that so much caffeine, which has a six- to nine-hour half-life, would interfere with his ability to sleep. Prescribing a sleeping pill for his insomnia without identifying the underlying cause would have been a mistake.

There are non-pharmacological treatments for insomnia that seem very promising, by the way. Cognitive behavioral therapy, or CBT, helps people recognize and change thoughts and behaviors that might be keeping them awake at night. A researcher named Dr. Gregg Jacobs at Harvard

Medical School has reported that CBT works better over both the short and the long term than sleeping pills do.

Sometimes executives simply have to function without much sleep. What are some strategies they can use to get by until they can go to bed?

Though there is no known substitute for sleep, there are a few strategies you can use to help sustain performance temporarily until you can get a good night's sleep. Obviously, executives can drink caffeine, which is the most widely used wake-promoting therapeutic in the world. Naps can be very effective at restoring performance, and if they are brief—less than a half hour—they will induce less grogginess upon awakening. Being in a novel or engaging circumstance will also help you stay alert. Exercise, standing in an upright position, and exposure to bright light are all very helpful. Human beings are amazingly sensitive to light. In fact, the color of light may also be important. Exposure to shorter wavelength blue light is particularly effective in suppressing melatonin production, thereby allowing us to stay awake during our biological night. Photon for photon, looking up at the blue sky, for example, is more effective in both resetting our biological clock and enhancing our alertness than looking down at the green grass.

While all these things can help an executive function in an emergency, I must reiterate that he or she should still not drive when sleep deprived, even if a cup of coffee or a walk on a sunny day seems to help for a little while.

Do you get enough sleep?

Like everyone else, I try to, but I don't always achieve it.

[1]*Dr. Czeisler is the incumbent of an endowed professorship donated to Harvard by Cephalon and consults for a number of companies, including Actelion, Cephalon, Coca-Cola, Hypnion, Pfizer, Respironics, Sanofi-Aventis, Takeda, and Vanda.*

Personal Progress Charts

Getting up to speed with your reading requires you to keep track of your progress. That's where the charts in this appendix come in handy.

One-Minute Timing Progress Chart

Reading Strategy	Words per Minute	Comprehension Percent
_____	_____	_____
_____	_____	_____
_____	_____	_____
_____	_____	_____
_____	_____	_____
_____	_____	_____
_____	_____	_____
_____	_____	_____
_____	_____	_____
_____	_____	_____
_____	_____	_____
_____	_____	_____
_____	_____	_____
_____	_____	_____
_____	_____	_____
_____	_____	_____
_____	_____	_____
_____	_____	_____
_____	_____	_____
_____	_____	_____
_____	_____	_____
_____	_____	_____
_____	_____	_____
_____	_____	_____
_____	_____	_____

3-2-1 Speed Drill Personal Progress Chart

Reading Strategy	Words per Minute	Comprehension Percent
_____	_____	_____
_____	_____	_____
_____	_____	_____
_____	_____	_____
_____	_____	_____
_____	_____	_____
_____	_____	_____
_____	_____	_____
_____	_____	_____
_____	_____	_____
_____	_____	_____
_____	_____	_____
_____	_____	_____
_____	_____	_____
_____	_____	_____
_____	_____	_____
_____	_____	_____
_____	_____	_____
_____	_____	_____
_____	_____	_____
_____	_____	_____
_____	_____	_____
_____	_____	_____
_____	_____	_____

Discipline Your Eyes Personal Progress Chart

Today's Date   **Reading Time**

Appendix D

Calculating Your Reading Speed

When you're trying to improve your speed reading skills, you need to know the number of words and the number of words per line to calculate your speed. I've provided that information for you on the articles in this book. In this appendix, I explain how you can determine this information on your own, should you want to perform timings on other material outside this book.

First, a few guidelines:

◆ The best reading material to use for self-timing has a standard column width, meaning it's the same width all the way down the page. Many novels fit this bill because there are rarely pictures or illustrations included that adjust the column width.

◆ Magazine articles and textbook chapters can be used, although you might need to make adjustments for lines that are shorter or longer because of photos or illustrations.

◆ Using articles on the web are great *as long as* you put them in the printable version. The printable version removes any ads or illustrations and standardizes the line width. It's also less distracting to read.

Determining the Average Words per Line

You have two options when it comes to finding the average words per line in a piece of writing:

Option 1:

1. Select a full line of print.

2. Add all the letters, punctuation marks, and blank spaces in that line.

3. Divide this number by 5.

Let's look at an example:

> Most evenings, I would rather eat than sleep.

The line total is 45. So 45 ÷ 5 = 9 words per line.

Option 2:

1. Select any consecutive 10 lines of print.

2. Count the number of words *per line* on each of the 10 lines (8 in line 1, 6 in line 2, 9 in line 3, etc.).

3. Add the number of words. Place a decimal point one place over from the right. If the number is 81 or 8.1, round it down to 8, making it 8 words per line. If the number is 97 or 9.7, round it up to 10 words per line. If the number is 65 or 6.5, you can round up or down. The difference isn't that substantial, although the words do add up.

Finding the Total Number of Words (Optional)

Now to determine the total words in the article or piece of reading in front of you:

1. When you have an average words per line, count the number of lines in the piece.

2. Multiply the number of lines by the average words per line. This is the total number of words in the piece.

Calculating Your Words per Minute

Now for the information you want to know—how many words per minute you read!

1. Read for 1 minute.

2. Count how many lines you read.

3. Multiply the number of lines read by the number of average words per line to get your words per minute.

Voilà!

Speed Tip

If you have the reading on your computer, paste it into your word processing program and use the word count feature to determine the number of words. The word count feature also calculates the number of lines, but be aware the counter includes blank spaces as well.

Index

CHECK OUT THESE BEST-SELLERS

More than 450 titles available at booksellers and online retailers everywhere!

ALPHA   idiotsguides.com